AN ARCHAEOLOGICAL HISTORY OF MONTSERRAT IN THE WEST INDIES

AN ARCHAEOLOGICAL HISTORY OF MONTSERRAT IN THE WEST INDIES

by

John F. Cherry and Krysta Ryzewski

OXBOW | books

Oxford & Philadelphia

Published in the United Kingdom in 2020 by
OXBOW BOOKS
The Old Music Hall, 106-108 Cowley Road, Oxford, OX4 1JE

and in the United States by
OXBOW BOOKS
1950 Lawrence Road, Havertown, PA 19083

Paperback Edition: ISBN 978-1-78925-390-0
Digital Edition: ISBN 978-1-78925-391-7 (ePub)

A CIP record for this book is available from the British Library

Library of Congress Control Number: 2019954228

Printed in Malta by Melita Press

Typeset in India for Casemate Publishing Services. www.casematepublishingservices.com

For a complete list of Oxbow titles, please contact:

UNITED KINGDOM
Oxbow Books
Telephone (01865) 241249
Email: oxbow@oxbowbooks.com
www.oxbowbooks.com

UNITED STATES OF AMERICA
Oxbow Books
Telephone (800) 791-9354, Fax (610) 853-9146
Email: queries@casemateacademic.com
www.casemateacademic.com/oxbow

Oxbow Books is part of the Casemate Group

Front cover: View of Montserrat approaching from the northeast by helicopter. Photo by Gregory Scott, 2018; reproduced with permission.

Back cover: (*left*) A large *adorno* from excavations at the Early Ceramic Trants site. Photo: John Cherry, by permission of David Watters; (*right*) Potato Hill and its steep sea-cliffs, between Carr's Bay (foreground) and Little Bay. Photo: John Cherry.

Contents

Preface

It is necessary to start by explaining how, when, and why this book came into being. When we began our research project—*Survey and Landscape Archaeology on Montserrat* (*SLAM*)—in January 2010, this small Caribbean island's future was uncertain. The Soufrière Hills volcano was then entering its fifteenth year of activity; well over half the island's population had left it for good, and its southern half had become an Exclusion Zone. In between major periodic eruptions, the volcano unleashed ash falls, pyroclastic flows, lahars, and earthquakes on an almost daily basis. Everyone kept one eye on the volcano as they tried to maintain some semblance of normalcy in their daily routines. That winter we watched anxiously as its dome grew taller and more threatening by the day; another volcanic event was imminent, but no one could predict exactly when it might happen. Scientists from the Montserrat Volcano Observatory took to the airwaves during their weekly program on local radio ZJB to discuss the real potential for a lateral blast and the catastrophic damage it could cause to the designated safe areas in the island's north. The volcano cast a cloud of urgency over every aspect of island life, including our archaeological fieldwork.

In the midst of this volcanic crisis, we were invited by the Montserrat National Trust to help locate and document the archaeological sites in the safe northern third of the island. Only a handful of sites in this hitherto sparsely inhabited part of the island had ever been the focus of archaeological investigation. The collective fear was that numerous sites were at risk of destruction by both the direct and indirect impacts of Soufrière Hills—that is, not only volcanic eruptions and collapses, but also cultural resettlement and development projects. So much of Montserrat's cultural heritage resources had already been devastated by the eruptions that totally buried the capital city Plymouth and destroyed virtually everything in the south of the island. A total loss of the physical traces of Montserrat's past was a real concern.

Thus in January 2010 we set out on the first of over 100 exploratory surveys to locate the traces of the island's past as they survived in building ruins, artifact scatters, man-made features, and other landscape modifications. Some of the areas into which we hiked, such as the high-elevation jungle of the Centre Hills, were so thickly covered in volcanic ash that they could have been mistaken for a winter wonderland. Remarkably, it was still possible to locate archaeological remains under these inhospitable conditions. Over the course of our first four fieldwork seasons we succeeded in assembling an inventory of 55 archaeological sites and hundreds of anthropogenic features, the vast majority of which were previously unrecorded.

Even more unexpected was the fact that the volcano became notably more quiet shortly after our fieldwork began, the last partial (but very destructive) dome-collapse occurring on February 11, 2010. For the past ten years the volcano has certainly remained active, but, fortunately, there have been no major eruptive events. And as a result of this lull, the island's landscape today has become one that is dramatically different from what we encountered in 2010. So too is the outlook of Montserratians towards their island's future prospects.

Today, in 2020, an entirely new capital town at Little Bay is beginning to coalesce, while new villages and numerous infrastructural developments have transformed the island's north into a bustling zone of activity. Freshly established industries, including geothermal energy and sand/ash mining, are capitalizing on the island's volcanic geology and the materials the volcano has produced over the past two decades. Ashfalls in inhabited areas have become uncommon, and residents, it seems, now conduct their daily lives without great concern about the volcano. Centre Hills, Silver Hills, and even parts of the Soufrière Hills are covered with rejuvenated forests and other vegetation. The ruins of buildings in Plymouth and those in former villages fairly close to the volcano, such as Molyneux, Long Ground, and Harris, are increasingly invisible as they become engulfed by tall and fast-growing grasses, ferns, and trees. Other settlements—for instance, Richmond Hill, Cork Hill, and Isles Bay—that were strictly off-limits in 2010 are now accessible to the public, and in some cases, becoming inhabited once again. Access to other areas of the Exclusion Zone continues to expand. Plymouth and its ruins—marketed as a "modern-day Pompeii"—have become a popular, if tightly regulated, destination for day-tripping tourists and foreign TV and film productions.

Like Montserrat, our own situation has also changed considerably over the past decade. Upon completing pedestrian survey of the north in 2013, we reoriented our research to focus on understanding the island's archaeologically-informed history between the period from AD 1000 to 1750. Our subsequent seasons of fieldwork have involved survey and excavation at five of the sites we located during our initial survey program: Potato Hill, Upper Blakes, Valentine Ghaut, Indian Creek, and Thatch Valley. As we delved more deeply into the historic archives, scholarly literature, and comparative artifact collections to interpret our findings, we came to realize that we had more questions than answers about Montserrat's cultural history. In fact, there existed no book of any sort that synthesized Montserrat's entire 5,000-year human past, as informed by the conjunction of both archaeological and historical evidence. Our book was born out of this absence in the scholarly and popular literature on Montserrat.

So here we present an archaeological history of Montserrat from the earliest known traces of human activity on the island, about 5,000 years ago, to the present. Although much of the information we incorporate in the following chapters was collected during our own research, the present book is not designed to showcase or summarize the *SLAM* project and its findings: that will be done elsewhere. Instead, we take an inclusive and holistic approach to assembling Montserrat's archaeologically-informed history by integrating contributions from all previous archaeological research on the island. Happily, nearly all of the other scholars who have worked on the island earlier are still around and have been able to provide us with information and guidance.

This is not the story of an isolated and remote island: Montserrat is shown rather to be a place intricately connected to the flows of people and goods that have travelled between Caribbean islands and across the Atlantic at various points in time, both Amerindian and historical. Despite its small size and seeming irrelevance, Montserrat has in fact always been networked into regional and global systems of connectivity. We interpret Montserrat's past through locally-based evidence, but also by following historical links off-island, incorporating data from other Caribbean islands and western European contexts to interpret local conditions. Beyond these comparisons, however, we do not engage at length in many of the current debates in circum-Caribbean and trans-Atlantic archaeology, which are beyond the scope and purpose of this volume.

Our narrative is unapologetically focused on Montserrat. One of the reasons we chose to write a Montserrat-centered book is because the island's small size and the quality of its archaeological data provide us with the rare opportunity to tell the story of a single place over the course of its entire human history. Another reason is that, in Caribbean archaeological and historical scholarship, Montserrat is often dwarfed in comparisons with islands such as Barbados and Jamaica, which, with the exception of their shared British colonial pasts, are quite distinct in terms of size, geography, history, culture, and their wealth of archival records. This book, by contrast, is an opportunity to appreciate Montserrat on its own terms.

Initially, we set out to write a popular book about Montserrat oriented at the (perhaps mythical) "educated general reader". But as we began to cull information from our own research, as well as from other archaeologists' previous projects, we realized that so much new archaeological data and previously unexamined archival records had come to light over the past decade that our energies were best directed at writing a somewhat more scholarly account of the island's history. We envision and hope that this book will appeal to a variety of specialists, including professional archaeologists, students of archaeology, heritage managers, museum workers, environmental scientists, historians, educators, architects, and preservationists. But, at the same time, we have also worked hard to write the book so that its content will be accessible to non-professionals, readers who for whatever reason simply wish to learn more about Montserrat's history and archaeology. With this latter audience in mind, we have made a deliberate effort to include striking imagery, box features, and straightforward language, avoiding jargon and technicalities so far as possible. Nevertheless, since this *is* a book rooted in archaeology, there are places in the text where mention of technical terms is necessary: we have not been able entirely to avoid mention of prehistoric groupings (*e.g.*, Saladoid) or references to the taxonomic system of Caribbean cultural sequences that Irving Rouse introduced many years ago. We offer our readers these technical terms and supporting scholarly references as opportunities to engage further with the region's archaeology. Or they can, if they wish, gloss over them and perhaps just retain them for Pub Trivia nights at the Isles Bay Beach Bar!

The majority of the book's ten chapters are organized chronologically and present Montserrat's archaeology and history at various points in time. Readers will notice that there are more chapters that focus on the island's post-1492 historic period than its considerably longer Amerindian history. This imbalance merely reflects a disparity in the level of available information. Artifacts, built structures, landscape features, and archival documents survive in far larger quantities for the period following European arrival in the Caribbean than for the millennia beforehand. The chronologically-organized chapters are bracketed by two chapters at the beginning and one at the end of the volume. Chapter 1 describes the general geographical, environmental, and vulcanological setting of the island, while Chapter 2 provides the history of archaeological research on Montserrat and the institutional settings in which it has taken place. The final chapter reflects upon Montserrat's cultural heritage in the context of the ongoing volcanic crisis and it considers how larger issues of heritage preservation may inform future approaches to protecting the island's past.

An underlying theme of this volume is resilience. It presents insights from the archaeological and documentary evidence on how the island's inhabitants have coped with often adverse conditions throughout the course of its history—hurricanes, volcanic eruptions, slavery, disease, invasions, and impoverishment—all while remaining proudly connected to heritage that celebrates the multicultural accomplishments of island residents. While compiling the research for this book, we had the opportunity in 2018 to co-design and co-curate an international exhibition entitled, *Trials, Tragedy & Resilience*. It celebrated the archaeology and history of the island in honor of the 250th anniversary of the attempted slave uprising on St Patrick's Day in 1768. Four versions of this exhibition were simultaneously displayed at the Montserrat National Museum in Little Bay, the Grosscup Museum of Anthropology at Wayne State University in Detroit, Michigan, the Joukowsky Institute for Archaeology and the Ancient World at Brown University in Providence, Rhode Island, and the Department of Archaeology and Heritage Studies at Aarhus University in Denmark.

Ultimately, this book positions archaeology as the primary basis for understanding Montserrat's human past in its entirety. It also serves as a vital reference to archival repositories worldwide that contain collections about Montserrat's history, and to archaeological reports and collections that are housed at the Montserrat National Trust and elsewhere. To assist those who might wish to conduct their own historical or archaeological research about Montserrat, the various sections of the bibliography at the end of the book should provide the necessary links. We hope that the information we share in this volume will be utilized both by our professional colleagues and by local stakeholders to preserve, protect, and learn from the past on Montserrat and indeed across the wider Caribbean region. Our Acknowledgements name all those individuals who have helped, in whatever way, to make this book possible. It is to our colleagues, friends, and helpers, mainly on Montserrat, but also beyond it, that we are most greatly indebted: this book is for them, and for all who love Montserrat.

Connemara, Old Town, Montserrat

Acknowledgments

One of us (KR) first came to Montserrat in 2006, as a participant in the Little Bay Estate archaeology project; our joint *SLAM* project began in January 2010, and since then we have conducted eleven consecutive seasons of fieldwork and research between 2010 and 2019. Over the course of these years, we have developed a real affection for the island and its people. What's not to like about a place with just one main road, no traffic lights, one gas station (sometimes two), and a single bank with an ATM? And, on an island with a resident population of less than five thousand, one gets to know a lot of people quickly.

All of our research on Montserrat has taken place under the auspices, and with the co-operation, of the Montserrat National Trust. Our first, and most important thanks therefore go to the successive Directors of the MNT with whom we have collaborated: Lady Eudora Fergus and Sarita Francis, OBE. They have been critical supporters, not only in approving our plans for fieldwork, but in contacting landowners, allowing access to artifacts and archival resources maintained at the Trust, and permitting year-long artifact loans for study purposes. Other members of the MNT Board have been equally helpful, especially Dulcie James (the current President of the Board). We have spent many hours working alongside Donna Henry, the Exhibition/Library Assistant at the Trust, and we have been supported in the archives, office, and in the bush by MNT staff Jean White, D'Andre Lee, Philemon (Mapie) Murrain, and Victor (Tumba) Brown. We offer these colleagues our heartfelt thanks for their time and assistance. We hope that we have repaid some of these debts by the assistance we have provided in cataloging the artifact holdings of the Trust, in co-organizing museum exhibitions and educational outreach activities, and in conducting various rescue excavations on behalf of the MNT.

We owe sincere thanks to the many other local officials, colleagues and agencies on Montserrat who supported our work and shared their resources with us over the years. They include former Governor HE Elizabeth Carriere; Director of Agriculture Melissa O'Garro and Elvis Gerald of the Ministry of Agriculture; former Chief Minister Reuben Meade; Laverne Rogers-Ryan, Director of the Montserrat GIS Centre, Physical Planning Unit; Rod Stewart and Adam Stinton of the Montserrat Volcano Observatory; Rose Willock of Radio ZJB; Neil How; the staff of the Montserrat Public Library; the Montserrat Rotary Club; and the Montserrat Animal Protection Society.

A benefit, perhaps, of the fact that archaeology on Montserrat is still a fairly young endeavor is that almost all of those who have ever been involved in Montserratian archaeology are still alive! This means that we know, and have been able to talk to, most of them. For their assistance, memories, and comradeship (both on and off the island), we thank David Watters, Lydia Pulsipher, Conrad Mac Goodwin, John Crock, Mary Beaudry, and Jessica Striebel MacLean.

Our own *SLAM* project has involved numerous undergraduate and graduate students, postdoctoral researchers, faculty colleagues, and local volunteers. We are happy to acknowledge here their significant contributions to the archaeological findings reported in this book. They include: Sue Alcock, Serena Alwani, Douglas Anderson, Emanuela Bocancea, C. Lorin Brace VI, Shawn Chittendon, Brendan Doucet, Samantha Ellens, Elissa Faro, Katherine Harrington, Jeffrey Howard, Kiera Kim-Freidell, Troy Deppermann, Beau Kromberg, Thomas Leppard, Rondell Meade, Laura McAtackney, Elizabeth Murphy, Alexis Ohman, Luke Pecoraro, Matthew Pihokker, Ian Randall, Miriam Rothenberg, Alexander Smith, Thomas Urban, Hank Villerot, Susan Villerot, and Athena Zissis. We are especially grateful to Miriam Rothenberg for her assistance in creating the maps for this book and Samantha Ellens for the artifact illustrations. Also to Ayla Çevik for careful proof-reading and preparing the index.

Most of our fieldwork took place in the north of the island, but our various residential bases (thanks to Susan MacLeod Edgecombe) have been in Woodlands, Olveston, and Old Town. So every day, we have passed by, and usually stopped at, the hilltop People's Place. With its self-proclaimed coldest beers on the island, its refreshing breeze, and John Fergus's unabashed welcome, this is a place that will linger in our memories for a very long time.

We worked hard to write this book in a way that is accessible and intelligible to readers who are not professional Caribbean archaeologists. In the process we solicited feedback from various audiences, including the peer reviews of our colleagues and our family members. Our thanks to Sue Alcock, Mary Daley ("Aunt Min"), Kaitlin Deslatte, Sarita Francis, Laura McAtackney, Sarah Sharpe, and David Watters for their comments on earlier drafts of this book.

Our work on Montserrat would not have been possible without the support of multiple funding agencies. We are fortunate that our archaeological research bridges the sciences and humanities, and so we have secured funding from several national and international agencies, especially the National Endowment for the Humanities (Collaborative Research Grant #RZ51674-14), National Geographic Society (Research and Exploration Grant #9610-14), National Geographic Society Waitt Family Foundation (#W86-10), National Science Foundation-Spatial Archaeometry Research Collaboration (SPARC; Data and Analytics Grant #1321443). We also acknowledge the continued support from our entities at our home institutions, including the Joukowsky Institute for Archaeology and the Ancient World at Brown University, and the Department of Anthropology and Office of the President at Wayne State University.

List of figures

Chapter 1

Chapter 2

Chapter 3

Chapter 4

Chapter 5

Chapter 6

Chapter 7

Chapter 8

Chapter 9

Chapter 10

1. Introduction: Montserrat's island setting

Montserrat stands at a most unusual moment in its history, one that—as we now know, from recent discoveries (presented in Chapter 3)—extends back nearly 5,000 years. The ongoing volcanic crisis that began in July 1995 has changed everything. The resident population has been reduced to one-third its previous size. More than half the island lies out of bounds in the Exclusion Zone, with formerly lively villages now abandoned and swamped by ash and the all-engulfing vegetation. Very many archaeological sites and other places of significance for cultural heritage have been destroyed or obscured in the south of the island (see Chapter 10). This book draws on the results of what archaeological work had taken place before the current eruptions, but it also relies quite heavily on information collected in the course of the present authors' *Survey and Landscape Archaeology on Montserrat* project. This project ran from 2010 to 2019, under the difficult conditions that currently govern life on the island.

Where Montserrat stands at the current moment needs to be placed within a much longer-term perspective. We provide here, by way of introduction, a brief account of various aspects of the geographical, environmental, and volcanic setting in which the archaeological history of Montserrat has unfolded over the past several millennia. Perhaps we can summarize this by saying that Montserrat is best characterized as a small, mountainous, volcanic, semi-tropical island. Each word in that description is important, and we try to explain why that is so.[1]

In British hands for all but two years since its European colonization in 1632, Montserrat is today a British Overseas Territory. It is the southernmost of the Leeward Islands of the Lesser Antilles in the eastern Caribbean (Fig. 1). The Leeward Islands' distinctive configuration—a convex volcanic arc—hints at the process of their formation: it outlines the boundary along which the oceanic crust of the South American Plate is being subducted under the Caribbean Plate, forming a number of volcanic islands in the process. No less than seventeen volcanoes are currently active along this plate boundary. One of them, the most devastating of the later 20th century, is the Soufrière Hills volcano on Montserrat.

Montserrat has an outline that could be described as pear- or teardrop-shaped, about 16 km north–south and 11 km east–west (Fig. 1). Like everything else on Montserrat, even its size has

[1] The dissertation of David Watters (1980: 107–137) contains a thorough environmental overview of Montserrat, much of which is still useful many years after it was written.

Fig. 1. Topography and place-names on Montserrat. (Map by Miriam Rothenberg; base map from Wadge 1988, provided by the Montserrat Volcano Observatory.)

Fig. 2. Montserrat's profile as seen from the northeast. (Photo: Gregory Scott.)

been affected by the eruptions since July 1995 of the Soufrière Hills volcano in the south. While the island's area currently measures about 102.5 sq. km, it is expanding and its surface area is growing, as a result of pyroclastic and laharic flows down the volcano's slopes and along various rivers and watercourses (known locally as *ghauts*) out to the ocean (see Fig. 27, Radio Antilles).[2] The most serious recent volcanic event, in February 2010, actually extended the shoreline at Trants on the eastern, windward side of the island by 650 m.[3] Utterly dwarfed by comparison with the large islands of the Greater Antilles such as Cuba and Hispaniola, Montserrat is also considerably smaller than either of its two closest inhabited neighbors, Antigua and Guadeloupe, each less than 50 km distant.

Whether one approaches the island by sea or air (Fig. 2), the features that stand out immediately are its several steep and rugged mountains, and its sea-cliffs. Montserrat consists of a series of

[2] Pyroclastic flows and surges (technically known as Pyroclastic Density Currents [PDCs]) are a dangerous mixture of hot volcanic gases and debris that travels down from the volcano at speeds of up to hundreds of kilometers per hour; a lahar is a volcanic mudflow consisting of a slurry of water, ash, and volcanic debris.

[3] Cherry *et al.* 2012: fig. 3.

north–south trending volcanic cones whose lower slopes descend below the sea, but at sea level itself they have been severely eroded to create cliffs, in places massive, that front much of the coastline. This is especially the case around the south and southeast coasts, along the northeast and northern tip of the island from Trants to Northwest Bluff, and from Carr's Bay southward to Old Road Bluff. Embayments or beaches forming viable anchorages scarcely exist along the windward side of the island, and they are only sporadic on the leeward side. So it is no coincidence that the chief towns of the island in early historical times were located at Stapletown in Old Road Bay and at Kinsale/Plymouth in Sugar Bay; or that the British in the 18th century constructed a system of defensive cannon batteries and forts along the leeward coast, since this was the only side of the island that enemy warships could be expected to approach.[4]

Volcanic geology

It was Montserrat's distinctive saw-tooth profile, as seen from both the east and west sides, that reminded Columbus, sailing by in 1493, of the jagged peaks of Montserrat (meaning "serrated mountain" in Catalan) above the Benedictine Abbey of *Santa Maria de Montserrat* near Barcelona in Catalonia, Spain. This visual effect is created by the three main volcanic complexes of the island—Silver Hills, Centre Hills, and Soufrière Hills—which are progressively younger in geological age and taller in height from north to south (Fig. 2).[5] Because their ages are so diverse—Silver Hills (active 2.6–1.2 million years ago), Centre Hills (active 954–550 thousand years ago), and Soufrière Hills (active from at least 250 thousand years ago, until the present), they have experienced very different degrees of erosion, affecting their relative altitudes and the amount of moisture they receive, and consequently their vegetation cover.

For example, although the summit of Silver Hills reaches only 403 m, it has a well-developed submarine shelf around it. It represents the very worn down remnant of what was once a more substantial volcanic massif, perhaps equivalent in size to Centre Hills or even the way Soufrière Hills looks today. Because the volcanic cone is so eroded, with poorly developed soils and little orographic rainfall, this northern part of Montserrat has throughout the colonial era always been characterized by a hard-scrabble way of life, with poor agriculture and far fewer residents than elsewhere on the island. On the other hand, the appropriately named interior mountains of Centre Hills present a very different aspect (Fig. 3). Being substantially higher (its summit at Katy Hill rises to 741 m), its upper reaches are often under cloud and mist, resulting not only in the development there of distinctive vegetational communities of Elfin Forest, but abundant rainfall that flows down the numerous watercourses to supply the modern-day settlements at lower elevations along its western and northern sides.

Good soils, plentiful water, and generally moderate slopes encouraged European planters to clear the native vegetation for their sugar cane fields a substantial distance up the slopes of Centre

[4] Akenson 1997; Crandall 2000.

[5] The literature on the volcanic geology of Montserrat, as might be expected, is now vast; the most accessible and still reasonably up-to-date summary, in its wider Lesser Antillean context, is that by Hincks *et al.* (2005). For stunning images of the erupting volcano and the devastation it has caused, see Odbert *et al.* 2011. More technical information can be found in (*e.g.*) Rea 1974; Roobol and Smith 1998; Druitt and Kokelaar 2001; Zellmer *et al.* 2003; Smith *et al.* 2007; Le Friant *et al.* 2008; Wadge *et al.* 2014. Real-time information and an archive of past scientific reports are available on the official website of the Montserrat Volcano Observatory (www.mvo.ms).

Hills (to elevations of 400 m or more), but these have now disappeared beneath regrowth of the neotropical forest. An area of about 12 sq. km of the Centre Hills is now maintained as a well-studied forest preserve.[6]

Fig. 3. Montserrat's Centre Hills, seen from the northwest. (Photo: John Cherry.)

Although there are other, geologically recent, but now extinct volcanic features that contribute to Montserrat's landscape configuration (such as the fairly low St George's Hill and Garibaldi Hill, immediately north and northwest of Plymouth), all eyes are now on the Soufrière Hills volcano, the only one that is currently, and catastrophically, active (Fig. 4). The curiosity of 18th- and 19th-century visitors to the island was stimulated by its various fumaroles, soufrières, sulphur springs, and hot pools, about which they wrote brief accounts.[7] Premonitory warnings of future activity came in the form of severe earthquakes that began in 1897 and continued for several years, as well as earthquake swarms in the mid-1930s, and again in the 1960s.[8] But since Soufrière Hills had not seen any major eruption during the colonial era, its coming to life so abruptly on 18 July 1995 took the island's people and their government by surprise. At the time of this eruption, this volcanic complex comprised five steep-sided andesitic lava domes, named Gage's (the oldest), Chance's, Galway's, Perche's, and Castle Peak. Their appearance has now been totally transformed by volcanic activity over the past two decades or more. Castle Peak was buried early in the 1995 eruptions, and the old domes that remain are now flanked by pyroclastic and laharic flows resulting from dome collapses, along with a variety of deposits arising from debris avalanches, pumice flows, tephra fallout, and other such processes.

Should this latest eruptive activity have come as a surprise? For how long had Soufrière Hills been dormant? We now have fairly good answers, as a result of scientific research that the recent eruption itself has prompted. Geological study of the stratigraphy of the volcanic deposits visible in the island's southeastern sea-cliffs, along with more than 40 radiocarbon dates, has allowed reconstruction of the eruptive history over the past 31,000 years.[9] In brief, the volcano was active until about 16,000 years ago, producing several distinctive types of deposits indicative of various kinds of eruptions, but seems then to have had a long period of dormancy that lasted until roughly 4,000 years ago. At that time, Soufrière Hills produced a dense andesite ash flow deposit up to 3.6 m thick; since this occurred centuries later than our first evidence of people on Montserrat (Chapter 3), this episode would have been devastating to anyone who might have been living there at the time (or perhaps may have discouraged settlement). Most recently, there occurred a phase

[6] Holliday 2009.
[7] *e.g.* the Irish doctor Patrick Browne, who lived on Montserrat 1765–1769: see Nelson 2001.
[8] Shepherd *et al.* 1971; Hincks *et al.* 2005.
[9] Roobol and Smith 1998.

Fig. 4. The Soufrière Hills volcano in June 2018. (Photo: Krysta Ryzewski.)

of smaller eruptions, well dated—from 770 to 200 years ago—by radiocarbon dates on abundant charcoal (including logs up to 3 m long). This date range of course overlaps with the early years of European colonization of Montserrat, but no surviving records mention volcanic activity, perhaps because it was fairly insignificant in scale. With the possible exception of Trants, no volcanic episodes have been encountered in archaeological deposits at any excavated site on the island.[10]

The modern cataclysm of the Soufrière Hills eruption unfolded with great speed.[11] A major dome collapse that sent a pyroclastic flow down Fort Ghaut and through the center of Plymouth on 3 August 1997 spelled the end for the already abandoned capital town (Fig. 5). And a massive pyroclastic surge on Boxing Day that same year devastated about one-tenth of the entire island in the south. The evacuations that took place during the early stages of the crisis hardened into an enforced and closely policed Exclusion Zone, still in place today. Its northern land boundary (there is also a maritime Exclusion Zone) has, at various times, extended from Trants on the east coast to as far north as Old Town, Olveston, and Salem on the west, although this northern limit has been subject

[10] On the ambiguous evidence from Trants, Petersen *et al.* 1999b.

[11] The major eruptive events, on a month-to-month basis, are set out in detail as a table in Hincks *et al.* 2005: 157–160.

Fig. 5. Devastation in downtown Plymouth caused by the Soufrière Hills volcano. (Photo: John Cherry, June 2018.)

to numerous modifications over the years, in response to changing risk assessments for the settled areas of the island (Fig. 1). At present (2020), with the volcano having been relatively quiet since 2011 and volcanic threat set at its lowest level, the boundary of the Exclusion Zone lies immediately north of Plymouth, and some residents are beginning to return to their properties in communities such as Cork Hill and Richmond Hill that have been off limits for many years. Tourist visits to a small part of Plymouth, in order to witness the spectacular devastation on display, have begun under strictly supervised conditions, and the town's jetty is again in use for the shipment of sand and ash.

A great deal is known about the Soufrière Hills volcano as a result of the establishment, immediately after eruptions began in 1995, of the Montserrat Volcano Observatory (MVO) which, since 2003, has occupied a purpose-built facility at Flemming's, in full view of the volcano. It conducts round-the-clock observations using seismic, deformation, gas emission, visual, and environmental monitoring methods. These data are used to set the level of threat (on a scale of 1 to 5), to define the boundaries of the terrestrial and maritime Exclusion Zones, and to provide scientific advice concerning the safety of its residents to the government of Montserrat.[12] Because the volcanic crisis

[12] In its early years, the MVO experienced growing pains, since the Montserratian government looked for definitive predictions and advice, but the scientific community was not of one mind about the data and their implications; this tension between government and science has been explored by Donovan *et al.* (2013).

has been so protracted and because rotating teams of scientists have continuously been collecting such a wide variety of data over so many years, it is probably the case that the Soufrière Hills is today the most intensively studied volcano in the world.

The impacts of Montserrat's volcanic crisis—geological, ecological, environmental, economic, demographic, social, political—have been well documented in numerous academic publications, TV documentaries, and now coverage on social media.[13] While of course less tragic than the nineteen deaths and massive disruptions to personal lives that the volcano has caused, the cultural heritage of Montserrat has also suffered greatly, in ways that will be apparent in all of the chapters that follow, and particularly in Chapter 10.

Climate and natural environment

Montserrat is situated at latitude 16°45'N and longitude 62°10'W. Its climate, therefore, is essentially tropical, driven mainly by the North Atlantic High-Pressure System and the Intertropical Convergence Zone. This means that the weather is warm year-round, with an average temperature of 26°C that varies during the year only within a 5°C range (although with considerable altitudinal variation). Humidity hovers around 75%. Atlantic currents flow westwards, passing through the gaps between the islands of the Lesser Antilles almost like a weir; these strong currents affecting the passages between the various islands almost certainly posed challenges for early Amerindian voyagers in canoes and may have had some impact on the patterns and processes of initial island colonization, as we discuss later. Winds too (the Northeast Trade Winds) blow predominantly from the east.

Unlike the relatively flat and low-lying uplifted limestone islands of the outer volcanic arc of the Lesser Antilles (such as Antigua, Barbuda, and Anguilla) that lack a mountainous topography to generate orographic rainfall, Montserrat is fairly well watered. Annual rainfall has varied from about 95 to 178 cm, with a mean of about 135 cm. It has a seasonal character, with the wettest period of the year generally falling in the months between October and January, and the driest in February through April. These figures, however, ignore the major impact that topography has on the distribution of rainfall, with the higher elevations receiving by far the most abundant precipitation. The upper reaches of the Centre Hills and Soufrière Hills average almost three times the rainfall that falls in the island's extreme north or along the south and southeast areas of the windward coast.

These "normal" conditions of course overlook the vulnerability of many of the islands of the Lesser and Greater Antilles to tropical storms and hurricanes (the official season for which starts at the beginning of June, although most hurricane events are later in the year). Montserrat has always been subject to these natural forces, and the chapters that follow enumerate many instances in recent centuries of the great damage caused by storms to buildings and livelihoods, as well as crops, livestock, vegetation, and wildlife. Modern, long-range weather forecasting and storm-tracking now provide fairly accurate predictions of a hurricane's severity and likely arrival time, allowing some measure of preparedness; but no such luxury existed for the inhabitants of Montserrat in Amerindian and colonial times, and levels of devastation were correspondingly greater. The last truly major hurricane to affect Montserrat was Hurricane Hugo in 1989, which destroyed

[13] For a journalistic account relatively early in the volcanic crisis and sharply critical of governmental responses, see Pattullo 2000. Local resident and cinematographer David Lea has produced an informative series of DVDs that includes much archival footage: see http://www.priceofparadise.com/.

or very seriously damaged as much as 98% of all the structures on the island, leaving most of its population at least temporarily without shelter or homes.[14] It was a double tragedy that the current volcanic crisis should begin only half a dozen years later, while hurricane recovery efforts were not yet fully completed.

Adequate rainfall, equable temperatures, and (in places) rich volcanic soils have resulted in a natural environment—at least aboriginally and prior to recent volcanic depredations—dominated by jungle, or, more technically, by wet and dry neotropical forest. There have been some not insignificant changes in climate in the region, even during the later stages of the Holocene, an epoch which encompasses the entirety of human life on Montserrat. Unfortunately, there currently exist no palaeo-environmental or palaeo-climatological data from the island of Montserrat itself and we can only generalize from evidence collected elsewhere. It is known, for example, that periods of drought and high hurricane frequency characterized the Archaic Age from 4300 BC onwards, with generally wetter and less stormy conditions throughout the past 2,500 years, but also considerable variability (wetter periods ca. AD 100, 400–600, and 1000–1400; drier intervals ca. AD 200–400, 700–900, and around 1600).[15]

Despite these variations, the likelihood is that the first visitors to Montserrat nearly 5,000 years ago would have been greeted by a landscape cloaked in green. One reason for this is that Montserrat is a small island. As with most such environments, it is "depauperate" (*i.e.* it has fewer species than a similar area of comparable size on a mainland landmass), particularly with regard to invertebrates whose swimming skills are limited or non-existent, making it difficult for them to cross the substantial water passages that have always separated Montserrat from neighboring lands (themselves also small islands). In particular, until introductions by both Amerindians and (especially) Europeans, there were no native grazing mammals to suppress plant and tree growth.[16] Things are very different today, not only because of several centuries of heavy exploitation of the landscape by colonial farmers, but also because of the severe effects of feral livestock on natural vegetation in what is now the Exclusion Zone.

In the past, and still largely today, ecological zones and their distinctive plant and animal communities were differentiated by altitudinal zones: mangroves and Littoral Forest growing around the coast, with Dry Forest inland, giving way to Mesic and Wet Forest at greater heights, and eventually the specialized plant associations of the Elfin Forest in the zone of near-continuous cloud cover (Fig. 6). Montserrat's biodiversity—about which relatively little was known, even as recently as a generation ago[17] —has now been intensively studied, not least as a result of a variety of collaborations by British and European institutions in partnership with the Montserrat National Trust (as described in Chapter 2). The impetus for such initiatives has arisen in part from the fact that the volcanic eruptions destroyed as much as 60% of the forest ecosystem, amongst other things creating a survival crisis for unique endemic species such as the Montserrat Oriole (loss of habitat) and the large frog known as the Mountain Chicken (disease) that has helped foster intensive fieldwork and garner widespread international attention. There is also the realization that—in the aftermath of the volcanic crisis, with little agriculture and a sluggish economy—ecotourism represents one viable

[14] Markham and Fergus 1989.
[15] Siegel *et al.* 2015; Hofman and Hoogland 2016: 12–13; Siegel 2018.
[16] Giovas *et al.* 2012; Fitzpatrick 2015: 320–322.
[17] As detailed in Watters 1980.

Fig. 6. Secondary regrowth of the neotropical jungle in the Centre Hills, and the difficult conditions it poses for archaeological survey. (Photo: John Cherry.)

path for future development and thus the natural environment warrants most careful husbandry. The same, of course, could be said of cultural heritage resources, as we argue in this book.

Montserrat, now and then

So far, we've briefly touched on some of the chief geographical, geological, and climatological factors that characterize Montserrat today, and that have affected its soils, vegetation, and animal life. But we should also ask: How different might Montserrat have looked at various times over the course of the past several thousand years of its human history?

Today, looking at the island from the air or in space imagery, the most striking feature is the brutal scarring of the verdant green neotropical forest landscape by extensive exposures of volcanic ash and rock, sometimes confined to flows down natural watercourses, but in some places (for example, on the coastal plain south of Trants on the east coast) fanning out to create huge expanses of an almost lunar landscape (Fig. 7). In some places within this zone of devastation, which occupies well over half the island, there appear to be areas of natural vegetation that have escaped the volcano unscathed: but appearances are deceiving. As just mentioned, large numbers of domestic livestock abandoned in the course of the hasty evacuation of the south roam the Exclusion Zone unchecked, and the depredation by uncontrolled populations of goats is preventing natural regeneration of forest, while feral pigs in the Centre Hills require culling in order to limit their seriously damaging impacts on the ecosystem. Parts of these now-abandoned landscapes, seen from the air, suggest an almost pastoral tranquility, with their lush vegetation of long grasses, bushes, and various invasive species that are rapidly reclaiming it. Yet that too is an illusion: beneath the vegetation lie formerly cultivated fields and terraces now drowned in ash, and through it one discerns the roofless shells of buildings in the villages that were overwhelmed by volcanic pyroclastic flows and ashfalls or set on fire by red-hot ballistic rocks.

Fig. 7. False-color image of Montserrat from space in the aftermath of the February 2010 eruptive events; red indicates healthy vegetation, gray denotes volcanic flows. (Image from NASA Earth Observatory, captured 26 February 2010. Retrieved from https://commons.wikimedia.org/wiki/File:Soufriere_Hills_Volcano_dome_collapse.gif on 18 February 2019.)

In the years before the 1995 eruptions began, settlement was spread very widely throughout the island. Its focus—commercial, social, and political—was of course the capital town of Plymouth (Fig. 8). Residential communities extended virtually unbroken along the west coast, extending from St Patrick's in the south to Carr's Bay in the north, with many villages scattered among the ridges on the lower slopes of the Centre Hills, along the road over the central saddle linking Plymouth with the former Bramble airport at Trants, and from there southwards down the windward coast as far as upland settlements such as Long Ground. The 1960s to 1980s, moreover, saw the expansion of population (albeit seasonal) with the construction of many relatively luxurious villas in several communities—Old Town, Olveston, Woodlands, and Spanish Point—serving expatriate visitors. Today, however, the situation could not be more different. By definition, of course, no one lives in the dangerous Exclusion Zone, nor are there residents anywhere along the east coast south of Lookout or in the northernmost Silver Hills area. The former population of twelve or thirteen thousand has been reduced to one of less than five thousand, crowded into a quite small portion of the island's northwest, and served by a government housed in temporary headquarters at Brades, pending development of the projected new capital town at Little Bay and Carr's Bay that proceeds at a gradual pace.

In the aftermath of the ongoing volcanic crisis, farming is now conducted on a quite modest scale: there are individual houses-gardens and many small plots, certainly, but few areas are given

Fig. 8. Plymouth, the island's capital town, in 1995 and 2018. (Photos: David R. Watters and Mike Schinkel.)

over to large clearances for agricultural fields. (Upper Blakes on the north slopes of Centre Hills, also a location important for its archaeological record that we discuss in Chapters 3 and 6, is one notable exception; see Fig. 20.) If we were to wind the clock back to the earlier decades of the 20th century, however, a different scene would be on display. Sea Island cotton was king from the early years of the 20th century (as a British Government-supported recovery effort after the devastating hurricane of 1899) until World War II.[18] Descriptions from the time refer to a landscape white with cotton on every side, and indeed the acreage under this crop rose from 2,700 in 1911 to almost 4,500 on the eve of World War II, a very high proportion of the total arable land available on the island. Yet going back to the mid-19th century, and especially its later decades, another Montserrat would have been apparent, one almost entirely dominated by its many square miles of lime orchards (Fig. 9)—as one visitor described it, a "vast garden … laden with the fruit of the lime or fragrant with its blossoms" (see Box K).

These were abrupt and rather short-lived transformations of the agricultural landscape of Montserrat. But they pale in comparison with the extent and severity of the changes effected by the introduction of slave-based, industrial-scale, sugar monocropping from the 1650s, aspects of whose story we relate in Chapters 6 through 8. To be farmed efficiently, sugar cane requires large fields cleared of all vegetation and planted in systematic rows, as well as tracks and roads to convey the cut cane stalks quickly to the processing works before they spoil. The imposition of this wholly artificial landscape on the natural environment of Montserrat's neotropical jungles, as on many other Caribbean islands in the 17th and 18th centuries, involved stupendous amounts of labor and effort, as well as the use of fire on an unprecedented scale. The felling, chopping, and ring-barking of trees was a continuous activity, and the smoke from charred logs and smoldering stumps probably resulted in lingering hazy conditions throughout the year. As a recent historian of fire in the Caribbean has written:

> Among the first sensations that some African slaves had of the Caribbean region, as they stumbled from the holds of slave vessels, were sights of smoky skies and smells from local clearing fires, initial sensual impressions that were in many ways accurate precursors of what the inferno of Caribbean slavery would be like.[19]

[18] Fergus 1994: 132–137.

[19] Richardson 2004: 28; Cherry 2018: 348–352.

At the height of the sugar-boom in the 18th century, some of these estates and their surrounding fields (at Locust Valley or Galways, for example) were established well up in the mountains at quite high elevations. But even in the earliest years of the industry, the sheer speed with which the natural landscape was demolished to make way for sugar is astonishing. We have visual proof of this in the 1673 Blathwayt map (see Box F) that—scarcely a generation after these clearances began—shows a mosaic of geometric cane fields already climbing high up the mountain slopes.

Fig. 9. An advertisement for Montserrat lime juice in The Bystander, *June 11, 1919.*

Were the landscapes on which the European planters wrought such destructive changes in their mad scramble for sugar-based profits themselves "natural"? And did they look like the secondary-regrowth forest that has in many areas now reclaimed land formerly cleared for sugar? As we discuss in Chapters 3 and 4, humans seem first to have set foot on Montserrat almost 5,000 years ago, although permanent settled village communities were probably not established until the middle of the 1st millennium BC. What impact did these Amerindians have on the environments that they exploited and on which they depended? For Montserrat, we lack data to answer this question, although we may guess that it was slight, considering that rather few prehistoric sites are known, and the population of individual settlements and of the island overall was probably quite modest. On other islands better information exists, most notably from a recent ambitious project in historical ecology that involved coring on multiple islands of the Lesser Antilles; it recovered data (such as pollen, plant phytoliths, molluscs, charcoal, and radiocarbon samples) that can speak to changes in the natural environment over long periods of time, including those that might be attributable to human hands. In some instances, the evidence points to the introduction of non-local plants and trees, the selective use or even "cultivation" of economically useful species, and sudden upticks in quantities of particulate charcoal that may indicate deliberate modification or clearance of the landscape with the help of fire. On a few islands, in fact, this evidence can be dated earlier than the current archaeologically accepted evidence for first colonization.[20] In other words, even thousands of years ago, once humans arrived on the islands, no environment remained entirely natural, and distinct changes would have been apparent—at least locally, in the vicinity of ancient settlements.

[20] Siegel *et al.* 2015; Siegel 2018; see Cherry 2018 for a summary.

This short discussion, in reverse chronological order, tries to drive home the point that we should not think of Montserrat's physical and natural environment as an unchanging, static backdrop against which its history and archaeology can be viewed. What has happened on the island, in terms of volcanic catastrophe in just the past generation, should suffice to disabuse anyone of that notion. But humans too create transformative effects, not always beneficial, and—as biogeographers have shown—on small islands these can have outsized impacts. We turn to the long-term archaeological history of people on Montserrat beginning in Chapter 3. But before we do so, we need first to give some account of the archaeological and historical heritage of the island: the information that now exists, the means by which it has been acquired, and the organizational structures for its preservation.

2. Archaeology and heritage on Montserrat

A little history of archaeology on Montserrat

The discipline of archaeology—at least, as a systematically organized historical science—is not very old. Of course, people in all ages have been aware of the physical traces of those who went before them. Antiquarians and a wide variety of other specialists in the material remains of the past have existed for hundreds, even thousands, of years, sometimes intervening on a large scale to retrieve objects for admiration, study, and display (for example, the excavations at Pompeii that began in the mid-18th century). But archaeology as we know it today is mainly a development of the 19th century, evolving hand-in-hand with the closely related field of geology, with which it shares many defining principles, such as the importance of context, dating, and the laws of stratigraphy. By now, archaeological investigations have taken place in every conceivable environment on earth, including the polar regions and the ocean depths. Nonetheless, the growth and spread of archaeological research has developed unevenly and at varying rates in different regions of the world.

This point is important to bear in mind when we turn to the archaeology of Montserrat and its wider context. In the Caribbean, while there were certainly some excavations and their publication in the late 19th and early 20th century (especially on the larger islands of the Greater Antilles), the widespread development of archaeology is something that happened only in the second half of the 20th century.[1] One index of that is the bibliography in the most recent synthesis of Caribbean prehistory, William F. Keegan and Corinne L. Hofman's book *The Caribbean before Columbus*, published in 2017: very few of its ca. 900 bibliographic references predate 1950, while over 80% are publications since 1980. Likewise, the body that represents the interests of Caribbean archaeologists—IACA, the International Association for Caribbean Archaeology, which organizes a congress on a different island every other year—was not formed until 1961.[2] On Montserrat, the non-governmental entity charged with the conservation and enhancement of the cultural and natural heritage of the island (the Montserrat National Trust [MNT], discussed

---

[1] Siegel 2013.

[2] These biennial meetings were initially termed the "International Congress for the Study of Pre-Columbian Cultures of the Lesser Antilles", but later expanded to embrace both the entirety of the Caribbean region and all periods of its archaeological history.

further below) was not established until 1970, and even today there is no professionally trained archaeologist permanently resident on the island.

An interest in the archaeological past of Montserrat is perhaps first seen early in the 20th century, when Seymour Wylde Howes, the owner at that time of the Trants Estate, created a collection of more than 1,000 Amerindian artifacts, gathered from the fields or found during the excavation of a number of burials. (Trants is the most thoroughly explored and best known of all the prehistoric sites on Montserrat, as well as an early and important sugar estate; we will refer to it frequently in the following pages.) Howes sold his collection to the Museum of the American Indian in New York City in 1924. It contained many ceramic *adornos* (see Box C), as well as hundreds of examples of beads manufactured from a wide variety of non-local stones (Fig. 10); the unique evidence these beads provided of an Amerindian "lapidary industry" at Trants prompted a brief publication that same year. The material was subsequently transferred to the Smithsonian's National Museum of the American Indian, where many years later it was studied and published by David Watters and Richard Scaglion.[3]

We know of no further archaeological activity on Montserrat until many decades later. In 1964, Walter Kenyon, from the Royal Ontario Museum (ROM), collected 395 potsherds and one shell item from the area at the mouth of the Belham River then being developed for the construction of a golf course (now totally destroyed by pyroclastic and laharic flows from the Soufrière Hills volcano). Lack of archaeological legislation allowed these finds to be taken to Canada and accessioned into the collections of the ROM, where they were studied 30 years later by James Petersen and David Watters; they noted among the sherds examples of White-on-Red (WOR) and Zone-Incised-Crosshatched (ZIC) styles, hallmarks of the Early Ceramic Saladoid prehistoric era.[4] Half a dozen years later, the British medieval archaeologist Colin Platt (University of Southampton), while on vacation on Montserrat, briefly excavated a test pit on the north side of the golf course, at the behest of the newly-established Montserrat National Trust. He retrieved both Amerindian and historic pottery, and filed a short report with the MNT.[5]

Almost another decade passed before the inception of two more formal, extended, research-driven archaeological projects: David Watters' survey of prehistoric sites in various parts of Montserrat (1978–1979), and Lydia Pulsipher and Conrad Mac Goodwin's excavations at the Galways Estate in southwestern Montserrat (starting in 1981). In the next few pages, to set the scene for later chapters, we summarize the archaeological work that has taken place over the

[3] Harrington 1924; Watters and Scaglion 1994; Watters 2010: 780.

[4] In this book, we have tried to limit the use of technical terms relating to archaeological cultures and their relative chronology, terms that are important to archaeologists, but probably tedious or confusing to non-specialists. Although our discussion of Montserratian prehistory is organized around its very broad division into the Archaic, Early Ceramic, and Late Ceramic periods, on occasion we need to be more specific. The mention here of the Saladoid series refers to the classificatory system introduced to Caribbean archaeology after World War II by Irving Rouse, in which peoples and cultures (referred to by the names of type-sites) are arranged in complex diagrams, with time on the vertical axis and space on the horizontal axis. Series names usually refer to characteristic types of artifacts (mainly pottery) found throughout a region or group of islands, often over fairly long periods of time. More local and shorter-lived expressions of material culture are described with sub-series names: thus, the Late Ceramic Age Troumassoid series that characterizes the Leeward and Windward Islands includes various sub-series (again named from type-sites), such as the Mamoran Troumassoid (after the Mamora Bay site on Antigua in the Leeward Islands) and the Suazan Troumassoid (after the Suazey site in Grenada in the Windward Islands). For an example of such taxonomic diagrams, see Rouse 1992: figs 14 and 15. Different classificatory schemes in Caribbean prehistory are described and critiqued in Keegan and Hofman 2017: 15–22.

[5] Watters 1980; Watters 2010: 781–782.

Fig. 10. Stone beads from the Trants lapidary industry, part of the Howes Collection now in the National Museum of the American Indian, Washington D.C.; among the raw materials identified are nephrite, diorite, turquoise, jade, serpentine, amethyst quartz, rock crystal quartz, and carnelian. (Modified from Watters and Scaglion 1994: fig. 16.)

course of the subsequent 40 years, starting with pedestrian surveys, and then turning to excavations (both research and rescue).

Surveys

Archaeologists are always on the lookout for sites and artifacts. For historical archaeologists working in the eastern Caribbean, the search has most often been driven by the desire to identify and document the remains of places listed or described in archival papers or indicated on maps and plans. One such documentation effort on Montserrat was the summary survey of plantation estates and their associated works throughout the island, conducted by the Oxford Archaeological Unit in 1995—fortuitously, immediately before many of them were buried, destroyed, or rendered inaccessible by the eruptions of the Soufrière Hills volcano, which began in July that same year.[6] Prehistorians, by contrast, have no such clues on which to rely, but have tended to focus their search for sites on coastal locations, knowing that on most islands of the Lesser Antilles the majority of Amerindian settlements have been found on or very near the shore, often where watercourses run down to the ocean. To give a Montserratian example, when the prehistorian Henri Petitjean Roget from Guadeloupe made a brief visit to the island in August 1978, he surveyed various areas of the coastline, with some success: he was responsible for the discovery of prehistoric remains at the Radio Antilles site at Old Fort Point in the extreme south of the island, the Little Bay site in the far northwest, and finds (including a human skull) of indeterminate date at Carr's Bay.[7]

Such work is not without value, but it is not led by clear research questions, nor does it aim at an island-wide understanding of the distribution, density, dates, and locational characteristics of sites. Quite different, therefore, was the survey project initiated by David Watters in the same year, as fieldwork for a doctoral dissertation at the University of Pittsburgh.[8] Characteristic of the so-called "New Archaeology" which dominated North American archaeology at the time his research was undertaken, there was an emphasis in Watters' fieldwork on hypotheses to be tested; an explicit, pre-formulated, multi-stage research design; the use of statistical sampling strategies; (mainframe) computer analysis of data; and so on. Watters' work on Montserrat was focused solely on prehistoric sites and, moreover, it was carried out in conjunction with a closely similar research design he employed at the same time on the utterly different low, limestone island of Barbuda. On both islands, he devised a scheme for pedestrian survey that involved examining a small sample of five 250 m-wide parallel transects laid out across the island east–west. Watters quickly came to realize that issues of inaccessibility, dense jungle, steep terrain, and poor ground visibility meant that the transect survey as originally planned could not be effectively implemented in a setting like Montserrat. He therefore limited his survey work to coastal areas and the lower flanks of the mountains. Ultimately he wound up including in his sample other known sites that did not fall within the survey transects. Even so, the total number of prehistoric sites discovered remained very small (five in all: Little Bay, Trants, Windward Bluff, Radio Antilles, and Dagenham Beach; see Fig. 21). He then moved to subsequent phases of his research design, involving test excavations, artifact analysis, and comparative evaluation of prehistoric settlement on Montserrat and Barbuda.

---

[6] *UPR* 30; Miles and Munby 2006.
[7] Watters 1980: 235–237; 2010: 784.
[8] Watters 1980.

Over 30 years later, a much more comprehensive regional survey project was undertaken by the present authors—the *Survey and Landscape Archaeology on Montserrat* (*SLAM*) project, whose fieldwork and research took place between 2010 and 2019.[9] Naturally, fieldwork in the aftermath of the 1995 volcanic crisis could only be undertaken in the northern portion of the island that lies outside the Exclusion Zone (whose boundary, however, has been somewhat relaxed in the course of the *SLAM* project: see Fig. 1), although the academic scope of the project was the whole island. A feature that distinguishes this project from almost all others in the Lesser Antilles (partly because it was jointly conceived by a prehistorian and an historical archaeologist) is that it concerns *all* periods of Montserrat's past, both before and after Columbus's world-changing arrival in the Caribbean in 1492. *SLAM*'s methods did not involve any formal sampling scheme, but simply a determined effort to survey all available parts of the island's north, to the extent that topography, accessibility, vegetation, and other factors allowed. The focus of data collection included not only sites (of which several dozen were newly discovered or further documented), but also hundreds of "features", a catch-all term for a wide variety of human interventions in the landscape, such as boundary walls, animal enclosures, rock-ovens, water-stones, field clearance cairns, lime kilns, small concentrations of artifacts, etc. (Fig. 11).

SLAM was designed as a multi-stage project. In its later phase, for example, attention was re-focused on the intensive examination—by further survey, excavation, geophysical analysis, geological sampling, and archival research—of three multi-period, microregional landscapes that had seen repeated occupation and activity during the long period from about AD 1000 to 1750 that saw settled Amerindian communities gradually impacted by, and entangling with, European settlers. While *SLAM* was initially conceived as a survey project, its goals led to research-oriented excavations at several sites (Valentine Ghaut, Indian Creek/Thatch Valley, Upper Blakes, and Potato Hill), as well as rescue archaeology, undertaken at the request of the MNT, at Rocklands, Glendon Hospital, and Gun Hill. Lastly, it is worth noting that, by comparison with the circumstances under which David Watters conducted his survey in the late 1970s, this 21st-century project was able to make use of a wide variety of advanced technologies for archaeological research—high-resolution satellite photographs, Geographical Information Systems, LiDAR imagery, and Unmanned Aerial Vehicles (Fig. 12). We briefly return to these methodological aspects below.

Excavations

Only four excavation projects on Montserrat have extended beyond one or two seasons of field-work—those at the plantation estates of Galways and Little Bay, the prehistoric site at Trants (which is also an important colonial-era estate), and at the historic sites atop Potato Hill (these excavations are discussed in more detail in Chapters 7 and 9).

Lydia Pulsipher and Conrad Mac Goodwin's work at Galways is perhaps the best known archaeological project on the island, largely because it ran for so many years and attracted many participants and visitors (even including the Rolling Stones while on the island in 1989 recording at AIR Studios). Excavations began in 1981 and continued into the 1990s, until they were brought to an abrupt halt by the 1995 eruptions whose impact on this part of the island

[9] Publications, unpublished reports, and conference presentations on the SLAM project are by now numerous. Among the more accessible overviews are Cherry *et al.* 2012; Cherry and Ryzewski 2014; Opitz *et al.* 2015; Ryzewski and Cherry 2012; 2015; 2016. Many articles and reports can be accessed via the project's website at: https://blogs.brown.edu/archaeology/fieldwork/montserrat/.

Fig. 11. Stone field-clearance cairns in the Old Quaw region of extreme northeastern Montserrat, an example of the many landscape features recorded by the SLAM project. (Photo: John Cherry.)

was especially devastating. The site is now believed to be either entirely buried or destroyed—at least, a low-level helicopter inspection of the site's location in 2018 could detect no remaining signs of this site.

Galways Estate was established by the Irish planter David Galway ca. 1660 and remained active as a sugar works until the mid-19th century. At about that time, a new sugar works was constructed several hundred meters downslope on land that was part of the original estate; this site ("Lower Galways") operated for sugar into the 1920s and also until World War II for cotton. Upper Galways was situated at relatively high altitude (ca. 350 m) above St Patrick's village, on the southwest flank of Soufrière Hills in a notably steep, arid, and relatively unproductive part of the island that was also the locus of Irish settlement from the 17th century. Clearance of vegetation from the site allowed it to be mapped in detail (see Box I), with scale drawings of individual structures. All of them were built in the 18th century, as indicated both by their elegant Georgian architectural style and masonry construction details and by excavated ceramics and glass which are mid-18th century at the earliest.

Fig. 12. Use of a drone to image excavations in progress at the 19th-century schoolhouse on Potato Hill in 2016. (Photo: John Cherry.)

No 17th-century artifacts have been found at the site, so exactly where David Galway established his original plantation is not known.[10]

No monograph or final report has yet appeared about the Galways archaeological project, and little of the artifactual assemblage has been studied or published.[11] Following a flurry of brief publications on Galways in the first several years of the project, Pulsipher's interests (as a cultural geographer) turned to related topics such as ridged-field agriculture, mountain gardens, slave provision grounds, and the informal slave market-economy. Goodwin, the project archaeologist, included a long and detailed chapter on Galways in his 1987 doctoral dissertation, and this provides the best information on the site, including its changing ownership between the 17th and 19th centuries, and technological modifications to the sugar works, illustrated with detailed drawings and photographs.[12]

A second Montserratian sugar estate at Delvins, about 4 km northwest of Galways, was also briefly excavated in the early 1990s by Jean Howson. In connection with her doctoral dissertation

[10] Goodwin 1987: 86 n. 6.

[11] The doctoral dissertation of Howson (1995) contains some quantified comparisons between ceramic assemblages from the Galways and Devlins estates, but none of it is illustrated.

[12] Goodwin 1987: 82–155. Shorter treatments of work at Galways: Goodwin 1982; Pulsipher 1982; 1983; 1991; Pulsipher and Goodwin 1982; 2001. More general articles on related topics: Pulsipher 1990; 1994; Pulsipher and Goodwin 1999.

she developed a comparative study of the internal economy of the plantation village in 18th and 19th century Montserrat, using archaeological data and historical sources from both Galways and Delvins. Limited archaeological testing took place at Delvins, comprising a number of small shovel-pits at regular intervals across the slope of the site, and six 3 × 3 ft test squares in an area thought to contain slave houses. The finds dated to the early 19th century and (in the case of the midden) the late 19th and early 20th century.[13] Building on Howson's earlier work, in 2019 Samantha Ellens began a new phase of excavations at Delvins as part of her doctoral dissertation research on the labor and economy of the post-emancipation citrus lime industry. Her excavations focused on the Great House's outbuildings, including a cistern and a kitchen, which may have housed late 19th-century laborers.

Investigations and excavations at a third sugar plantation in Little Bay in the island's extreme northwest have taken place over a number of years, with active fieldwork ending in 2012. Interest in this site began in 1981, when Lydia Pulsipher equated the ruins with those of the "house and plantation" of Captain William Carr, indicated on the famous 1673 *Blathwayt Atlas* map of Montserrat (see Box F).[14] This identification has since been questioned: Carr's plantation disappears from archival records by the end of the 17th century, no material predating the middle of the 18th century has been found in excavations at the Little Bay Estate, and the available documentary records indicate clearly that ownership of this estate in the 18th century was in the hands of several generations of the Piper and Allen families.[15] Given the topography and limited hospitable terrain in the Carr's Bay/Little Bay area, it is quite possible that the later managers of the Little Bay Estate reconfigured lands that were once part of Carr's plantation, in the process erasing traces of 17th-century dwellings and other structures. Nonetheless, because this heritage site lies squarely in the midst of proposed construction for the new capital town to replace Plymouth, efforts were made to preserve, study, and publicly interpret it. One significant step in March 2007 was the transfer from the Crown to the MNT, as a heritage site, of a 1.4-acre parcel of land containing the core of the 18th-century Little Bay Estate.

Limited test excavations were conducted here by Lydia Pulsipher and Mary Beaudry in 2005, and again in 2006–2007. Some of these test pits lay uphill from the main estate structures, in an area thought to be the location of slave residences, but lying outside the protected zone of the heritage site. This led to further rescue excavations with a larger crew in March 2007, but attempts to preserve this late 18th-century enslaved village were not successful (see Chapter 8). In the following months, it was bulldozed in preparation for road-building, although in the end a change of plan resulted in no road being placed there; today the area of the (destroyed) former village lies downslope from the road that connects the Cultural Centre and the Social Security Building.[16]

Beginning in 2010, excavations directed by Mary Beaudry, and from 2011 by her graduate student Jessica Striebel MacLean, were focused on the structural remains within the protected area of the Little Bay Estate. This work (the Little Bay Archaeology and Heritage Project) took place with significant involvement of students from the USA and Slovenia, as well as 6–10 students from the Montserrat Secondary School, and it was also supported by a Site Preservation

[13] Howson 1995: 81–127.
[14] Pulispher 1986: 67; 1987.
[15] *UPR* 10.
[16] *UPR* 6.

Grant from the Archaeological Institute of America (Fig. 13). Much of these efforts were directed at the full excavation of the Great House, which became the focus of MacLean's 2015 doctoral dissertation.[17] In addition to excavation, the site was also mapped in detail by Luke Pecoraro using differential GPS and subjected to a geophysical survey conducted by Thomas Urban. The outcome of all these investigations demonstrated that the plantation was constructed in the mid-18th century and saw various modifications before its destruction by fire in the final quarter of the century.

Fig. 13. Excavation of the Great House at the Little Bay Heritage Site, with volunteers from the Montserrat Secondary School. (Photo courtesy of Jessica Striebel MacLean.)

Unlike these historic plantation sites, no standing structures mark the major prehistoric site at Trants, but its extent and the abundance of artifacts on the surface (or brought to the surface by the plow) must mean that it had to have been obvious to the many generations of owners of the Trants Estate, whose buildings partly overlie it (Fig. 14). Trants is the most significant and thoroughly explored prehistoric site on Montserrat. We discuss it in more detail in Chapter 4 and elsewhere, and here we merely outline the various phases of work there. Serious exploration was begun by David Watters in 1979–1980, with a surface survey followed by excavation of a single 2 × 2 m unit; though modest in scope, this work yielded valuable data for studies of (for example) vertebrate fauna and pottery clay compositions.[18] Trants was revisited several times during the 1980s, leading on to a larger and more systematic project in 1990, directed by David Watters and James Petersen as a collaboration between the Carnegie Museum of Natural History and the University of Maine at Farmington. Excavation of 29 small test pits along "corridors" across the site, together with three 1 × 1 m excavation units, produced a much-enhanced understanding of the size and configuration of the site, and far larger artifactual and faunal samples. Additional ^{14}C dates showed Trants to be a very long-lived settlement (between about 480 BC and AD 420). Results were reported in a series of articles.[19]

Meanwhile, plans were being developed for extensions to the W.H. Bramble (also known as Blackburne) Airport that lay immediately to the east of Trants. In Spring 1995, the UK Overseas Development Administration funded a 17-week mitigation project to identify all sites within the airport development area and evaluate their significance.[20] At Trants itself, further test pit

[17] MacLean 2015. In the absence of a final site report, this dissertation is the best source for structure and site plans, but it does not include comprehensive artifact inventories. Some artifactual data from the Little Bay plantation is curated in DAACS, the Digital Archaeological Archive of Comparative Slavery (https://www.daacs.org/).

[18] Watters 1980; Steadman *et al.* 1984; Donahue *et al.* 1990.

[19] Watters 1994a; Reitz 1994; Watters and Scaglion 1994; Petersen 1996; Crock and Bartone 1998.

[20] Watters and Petersen 1999; for interim reports, see *UPR* 29.

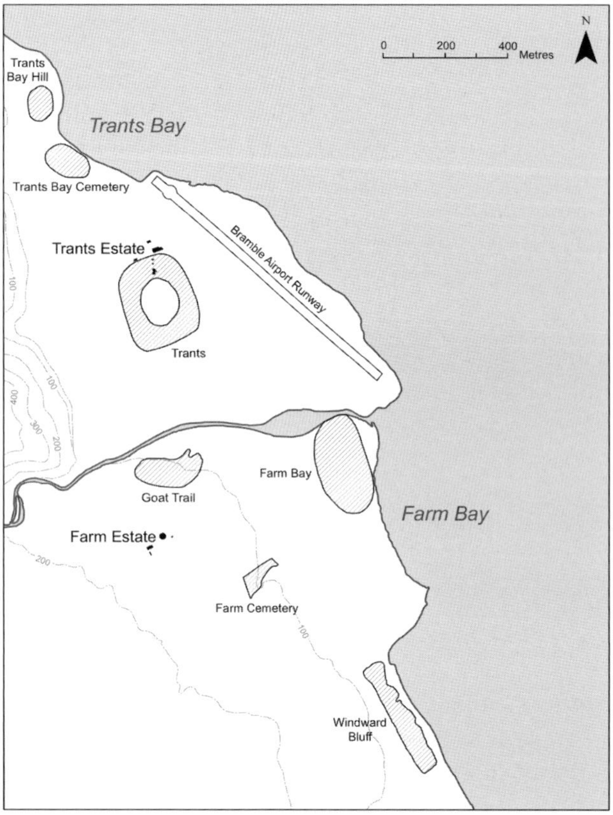

Fig. 14. Map of archaeological sites in the area of Trants in northeastern Montserrat. (Map by Miriam Rothenberg, based on data provided by David Watters.)

corridors were examined, along with additional closely-spaced excavation pits, the excavation of five long backhoe trenches cutting down through cultural deposits into geological strata beneath, and the mechanical stripping of an area of ca. 600 sq. m. This work showed the site to be slightly larger than previously thought (ca. 6.2 ha) and confirmed the settlement's configuration as oval-shaped, but with a different long-axis orientation. Features revealed included post-holes, pits, and seven human burials, widely distributed across the site. Within the wider zone of the airport development (Fig. 14), three new Late Ceramic prehistoric sites were located and tested, at Trants Bay Hill (north of the airport) and Farm Bay and Goat Trail (both immediately south of the Farm River, which ran to the south of Trants). In addition, historic-era sites were identified at Trants Bay Cemetery (perhaps the Trants Estate slave cemetery, where the skeleton of a young, adult male of African ancestry had been excavated in 1984), at Farm Cemetery (mid-18th century), and Canadiana (historic, but date unknown). The eruption of the Soufrière Hills volcano, beginning on 18 July 1995, terminated both archaeological research and airport expansion activities, and the Bramble Airport had to be abandoned in 1997. Catastrophic pyroclastic flows in February 2010 have left this entire area blanketed under many meters of ash, rock, and huge boulders (see Fig. 104).[21]

A variety of other short-term (sometimes rescue) excavations can be mentioned much more briefly.[22] These have been variable in quality and lacking in detailed documentation, although in some cases there exist short reports in the files of the MNT, with associated materials stored at the Montserrat National Museum in Little Bay. For example, in 1983 Liz Zabawski Gundy (a Peace Corps volunteer working with the MNT in the early 1980s) excavated at the 18th-century gun battery at Bransby Point, Montserrat's westernmost extremity, in order to unearth and remount several cannons.[23] Another volunteer, Bob Bell, conducted salvage excavations in 1984 at a late prehistoric site at Dagenham Beach in the town of Plymouth, where

[21] Watters and Norton 2007; for views of the Trants site before and after the 2010 pyroclastic flows, see Cherry *et al.* 2012: fig. 3.
[22] Much of this information is compiled in Watters 2010.
[23] *UPR* 2.

three units produced artifactual and human skeletal remains, the latter studied for a report to the MNT by Robert Mann.[24] In 1978–1979, as part of his survey for prehistoric sites on Montserrat, David Watters made surface collections at the Radio Antilles site in the island's extreme south, following up with the excavation of two test pits in 1979, and further collection of both prehistoric and historic materials in 1990. Shortly afterwards, in 1981, he dug test pits at the prehistoric site previously discovered by Henri Petitjean Roget near the coast in Little Bay, conducting further investigations along with James Petersen in the early 1990s; this site has now been totally destroyed by road construction. A more difficult piece of salvage fieldwork, spearheaded again by Watters, took place in 1979 at the Harney Site near Bransby Point, a later 18th-century cemetery disturbed by workers digging foundations for a house (see Chapter 8). Although excavation lasted only a few days and the site was very disturbed by construction activities, skeletal remains of 17 individuals and associated artifacts were of sufficient interest to result in several published papers on this site (which was interpreted as a slave cemetery).[25] Lastly, we again mention the range of excavations undertaken as part of the *SLAM* project under the auspices of the MNT between 2011 and 2017 at prehistoric and historic-period sites at Valentine Ghaut, Indian Creek, Thatch Valley, Upper Blakes, and Glendon Hospital, and historic sites at Rocklands, Gun Hill, and Potato Hill.

Sources of evidence for an archaeological history of Montserrat

In the popular imagination, archaeologists just dig. But even this brief sketch of how archaeology has developed on Montserrat makes it clear, we hope, that they do much more than that. And, for a variety of reasons, doing archaeology can be complicated, and the outcome sometimes less than ideal. Let us explain.

Sometimes, to be sure, an excavation project, undertaken primarily for research purposes, may continue for a number of seasons of fieldwork spread over a period of years: excavations at Trants began in 1979, for example, and at Upper Galways in 1981, both involuntarily terminated only by the start of the volcanic crisis in 1995. Such projects entail not only the painstaking process of contextual, stratigraphic excavation at the site, but also mapping, drawing, and other types of documentation; cleaning, photographing, drawing, and studying the artifactual finds in the comparative framework of what is known from other sites; and, in the case of historic-era sites, searching for maps, plans, drawings, archival documents and other historical records that may shed light on the site and its occupants. At some other sites, a research-driven excavation may be of much shorter duration, although these same standards of practice apply. This may be because the site is small or shallow, or it does not warrant the long-term investment of resources, or—most often—because of constraints of time, personnel, or funding. Examples on Montserrat include the excavations undertaken at the prehistoric sites of Radio Antilles, Little Bay, and Indian Creek. Sometimes, brief, small-scale digs may occur at the same site over several years, as was the case at Valentine Ghaut, where coastal erosion progressively revealed several midden-pits that merited immediate excavation before their inevitable destruction by the next season's storms.

---

24 *UPR* 3; *UPR* 4.

25 Watters 1981; 1987; 1994b; Mann *et al.* 1987; Petersen and Watters 1988; Petersen *et al.* 1999a.

Yet much of our knowledge of Montserrat's archaeology has come from necessarily hasty interventions at sites being damaged or threatened with imminent destruction. Here, archaeologists must make the best of things in less than ideal circumstances. David Watters gives a vivid description, for example, of conditions at the Harney Cemetery site, where a small team of local volunteers had to work in cramped builders' trenches, with very limited time to attend to each next burial brought to light by the construction workers.[26] As discussed below, a particular difficulty in dealing with the urgent needs of rescue archaeology on Montserrat is that there is no permanent archaeologist on the island. The MNT has always needed to rely on help from visiting archaeologists to attend to these situations.

For archaeology, the volcanic crisis of the past two decades has had doubly unfortunate effects. On the one hand, as David Watters and Gillian Norton have documented in detail (see Fig. 103), large numbers of sites, both historic and prehistoric, in what is now the Exclusion Zone have been buried, damaged, destroyed, or rendered inaccessible for the foreseeable future.[27] On the other hand, the forced movement of population to the island's north and the creation of new refugee settlements there (at Lookout, Drummonds, and Davy Hill; see Fig. 101), the building of roads and other infrastructure to serve their needs, and especially the extensive construction projects associated with the development, from scratch, of a new capital town at Little Bay/Carr's Bay have led to damage or destruction (or the threat of destruction) to many sites. It is difficult, if not impossible, to forestall these impacts on archaeological resources, if there is no clear prior knowledge of where archaeological remains are to be found in the first place. Indeed, it was the lack of maps or up-to-date lists to provide such knowledge that served as one catalyst for the inception of *SLAM*—which, while primarily a research-driven, multi-period, regional survey project, also aimed to provide information to the MNT and the government's Physical Planning Unit in order to help limit archaeological damage. Survey archaeology, just as much as excavation, can be undertaken for rescue purposes.

These good intentions notwithstanding, development has continued to have negative effects on the preservation of Montserrat's heritage. Several sites in the north have been impacted or completely destroyed by development-related activities over the past decade, including the aforementioned prehistoric site and enslaved laborers' village site at Little Bay, as well as part of an 18th-century structure on top of Potato Hill, an 18th-century Gun Battery at the south end of Carr's Bay, and an Archaic-period site at Upper Blakes. Such events are likely to continue, in the absence of an archaeologist on hand to consult and advise. But we reserve a more detailed discussion of the impacts of development and volcanic activity on the preservation of archaeological heritage sites until Chapter 10.

So far as recording and expanding knowledge of the history and heritage of Montserrat is concerned, there are two welcome advances worth briefly noting here. First, archaeology itself has not stood still over the course of the roughly half century of archaeological endeavors on Montserrat, and fieldwork on the island today is conducted with the assistance of methods, resources, and technologies undreamt of in the 1970s. It takes an effort of imagination to appreciate that landscape survey at that time took place without the availability of hand-held global positioning system (GPS) devices, high-resolution satellite imagery, or laptop computer-based geographical information systems (GIS), all of which are now ubiquitous and affordable. Accurately recording the location of a site in the landscape then required diligent map-reading skills (although the available maps for Montserrat, produced by the UK Ordnance Survey, were excellent).

---

[26] Watters 1987.
[27] Watters and Norton 2007.

In the past decade of work on Montserrat, a variety of technological innovations has been deployed for archaeological purposes. These include: the use of differential GPS for high-resolution mapping of the Little Bay Estate and numerous other sites recorded by the *SLAM* project; geophysical survey techniques to detect and plot sub-surface structures at the Little Bay Estate; the aerial imaging of several historic and prehistoric sites using a drone; the analysis and ground-truthing of LiDAR imagery, especially in the Centre Hills (see Box A), but now also elsewhere in the Exclusion Zone; photogrammetric modeling and 3-D imaging of both site features and individual artifacts; the use of advanced relational databases to record project data and museum holdings; and, of course, the general environment of the internet and the access it provides to relevant information of all kinds, including searchable databases such as DAACS, the Digital Archaeological Archive of Comparative Slavery.

The other development that is important to touch upon here concerns the historical archival resources of relevance to Montserrat. Inevitably, almost four centuries of British governance of the island have left a rich and detailed residue of official documents, letters, reports, and statistical summaries. Most of them are today to be found in official repositories in the United Kingdom, such as the British Library, the Foreign and Commonwealth Office, and, especially, the National Archives at Kew in London. These, together with other important archives such as the papers of 17th-century Governor William Stapleton and his descendants (now in the Rylands Library at the University of Manchester), have provided the main sources of evidence on which those writing on Montserrat's earlier history have drawn.[28]

Montserrat too, of course, has its own records. Unfortunately, the hasty evacuation of Plymouth in the mid-1990s led to these being in some cases abandoned and subsequently destroyed, or else dispersed to inadequate facilities in the north. The principal archives are held by the Montserrat Public Library and the MNT,[29] but other documents in abundance have recently been retrieved from poor storage by the Registrar's Office, while significant records held by various churches on the island are only now beginning to be explored. Impetus for the recovery, conservation, proper storage, and digitization of these archival resources was provided in 2014 by a pilot project of the Endangered Archives Programme of the British Library, working in collaboration with the MNT.[30] This work is ongoing, resulting in an ever-growing body of digitized historical documents that have not previously been available for the study of Montserratian history. Important materials have also newly become available, such as the collection of documents, letters, maps, and photographs relating to the Sturge family, prominent on the island in the later 19th and early 20th centuries.[31] Other off-island archives, too, have increasingly been brought into play, such as those in the Lamont Library at Harvard University and in the Antigua and Barbuda National Archives.[32] In short, a new

[28] *E.g.* Wheeler 1988; Fergus 1994; Akenson 1997.
[29] Archival records in both the Montserrat Public Library and the Montserrat National Trust have been studied, as part of the *SLAM* project, under the primary direction of Laura McAtackney; summaries of this work can be found in *UPR* 18; *UPR* 19; *UPR* 28.
[30] https://eap.bl.uk/project/EAP769. The online report on the EAP pilot project provides an in-depth account of surviving archives and the work that was carried out to assess, list and re-house the material, together with access to digitized documents that have so far been made available.
[31] *PS MNT* 61.
[32] Antigua was the seat of the Governor of the British Leeward Island Colonies who had responsibility for Montserrat and thus served as the go-between for correspondence and dispatches to and from London and the Governor and House of Assembly on Montserrat.

Box A: Airborne LiDAR on Montserrat

Archaeological survey on Montserrat is very challenging. Much of the island is covered with tropical forest (mostly secondary re-growth, following the abandonment of colonial-era sugar cane fields) or with dense, tangled stands of thorny acacia bushes and manchineel trees that ooze a sap that causes dangerous skin-burns. The ground surface, too, often offers very limited visibility, on account of leaf litter or thick deposits of volcanic ash. How helpful it would be if these impediments to archaeological inspection could somehow be removed!

LiDAR (short for Light Detection and Ranging) offers one way to do so. Data are captured by an airborne vehicle—usually a light aircraft, but now often a drone—which emits pulsed laser light towards the ground many times per second. Some of these signals hit the top of the jungle canopy or bushes in the understory, but others penetrate all the way down to the ground. Differences in laser return times and wavelengths, recorded by sensors in the aircraft, measure the relative distance to the target and can be used to make digital 3-D representations of the earth surface. It is thus possible, digitally, to strip away all vegetation to reveal a "bare earth" image, although it is often more informative to use the data "point cloud" to model features both on and close to the ground surface. LiDAR technology has been used to spectacular effect, garnering major media attention, in recent years in the jungles of Central America, where for example the unsuspected extent and complexity of Mayan centers have been revealed with startling clarity.[i]

The Montserrat Volcano Observatory in 2010 commissioned the collection of LiDAR imagery over the southern two-thirds of the island for the purpose of monitoring volcanic risk—specifically, the development of more precise models to predict the likely impacts of future volcano collapses. The *SLAM* project was generously allowed access to these data and it used them to explore the landscapes of sugar estates high in the forests of the Centre Hills. Color images of the processed data were used to help guide fieldwalkers to possible human-made features for in-person verification (sometimes called "ground-truthing") during subsequent survey hikes.

Dozens of previously unknown landscape modifications were recorded with the assistance of processed LiDAR imagery at the Waterworks, Locust Valley, and Fairy Walk estates. They included walls, terraces, trackways, ditches, ponds, built structures, even stone windmill towers

Fig. 15. LiDAR cross-section of the windmill tower at Fairy Walk. (Image created by Athena Zissis.)

standing as high as 8 m (Fig. 15). In addition, LiDAR made it possible to examine detailed 3-D images of sugar estate works in areas overrun by pyroclastic flows and still far too dangerous to visit, such as at the Bugby Hole Estate (Fig. 16).

This work on Montserrat represents the first use of airborne LiDAR for archaeological research purposes anywhere in the Caribbean.[ii]

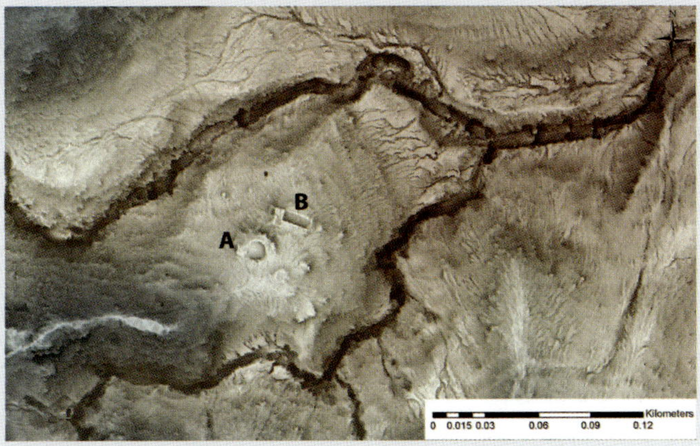

Fig. 16. LiDAR view of the Bugby Hole Estate sugar works. The base of a windmill tower (A), a boiling house (B), and other built structures nearby are clearly visible, even though the ground is covered with ash and obscured by trees felled by pyroclastic flows. (Image created by Rachel Opitz and Miriam Rothenberg.)

[i] *e.g.* Chase *et al.* 2010; 2011.
[ii] Opitz *et al.* 2015.

era is opening up in terms of the quantity and variety of primary records that are available for the study of Montserrat in the colonial period. We draw on them where appropriate in our account of Montserrat's archaeological history.

Archaeology and heritage management on Montserrat

We turn lastly to a brief consideration of the organizational structure of archaeology and cultural heritage management on Montserrat: how it has developed and how it looks at present.

No formal body nor any legislation seems to have existed to protect and preserve Montserrat's cultural heritage until about fifty years ago. That changed with the creation, by statute, in February 1970 of the Montserrat National Trust, then based in the former capital town of Plymouth. Both the name and the objectives of the MNT obviously derive from its English parent organization, The National Trust for Places of Historic Interest or Natural Beauty (to give its name in full), established in 1895 and now one of the largest landowners in the United Kingdom. National Trust bodies exist on a number of the other Caribbean islands that remain British Overseas Territories (Anguilla, Bermuda, British Virgin Islands, Cayman Islands, and Turks and Caicos) or that were formerly British colonies (*e.g.* Jamaica, St Lucia). These, and other preservation societies in the Caribbean, have recently begun to hold joint conferences to discuss challenges and present successes in developing a sustainable heritage economy.

All of these entities are not-for-profit non-governmental organizations. They have as their core mission the twin goals of protecting, preserving, and promoting for present and future generations (a) cultural and historic heritage, and (b) natural biodiversity. To quote the MNT's mission in full:

> The Trust's main objectives are: to conserve and enhance the beauty of Montserrat; to preserve and rehabilitate historical sites, including but not limited to buildings, monuments, documents, chattels etc.; to preserve the fauna and flora of Montserrat; to make the public aware of the value and beauty of the island's heritage; to pursue a policy of preservation and act in an advisory capacity; to acquire property for the benefit of the island; to attract funds by means of subscriptions, donations, bequests and grants for the effective carrying out of these objectives; to compile photographic and architectural records of the above.[33]

These are ambitious aims for an organization whose operating income is small, derived from funds provided by the Government of Montserrat, fund-raising events, donations, membership fees, projects, and occasional grants from British or European Union agencies. It suffices to support only a small staff, at present comprised of an Executive Director, an Office Manager, an Exhibition/Library Assistant, and two Gardeners/Trail Guides, plus assistance from a few interns and temporary placements. Organizational oversight is provided by a volunteer ten-person Executive Board, whose members also staff several more specialized committees that function to promote the MNT's mandate. Only one of these—the Historical, Archaeological, and Museum Committee—directly concerns cultural heritage.

The MNT's limited resources have never allowed the luxury of a professionally-trained archaeologist or heritage specialist on its staff (nor is any such person employed by the Government of Montserrat). In its early days prior to the 1995 volcanic eruptions, the MNT established and maintained a modest archaeological and historical museum on the three floors of the former sugar estate windmill at Richmond Hill on the northern edge of Plymouth, overseen by a separate Museum Head (Fig. 17). This older museum was evacuated during the early stages of the volcanic crisis in 1996, with help from MNT volunteers, assisted by several overseas and regional organizations, including the Museums Association of the Caribbean (founded in 1987). The MNT itself relocated to a new building in Olveston that offers limited exhibition and storage space, and it was not until 2012 that a purpose-built new Montserrat National Museum was opened, in a space immediately adjacent to the cricket pitch and the Little Bay Heritage Site, as part of the development plans for the new island capital at Little Bay/Carr's Bay (see Figs 107 and 108). This has been a welcome addition: all of the archaeological materials held by the MNT were transferred to storage at the Museum in 2017, and a variety of rotating exhibitions on aspects of the heritage and history of Montserrat has been on display over the past several years. At the same time, no additional financial support for maintaining the Museum has become available to the MNT, which must now split its activities between its headquarters (and associated botanical garden) in Olveston and the Museum in Little Bay.

Much of the MNT's time and effort, therefore, is devoted to natural, rather than cultural heritage—the ongoing, daily tasks of maintaining and developing its botanical garden, keeping open the network of nature-hiking trails in the Centre Hills, mounting exhibitions on biodiversity, organizing an annual Flower Show, developing a plant nursery to promote the propagation and planting of native species on the island, and many other such activities. In light of its close relations with organizations back in the United Kingdom, the Trust also regularly collaborates with and hosts research teams from the Royal Society for the Protection of Birds, Kew Gardens in London, and the Durrell Wildlife Conservation Trust in censuses of flora and fauna, and efforts to recuperate critically endangered populations such as the Montserrat Oriole and Mountain Chicken.

[33] MNT website at http://montserratnationaltrust.ms/about-us/.

A recent partnership with the Waitt Institute, the Blue Halo Initiative, is intended to help develop sustainable policies for the conservation and management of marine life in Montserratian waters.

Fig. 17. The Richmond Hill historic windmill, used as a museum until the evacuation of Plymouth in 1996. (Photo by John Cherry.)

Relatively little attention, however, is paid to the preservation (let alone the acquisition) of historic properties or the protection of archaeological sites, and the MNT conducts no archaeological activities on its own account, not having trained staff to do so. Almost all research is currently conducted by off-island archaeologists. It takes place under the eye of the MNT and by permission of its Director, who affords assistance in many ways (for example, by arranging connections with relevant government officials or local landowners). Foreign archaeologists have, over the past forty years, been responsible for identifying 119 archaeological sites around the island, each with a unique inventory number assigned to it by the MNT, and accompanying documentation about the location's setting, material remains, and age. Of the sites identified to date, 55 have been further examined in some capacity, and artifacts from these investigations are curated at the Montserrat National Museum.[34] In short, long-standing collaborations between the MNT and foreign researchers have been mutually beneficial: new sites are discovered and explored, the Montserrat National Museum's collections are augmented, and the expertise of professional archaeologists has not infrequently been co-opted to take preventive action at local sites which are threatened by development or to assist in the development of exhibitions.

[34] The entire collection of artifacts then stored at the MNT (now at the National Museum) was examined in 2011, resulting in the re-bagging and re-boxing of materials, and the creation of a new database for the MNT's use; for details, see *UPR* 8.

Lastly, what are the laws that govern cultural heritage and archaeological activity on Montserrat? They are to be found in Chapter 8.03 of the Laws of Montserrat, the Physical Planning Act and Subsidiary Legislation, which came into force in May 1996 and was revised in 2002 and again in 2008.[35] Part VI (Sections 35–55) concerns "Historic Buildings, Historic Sites, and Artifacts". It prescribes a "Planning and Development Authority" (a board comprised largely of heads of government departments, chaired by the Permanent Secretary in the Ministry responsible for the environment), which—in consultation with the MNT and other knowledgeable bodies or persons—is charged with drawing up a list of buildings, sites, and artifacts "which appear to be of special architectural, historical, traditional, cultural, archaeological, or palaeontological interest", accompanied by a map and descriptions (Section 35.1). The Act goes on to enumerate regulations governing such matters as acquiring or modifying historic buildings, undertaking archaeological excavation, and exporting artifacts from Montserrat.

The Physical Planning Act has more than a whiff of cumbersome and unenforceable legislation drawn up by civil servants back in the United Kingdom with little knowledge or appreciation of actual circumstances on Montserrat. To give one example (Section 47), a person accidentally discovering an artifact is required to report it to the Authority within 7 days, or face a fine of $1,000 or imprisonment for 3 months. Since the collection of archaeological finds on Montserrat is a practice going back at least to the early years of the 20th century and many Montserratians today have collections in their personal possession (sometimes on open display in their homes or offices), it is obvious that Section 47 has never been enforced. Likewise (under Section 46), anyone wishing to conduct excavation must be granted a permit by the Governor in Council, after consultation with the Authority and the MNT to ensure that the work is necessary in the national interest and that the person has appropriate qualifications and experience. So far as we know, these steps have never been followed and, in any case, as described earlier in this chapter, rather few excavations have ever taken place on the island. The Physical Planning Act has been more honored in the breach than the observance, and it seems to us to have little relevance to current archaeology and heritage on Montserrat.

In this chapter, we have sketched the development of archaeological enquiry and fieldwork on Montserrat, touched on what this fieldwork has entailed and how it has changed over the years, and outlined the structures and mechanisms that govern heritage research and preservation. We can now turn to give an account of the archaeological history of the island, beginning—as is appropriate—with the very earliest evidence of a human presence on Montserrat.

---

35 Physical Planning Act 2008.

3. First humans on Montserrat

Islands are among the last environments on earth to have been visited or settled by humans. In many parts of the world, in fact, the peopling of islands did not happen until the Holocene—that is, during the last 10,000 years—an epoch characterized by rising sea levels and the current warmer period following the last glaciation. There are exceptions, of course. Archaeological evidence found on Flores (Indonesia) is more than one million years old; the latest discoveries in Australia show Aboriginal people, who would have needed to cross water to reach it, to have been there for at least 65,000 years; earliest human movements into Near Oceania began about 40,000 years ago.[1] Some of the larger islands in the Mediterranean have likewise produced indications of human occupations that are tens of thousands of years old and, in one instance (Crete), perhaps even well over a hundred thousand; but in some of these very early examples, the evidence is ambiguous or controversial.[2] At the other end of the temporal spectrum, islands in the mid- and south Atlantic, or in Remote Oceania (such as Hawai'i, Easter Island, and New Zealand) were discovered and settled only within the last millennium or so.

This is the backdrop against which we should consider the current evidence that humans did not move to any Caribbean island until relatively recently, about 7,000 years ago; but of course the peopling of the North and South American continents as a whole happened earlier, about 15,000 years ago. The first island in the Caribbean to be settled prehistorically was Trinidad, where the sites of Banwari Trace and St John date to about 8,000–7,800 years before the present (6000 BC or later). This evidence is slightly misleading, however, since sea levels were still rising at that time and the island could probably have been reached without the use of watercraft. The real settlement of the Antilles began sometime between 7,000 and 5,500 years ago (5000–3500 BC), the earliest sites being on Cuba and Hispaniola. This "Lithic" or "Archaic" Age (the two terms are now generally conflated) lasted an extraordinarily long time, until and even after horticulturalists

[1] Kirch 2010; Dennell *et al.* 2013.

[2] Strasser *et al.* 2010; Leppard and Runnels 2017; Cherry and Leppard 2018.

began to arrive in the area in the middle of the 1st millennium BC.[3] Archaic-period settlement sites in the Lesser Antilles are still rather few in number and they have very disparate dates; examples are mainly in the northern islands, including Anguilla, Antigua, Barbuda, Nevis, Saba, St Kitts, St Maarten, and St Thomas.[4]

How does Montserrat fit within this picture? What, when, and where on the island is the earliest evidence of human activity? Who were these people and where did they come from? Until very recently, the answer to such questions would have pointed to the Trants site on the northeastern coast, close to the former (now destroyed) Bramble airport. As noted in Chapter 2, excavations conducted there in the 1980s and 1990s by David Watters and his colleagues revealed a long-lived, Amerindian agricultural settlement first established around the middle of the 1st millennium BC.[5] Trants became a well-known site, often mentioned in the Caribbean archaeological literature, because its oldest radiocarbon date of ca. 2,450 years ago (500 BC) put it among the earliest known examples of the influx of pottery-making horticultural people who began to colonize some of the eastern Caribbean islands, almost certainly from northeastern coastal South America, during the 1st millennium BC.[6] We discuss the Trants site in more detail in the next chapter.

But we now know, based on recent findings, that humans were present on Montserrat more than 2,000 years before Trants was first settled. As is more often the case in archaeology than we sometimes care to admit, serendipity played an important role in this new discovery.

When our *SLAM* project began its work on the island in 2010, we noticed among the archaeological materials curated by the Montserrat National Trust a small box of uncatalogued artifacts that included a few large flakes and blades (*i.e.* sharp-edged flakes, more than twice as long as wide, with roughly parallel edges) that were clearly made using the distinctive gray-brown chert that is to be found on Long Island off the northeastern coast of Antigua (see Box B). Unfortunately, all that was known about these artifacts was that they had been found somewhere in the Centre Hills, an area of over a dozen square kilometers of steep and relatively inaccessible jungle-covered slopes (Fig. 3). A more systematic survey of the National Trust's collections a year later,[7] however, brought to light a small bag containing similar lithic materials, but this time with an accompanying note indicating that they had been collected in 2000 by David Watters at a garden plot on the northeastern slopes of Centre Hills. The co-ordinates provided in the note allowed this findspot to be relocated.[8]

This location (Upper Blakes) is rather unusual, by contemporary Montserratian standards. Following the devastating (and ongoing) volcanic crisis that began in July 1995, Upper Blakes became one of the very few locations on the island where open-field agriculture is conducted over

[3] Hofman and Antczak 2019.
[4] For the most recent overviews of the early settlement of the Caribbean, see Fitzpatrick 2015: 307–311; Keegan and Hofman 2017: 23–50.
[5] Watters 1994a; Watters and Petersen 1999.
[6] Fitzpatrick 2015: table 1. The radiocarbon dates from Trants are presented in Watters 1994a: 283–289, table 2; Haviser 1997: 61.
[7] *UPR* 9.
[8] This discovery is briefly mentioned in Watters 2010: 783–784.

Box B: Long Island, Antigua: Montserrat's source of Chert

The Lesser Antilles, the distinctive curved chain of islands in the eastern Caribbean, form a volcanic arc, where the oceanic crust of the South American Plate is subducting under the Caribbean plate, forming a string of volcanic islands (Fig. 1). Seventeen volcanoes—including, of course, Soufrière Hills on Montserrat—are currently active. In many parts of the world, volcanoes produce the (usually) black, shiny glass called obsidian which, when fractured, provides edges as sharp as surgical steel. The volcanic geology of the Caribbean, however, is not conducive to its formation, and major obsidian flows are not known on any island.[i] Had tool-quality obsidian been generally available, we can be sure that Amerindian peoples would have made use of it; but only traces of poor-grade material has been found in proximity to their sites to date.

Other types of stone, therefore, served as raw material for tool-making. The most important of these is chert (also called flint), and the pre-eminent source of tool-quality chert in the Lesser Antilles is found on Long Island, just off the northeast coast of Antigua (Fig. 18). Chert occurs here because—unlike Montserrat, which is almost entirely volcanic—Antigua has a more mixed geology, with both volcanic rocks and uplifted limestone strata within which the chert formed. While chert originates in various parts of Antigua, very homogenous chert that was highly suitable for making tools occurs in greatest abundance on Long Island, especially at the appropriately named Flinty Bay on its northern coast. A Dutch team from Leiden University investigated archaeological sites and chert resources on Long Island in the late 1980s, and carried out excavations at Flinty Bay—in the nick of time, before resort and villa development obliterated what was left to be seen. They reported enormous quantities of flaking debris—the byproducts of people in the past making large cores from raw nodules of the distinctive gray-brown-yellowish chert. After initial processing, people transported the chert cores away from Flinty Bay for further working and use elsewhere.[ii]

Fig. 18. Long Island, Antigua; most travelers flying to Montserrat from the airport in Antigua pass close by Long Island on the left side of the aircraft. (Photo: Krysta Ryzewski.)

The existence on Antigua of this abundant source of superior-quality chert seems to have been known even to the first settlers

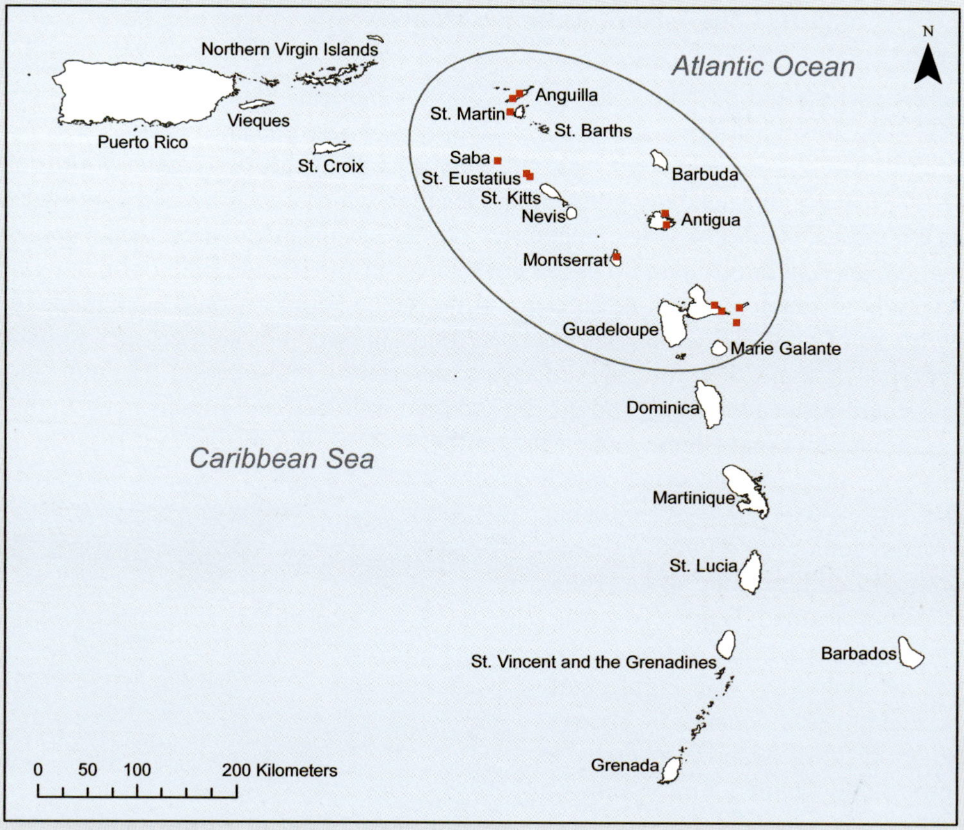

Fig. 19. Map showing the distribution of Long Island chert in the northern Lesser Antilles ca. AD 850–1250. (After Knippenberg 2006: fig. 6.3, adapted and updated by Miriam Rothenberg.)

in the eastern Caribbean, since it is found at a number of the earliest Archaic-period sites (among them, now, Upper Blakes on Montserrat). Another Dutch archaeologist, Sebastiaan Knippenberg, has in recent years studied the distribution of Long Island chert, as well as other stone materials, at sites (mainly of Ceramic Age) throughout the Lesser Antilles, backing up his identifications with scientific sourcing of the raw materials using techniques such as neutron activation analysis and petrographic thin-sections.[iii] It is clear that crucial raw materials such as chert were not available everywhere and had to be obtained from other islands, either by trade and exchange, or by mounting a canoe expedition to acquire it at the source itself. The changing patterns in the occurrence of Long Island chert over time go a long way towards mapping networks of inter-island relationships and the mechanisms that underlie them (Fig. 19).

[i] Christian Stouvenot has informed us that a small, localized outcropping of dacitic obsidian exists on Guadeloupe which is currently under investigation.
[ii] Van Gijn 1993.
[iii] Knippenberg 2006; 2011.

Fig. 20. View to the north over the cultivated fields of Upper Blakes. (Photograph: John Cherry.)

an extensive area. The agricultural land contains two dozen vegetable fields, all cultivated by hoe in a bank-and-furrow system (Fig. 20). The lack of weeds and other obscuring vegetation as a result of continuous and intensive cultivation produced excellent surface visibility conditions that allowed a thorough archaeological surface survey of the entire field system in 2012, with partial re-examination in 2016 and 2017.

The landscape setting of Upper Blakes is also anomalous (Fig. 21). On islands of the Lesser Antilles, the vast majority of Amerindian sites are on, or very close to, the coast. The Upper Blakes site, by contrast, lies well inland, in the foothills of the Centre Hills, and at fairly high elevation (well over 300 m above sea level). It is on a ridge, demarcated by two deeply incised *ghauts* (watercourses), that begins high in the Centre Hills and ends, much lower down, at the historically important colonial-era plantation site of Blakes Estate. The cultivated lands of this estate evidently continued a long way upslope to its south. Several of the surveyed fields at Upper Blakes contain abundant historic-era artifacts, mainly of mid- to late 18th-century date, and it seems likely that this was an area once occupied and cultivated by enslaved laborers on the Estate.[9] We deal with this phase of Montserrat's archaeological history in Chapters 6–8; here we focus only on the remains that date to a far more remote era, over 4,000 years earlier.

---

[9] *UPR* 23; Cherry and Ryzewski 2019; Ryzewski and Cherry 2019.

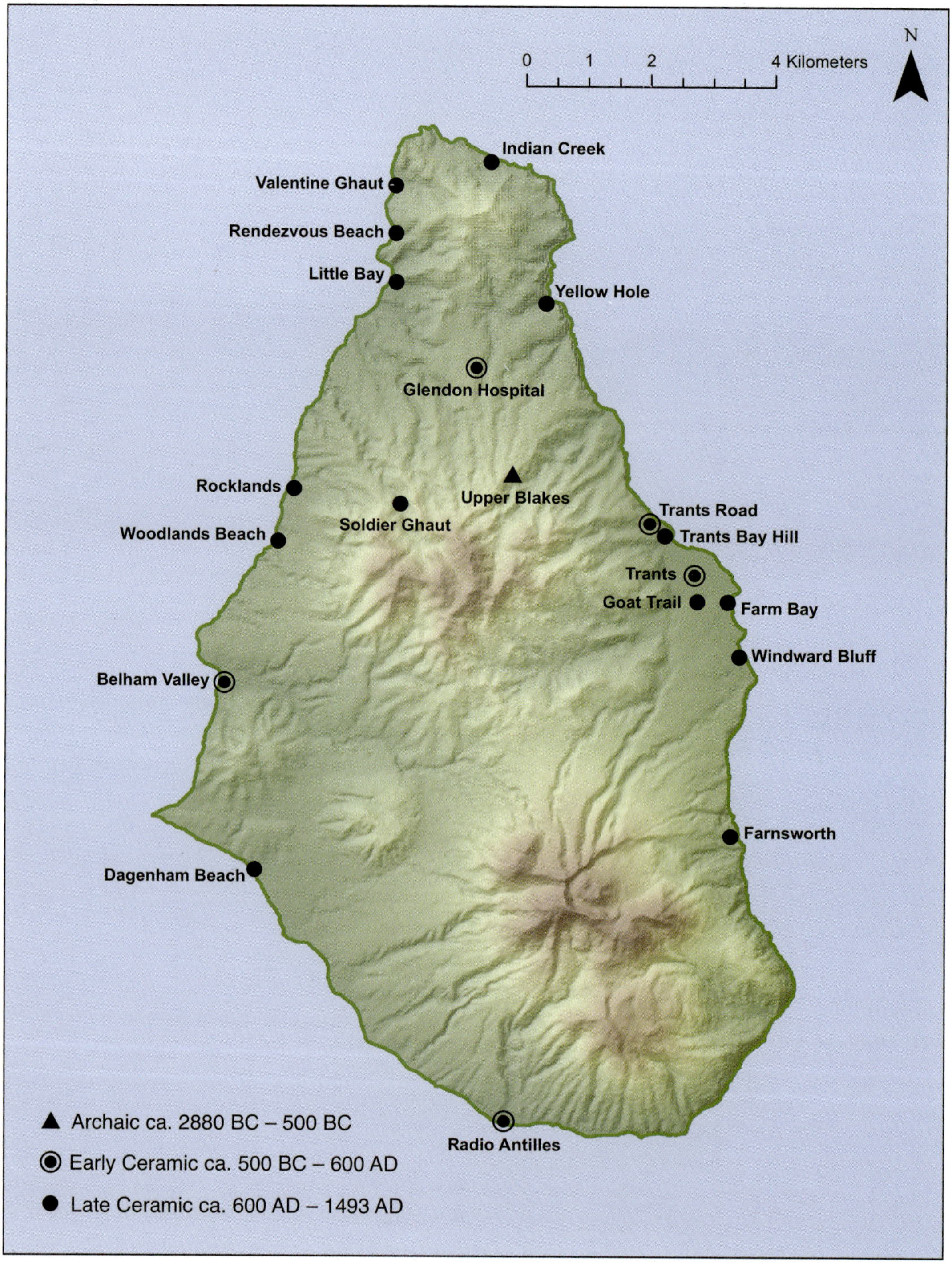

Fig. 21. Map of Montserrat, showing all known prehistoric sites of Archaic, Early Ceramic, and Late Ceramic date. (Map by Miriam Rothenberg; base map from Wadge 1988, provided by the Montserrat Volcano Observatory.)

What makes Upper Blakes the earliest known archaeological site on Montserrat?

Upper Blakes is almost certainly a special-purpose site, not a place of permanent settlement. Survey (and four excavated test pits) recovered no groundstone, bone, shell, or coral tools, no plant or animal remains, nor any prehistoric pottery. The sole category of find was chipped stone (lithics)—a large collection of 722 pieces, most (probably all) of chert from Long Island, Antigua. These artifacts were found widely scattered across the fields of Upper Blakes, but with a markedly dense concentration in one specific area (Field 2, Feature 206) that was evidently an *in situ* knapping area. What can be inferred from these finds and how can they be dated?

To turn to the latter question first, we have an absolute date for the site. A probe beneath the modern ground surface at the center of Feature 206 retrieved a sample of charred organic material that was submitted for radiocarbon analysis. The result, after calibration, is a date that has a 95% likelihood of falling between 2880 and 2625 cal BC.[10] This is over 2,000 years older than any other site currently known on Montserrat. In fact, it is among the earliest dates reported from anywhere in the Lesser Antilles for the first Archaic phase of colonization and settlement.

One would wish for more than a single radiocarbon date from a site of such significance both for Montserratian history and the wider framework of eastern Caribbean prehistory. Still, the lithic finds themselves can tell us a great deal about their technology, likely age, resource exploitation, inter-island voyaging, and more.[11] To begin with the obvious, this industry employs raw material brought in from elsewhere (Antigua): Montserrat, being an entirely volcanic island, has no usable chert sources. (Whether people resident on Montserrat traveled to Antigua to collect chert, or people from Antigua crossed over to Montserrat bringing it with them, is a matter discussed below.) It is certain, however, that knapping took place on the spot at Upper Blakes. How can we be sure? The majority of the lithics still show parts of the original exterior surface (the *cortex*) of the raw nodule, and unmodified lumps of chert weighing nearly one-third of a kilogram have been encountered. Equally telling is the fact that survey and test excavations have recovered numerous minute waste flakes from knapping (*débitage*), many weighing less than one-tenth of a gram. Neither finished tools, nor prepared cores or nodules from which later to produce flakes or blades, seem to have been brought to the island: in other words, a raw material foreign to Montserrat was being worked on the spot, without any prior preparation.

What was being manufactured at Upper Blakes, and for what purpose?[12] There are no finished tools—projectile points, scrapers, or piercing/boring tools, for example—among the finds, although if such items once existed, they could have been removed for use elsewhere. The main goal of the knapping process seems to have been to produce sharp-edged flakes and (especially) blades, including unusually long, wide blades that archaeologists refer to as *macroblades*. One complete example from Upper Blakes measures 16 cm in length (Fig. 22).

Blades such as these could have been employed in hunting and butchering animal prey, but (perhaps more likely) for making other tools from organic materials and for processing foodstuffs. In short, this is what a chipped-stone specialist would describe, in technical terminology, as a classic instance

[10] The ^{14}C date returned by the Beta Analytic lab (Beta-451179) is 4160 ± 30 BP, or, using the INTCAL13 calibration curve at 95% probability (2σ), cal BC 2880–2830, Cal BC 2820–2625.

[11] Even before an absolute age for the site was obtained via ^{14}C-dating, the Archaic age of the lithic assemblage was sufficiently clear to justify publication of a short note about the site's significance: Cherry *et al.* 2012.

[12] For technical details of the Upper Blakes lithic technology, including a coarse quantitative overview of the constituent parts of the assemblage, broken down by find context, see Cherry and Ryzewski 2019: 232–240, table 17.1.

of a direct-percussion, prismatic, blade-core technology. We can say this on the basis of various tell-tale items among the finds: trimming flakes to prepare the cores; examples of rejected, exhausted or "test" cores; blades and blade-flakes with characteristic wide striking-platforms; and a variety of waste (flakes, chunks, spines, shatter, and micro-débitage) created along the way. These are signs of ancient knappers who were well versed in the techniques of producing blades from cores in a standardized and efficient manner. They also knew how to make useful, sharp-edged flakes in simpler ways.

Fig. 22. Lithic artifacts from Upper Blakes: a selection of blades, with (top left) a prismatic blade core from Feature 206 and (right) a complete macroblade from Area 5. (Photographs: John Cherry.)

As always, the archaeologist looks around to ask where else similar discoveries have been made. The nearest answer comes from the neighboring island of Antigua, where more than forty Archaic sites are known (far more than on any other island in the Lesser Antilles), many of them discovered by the prominent Antiguan archaeologist, the late Desmond Nicholson.[13] Some of these sites are as old as, or even older than, Upper Blakes and they too have blades, although the Antiguan blades are generally smaller and made by a rather different technique.[14] Interestingly, big blades quite similar to those from Upper Blakes were found many years ago at Flinty Beach on Long Island, Antigua (the site has now been largely destroyed by development)—the source of the raw material used on Montserrat.[15] There are a good many sites of Archaic date elsewhere in the Lesser Antilles that have no blades at all. Macroblades, like those from Upper Blakes, have tended to be found on other islands at interior, high-altitude sites that may have served special functions.[16] These sorts of tools, struck from prismatic cores, are most common at very early sites in Cuba and Hispaniola, where they were probably used for processing marine and smaller terrestrial animals, woodworking, and making other tools, and many of these sites lack finds of shell or ground stone, being described as simple lithic scatters or knapping areas (just like Upper Blakes).

Montserratian colonization or visitation?

Now we come to what used to be called the "$64,000 question": do the Upper Blakes artifacts signal the first colonization of Montserrat by humans, or, rather, one or more visits to the island by people living elsewhere? And how could we tell the difference? You may have ideas just

[13] Davis 1974; 2000.
[14] Davis 1993.
[15] Van Gijn 1993.
[16] For example (aside from Upper Blakes), at The Level on Saba and Capesterre Belle Eau on Basse Terre, Guadeloupe (Hofman and Hoogland 2016: 41); but they have also been found at coastal sites such as Jolly Beach and Flinty Beach, both on Antigua.

as valid as our own, since the scantiness of the evidence means we are entering the realm of speculation here.

Let's first review the relevant information. Perhaps the most striking fact is that Upper Blakes is a site yielding chert finds only. It lacks any evidence of marine or terrestrial shell, bird, fish, or animal bone, or ground stone artifacts, let alone signs of refuse pits ("middens") or built structures. Although excavation might make matters clearer, this does not look like an established settlement where people actually lived, either permanently or temporarily. We can also rule out the possibility that Upper Blakes was a special-purpose site (whatever that purpose may have been) associated with pottery-making, farming communities living elsewhere on Montserrat: not only is the ^{14}C date far too early, but (as discussed in Chapter 4) those later Amerindian people did not employ blade-core technologies for manufacturing chipped-stone tools. Of course, it could be supposed that there *did* exist other residential sites of Archaic date elsewhere on the island, but, if so, it is noteworthy that the relatively thorough survey of the entire north of the island by the *SLAM* project has not found the slightest trace of them, nor did earlier work encounter such places or material. (Maybe evidence in what is today the Exclusion Zone was overlooked, but the question is now moot: further exploration there is impossible and, in any case, the archaeological record is either destroyed or permanently obscured by volcanic deposits.)

Two clear facts seem the most important to account for. First, the finds at Upper Blakes are predominantly composed of Long Island chert and, second, the evidence indicates that chert was brought in from Antigua as raw material and knapped on the spot. This opens up two possible interpretations. One is that Upper Blakes represents a visit to Montserrat by Archaic people otherwise normally resident on Antigua. An alternative hypothesis is that Archaic people living on Montserrat itself traveled both to and from Long Island to obtain chert. The considerations just mentioned—that Upper Blakes seems to be a special-purpose, non-residential site, and that no other Archaic settlements are known on Montserrat—in our view make this second possibility less likely (and certainly not demonstrable).

This inference, in turn, raises a further issue worth discussing here. The evidence presented in this chapter, even if from a single site on Montserrat, allows the conclusions that humans were present on the island during the Archaic period and that this evidence, dramatically, pushes back the earliest history of Montserrat by more than two millennia. But does this mean that Montserrat was "colonized" almost 5,000 years ago? All too often, archaeologists have assumed that the colonization of an island is indicated by the earliest signs of a human presence. In some cases, incidentally, this can be signaled not by sites and artifacts, but by indirect proxies, such as the evidence—found by coring of sediments—of sudden up-ticks in particles of charcoal (perhaps indicating deliberate landscape clearance by people using fire) or an increase in the pollen of economically useful plant and tree species (suggesting selective human intervention in the natural environment).[17] But that word "colonization" can indicate different degrees of investment in a new insular environment. At one extreme, it might indeed refer to permanent settlement (although perhaps with periods of abandonment and resettlement). At the other extreme, it might mean only that there are unambiguous signs of a human presence on the island, at least once. In between, we might envision repeated, perhaps even seasonal, visits to an island from other nearby islands or the mainland, but without any evident attempt to colonize it permanently.

[17] Siegel 2018.

Viewed in the context of this spectrum of possibilities, and given the sparseness of the data, we currently favor the conclusion—conservative though it may be—that Montserrat was only *visited* during the 3rd millennium BC, but not permanently *colonized* then. Whatever the case, to judge from the currently available evidence, it does seem that Montserrat may not have witnessed any human presence for an extraordinarily long time after footprints were first visible on its beaches (perhaps, as suggested in Chapter 1, renewed volcanic activity may have served as a deterrent). In other words, true colonization was probably not a development until more than 2,000 years after the lithics were knapped at Upper Blakes.

4. New peoples, new ways of living: the Ceramic Age on Montserrat

The first horticulturalists on Montserrat: the Early Ceramic Age

About 2,500 years ago, more than two millennia after people first set foot on Montserrat, new groups arrived on the island, this time to settle permanently. This movement marks the start of what is generally referred to as the "Early Ceramic Age", which lasted for around 1,000 years. Why these migrations into the islands of the Lesser Antilles happened when they did, so long after many of them had already been colonized by Archaic peoples, is not yet clear. Judging from dates of the earliest Ceramic Age sites, however, it seems clear that these movements happened quite rapidly, in a development that eventually came to encompass virtually all of the islands of the Lesser Antilles, from Trinidad in the south all the way north to Puerto Rico, in the eastern Greater Antilles.[1]

The main origin of these colonists was the Middle and Lower Orinoco River basin of modern-day Venezuela. In fact, archaeologists refer to the "cultural complex" (that is, the distinctive pottery and other material culture) of these early horticultural settlers as *Saladoid*, after the site of Saladero in Venezuela where such finds were identified and described half a century ago.[2] There is less agreement about the patterns and processes by which Early Ceramic Age groups moved out into the islands of the eastern Caribbean from the Orinoco basin and other coastal areas of northern South America. Looking at a map, and being told that the earliest insular Saladoid sites are on Trinidad, one might imagine a steady northward movement through the Windward and Leeward islands, with settlers paddling from one to another in a stepping-stone manner, until eventually reaching (and, apparently, stopping at) Puerto Rico. But this does not accord with the evidence we have at present, which indicates that islands in the northern Lesser Antilles—including Montserrat—were settled first, and those south of Guadeloupe were then colonized only some centuries later. Although there may be some biases in the differential preservation of evidence, it has been suggested that the channels between the islands may have been hard to navigate by canoe, because of the swift westward Atlantic currents that flow through them. Computer simulations of canoe travel have indicated that wind and current conditions would likely have made paddling and drifting directly

[1] Fitzpatrick 2015: table 1 provides an up-to-date list of dates (in ^{14}C-calibrated years before present) for initial colonization and earliest Ceramic Age colonization of the major islands of the Caribbean.

[2] Cruxent and Rouse 1958–1959. For the use in this chapter of technical classificatory terms such as "Cedrosan Saladoid" or "Suazan Troumassoid", see the explanation provided in Chapter 2, n. 4.

to the northern Caribbean less problematic, and it may have been from there that the Leeward islands were initially populated; this is known as the "Southward Route Hypothesis".[3] But more sites, more dates, and other forms of evidence (such as aDNA genetic data from skeletal samples) are needed to resolve this issue.

From whatever direction they may have arrived, however, the first Early Ceramic settlers on Montserrat were among the first to colonize any of the Leeward Islands, according to radiocarbon dates from both Trants and Radio Antilles (Fig. 21) that reach back to about the middle of the 1st millennium BC. As a result of the intermittent investigations over a 15-year period at Trants (as summarized in Chapter 2), and despite the lack of large-scale open-plan excavation, it is this site that gives us our best idea of settlement organization, subsistence, and production activities on an Early Ceramic Amerindian settlement on Montserrat. Preservation of faunal remains was excellent, and the relatively deep stratigraphy was intact.

Trants was a large village, a little over 6 ha in size, located close to the ocean and just north of the Farm River, on the largest expanse of flat terrain to be found anywhere on the windward coast of Montserrat (Fig. 14). The settlement was laid out in an approximately oval arrangement, measuring about 275 m × 225 m, and aligned roughly north–south. The center of the oval had a markedly lower density of remains, suggesting an open area, perhaps even a plaza, surrounded by houses and their associated middens, an arrangement that is also confirmed by soil analyses. Remarkably, this community layout seems to have continued unchanged for nearly 1,000 years. Villages organized according to circular, oval, or concentric arrangements are not uncommon at Amerindian settlements in the Amazonian rainforest, as well elsewhere in the Lesser Antilles during the Early Ceramic period, their central areas sometimes being used for burials and, perhaps, ritual activities.[4] Excavations at Trants in 1995 did indeed encounter seven human burials, both primary and secondary, but these were scattered rather widely across the site rather than confined to the plaza; the best preserved example had associated grave-goods including a deliberately "killed" pot (that is, complete, but missing its base that has been removed), a coral rasp, a shell celt, and other pottery sherds.

A good deal is known about the subsistence practices of the inhabitants of Trants village as a result of careful analysis of vertebrate bones. As might have been predicted, given its setting in the landscape (which is typical for Ceramic Age sites on Montserrat and many other islands), the faunal samples indicated an almost equal reliance on land animals and a variety of reef fishes. Terrestrial vertebrates included two species of rice rats that were indigenous to the island but are now extinct, as well as agouti and dog, both introductions from the South American mainland. Several types of lizard (including iguanas) were represented, as well as a variety of bird species (duck, gallinules, pigeons, doves, and small passerines, the latter at a surprisingly high percentage given their size). Among the marine resources were sharks and other bony fishes probably taken from inshore waters, and a wide range of species associated with coral reefs or rocky bottoms (such as groupers, jacks, snappers, grunts, wrasses, and parrotfish); fish from off-shore, deeper waters seem hardly to have been exploited. Sea turtles were present in small numbers, and land crabs were abundant. In general, most of the animal remains come from habitats nearest to the settlement. Less is known about the organic component of the diet at Trants, but it should be remembered that they

[3] Callaghan 2001; Fitzpatrick 2006; 2013.
[4] Siegel 1989; Petersen 1996. Watters 1994a: 291–292 discusses parallels for oval-configured sites.

were farmers, probably—to judge from more recent evidence from other sites—growing native and introduced crops such as manioc, maize, sweet potato, marunguey, cocoyam, peanuts, the common bean, chili peppers, jack bean, wild yam, and achira; they would also have been exploiting edible and economically useful forest products.[5]

Fig. 23. Examples of sherds with white-on-red decoration from Trants. (Photo: John Cherry, by permission of David Watters.)

By far the most abundant artifact, both from excavation and on the surface, is pottery in the so-called Cedrosan Saladoid style—thin-walled, well-fired, beautifully constructed ceramics made (mostly) of local clays, some of them decorated with attractive designs (Fig. 23). These are mainly the kinds of finds that have drawn generations of pot-hunters to Trants. The chief modes of decoration include white-on-red designs (known as WOR), or black-on-red, or white-and-black-on-red, together with incised decoration, especially zone-incised-crosshatching (known as ZIC). WOR and ZIC pottery is very characteristic of Early Ceramic sites, although sometimes only one or the other is found; at Trants, though, they co-occur throughout the site's very long occupation and might possibly have been used in different (perhaps ritual) contexts. Vessels occur in a wide range of shapes for different functions—plates, bowls, pots, flat griddles for cooking tubers, and so on—but more than 90% of them are undecorated. A very frequent feature is the addition of ceramic *adornos* (see Box C) to the vessel's rim or handle, in the form of elaborately modeled human faces, animal and bird heads, or sometimes hybrids of the two, although non-representational decoration also occurs. Adornos are a frequent find at Trants.

Items of stone are also very common. Flakes and waste material of Long Island and other chert sources indicate the need for sharp-edged tools for cutting and scraping, but these were made very simply (using a hard hammerstone to strike flakes from a cobble, in a rather unsystematic manner). There are no blades, and the sophisticated technology that had been used at Upper Blakes 2,000 years earlier was either not known to, or not needed by, the villagers at Trants.[6]

It is the extensive and well-developed lapidary industry that has attracted the most interest in Trants (Fig. 10). Stone beads and pendants, and the waste from making them, are common—both in the early 20th-century Howes collection and from the excavations in the 1980s and 1990s. The range of raw materials, nearly all of them exotic to Montserrat, is extraordinary, including carnelian, diorite, amethyst, rock crystal, several kinds of jade, serpentine, and turquoise. Moreover, the patterns this industry reveals are telling. For example, 65% of the bead débitage and 88% of the bead blanks found

[5] Reitz 1994; Dukes and Reitz 1995; Newsom and Wing 2004; Fitzpatrick 2015: 312–313.

[6] Crock and Bartone 1998; these authors' suggestion that lithic flakes at Trants were used as teeth on manioc grating boards now seems less likely, since archaeobotanical evidence for manioc is in fact rather rare, while there is increasing evidence that maize was a staple (see Mickleburgh and Pagan-Jimenez 2012).

Box C: Ceramic *Adornos*

Amerindian peoples of the Ceramic Age in the Lesser Antilles created imaginative representations of humans and other animals in the natural world around them. These appear in various media: white-on-red depictions on Saladoid pottery, entire vessels in animal form (a turtle bowl or bat censer, for instance), or free-standing carvings. By far the most common category, however, are *adornos* (the Spanish word for decorative additions). *Adornos* are small models in clay attached to pottery vessels, most often at the rim, but occasionally to a handle or elsewhere. Thousands of examples are known, both from excavations and from private collections that have been transferred to museums. From examples whose archaeological context is known, but also on purely stylistic grounds, *adornos* were most common in Saladoid decorative idioms of the Early Ceramic Age. Their use, however, persists throughout Caribbean prehistory, as seen, for example, by an example from the surface at the very late prehistoric site of Indian Creek on Montserrat (Fig. 24).

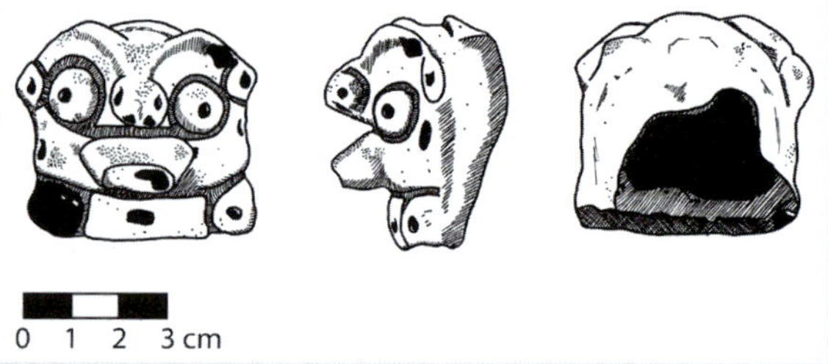

Fig. 24. Ceramic adorno *from the Late Ceramic Indian Creek site, northern Montserrat. (Drawing: Samantha Ellens.)*

Fig. 25. A large adorno *from excavations at the Early Ceramic Trants site. (Photo: John Cherry, by permission of David Watters.)*

An excellent recent study by Lawrence Waldron of zoomorphic representations in Saladoid pottery[i] demonstrates the very wide range of animals depicted in sufficient detail to allow secure identification. They include many species of mammals (armadillos, opossums, dogs, anteaters, monkeys, manatees, bats), birds (owls and other nightbirds, vultures, pelicans and wading birds, ducks, parrots, macaws), and several classes of reptiles and amphibians (snakes, lizards, crocodilians such as the Caribbean caiman, frogs, and turtles). Sometimes the figures represented in *adornos* are too generic for a specific identification. And occasionally, too, *adornos* seem—to our eyes, at least— to display a deliberately quirky sense of humor (Fig. 25).

Fig. 26. *A selection of* adornos *from excavations at the Early Ceramic Trants site. (Photo: John Cherry, by permission of David Watters.)*

Many *adornos* appear to be hybrid forms, created with seemingly intentional ambiguity, to include attributes of more than one species. This ambiguity allows an *adorno* to transform itself as the vessel is rotated or inverted—an anthropomorphic *adorno* becomes a crawling turtle when recumbent, or a turtle head takes on the attributes of an armadillo when seen from above.[ii] These subtle transformations speak to the highly symbolic content of adorned vessels and their shape-shifting and species-transgressive mythological and ceremonial significance (still important for tropical lowland Amerindians of South America in modern times).[iii]

Montserrat is notably well represented by ceramic *adornos*. The Early Ceramic site at Trants has produced hundreds of examples. Figure 26 illustrates a small selection (not yet studied or published) from excavations there in the 1990s. Many others in the Howes collection (see Chapter 2), now in the National Museum of the American Indian, were examined by Waldron. Among items found in this unsystematic assemblage from Trants, he reported the most popular animals to be turtles (with 58 examples), followed by owls, parrots, dogs, frogs, and bats.

[i] Waldron 2016.
[ii] Waldron 2011: figs 3–4.
[iii] Roe 1995. Also important for this interpretation are the ritual and mortuary contexts from which adorned vessels have been excavated, and the works of conquest-era writers describing later Taíno ceremonialism, mythology, and cosmology.

at Trants are carnelian, but finished beads of carnelian amount to only 1%—in other words, a lot of effort was put into making carnelian beads, but these clearly went elsewhere via trade and exchange with other communities. Other settlements, such as Pearls on Grenada, show a complementary pattern: finished carnelian beads (perhaps made at Trants?) and lots of amethyst waste (from making the finished amethyst beads such as those found at Trants?). The populations of both individual settlements and entire islands were probably quite small at this time, and long-term survival depended on relationships with other communities where mates could be found. The widespread exchange of exotic stone ornaments serves as just one proxy indication of the social significance of such networks linking communities dispersed widely throughout the Lesser Antilles.[7]

[7] Knippenberg 2006; Hofman and van Duijvenbode 2011; Mol 2013; 2014.

Fig. 27. The landscape setting of the now-destroyed Early Ceramic site of Radio Antilles in 1995 (left) and 2018 (right). (Photos: David Watters [left], John Cherry [right].)

The village at Trants seems to have persisted in the same spot and relatively unchanged for a period that lasted as long as eight or nine centuries. Its inhabitants were not isolated: the networks to which they were connected would have brought to the island raw materials, finished objects, influences and ideas, and even new people. One possible sign of this at Trants could be the occurrence there, in small quantities and alongside ceramics of standard Saladoid types, of pottery in the so-called Huecoid style (named after the site of La Hueca in Puerto Rico) with decoration that includes incised curvilinear zones, often filled with cross-hatching or punctation; the origin, spread, date, and distinctness of Huecoid pottery, however, are matters that archaeologists have argued over for years.[8]

The people who lived at Trants were certainly not alone on the island. Surface collections and two excavation units at the Radio Antilles site in the island's extreme south suggest that this too may have been the location of a substantial settlement of a comparably early date. The pottery finds are very similar to those from Trants and, of the three radiocarbon dates obtained, the earliest (440 BC, uncorrected), is equivalent to the second oldest date from Trants, the other two also being early (260 and 170 BC, uncorrected).[9] These dates confirm that the settlement at Radio Antilles was established at roughly the same time as Trants, and co-existed with it for several centuries. It was situated by the ocean on a relatively flat, triangular piece of land at the mouth of the White River, but repeated pyroclastic flows down the river bed since 1995 have annihilated the site and even extended the shoreline farther out to sea (Fig. 27); so we will never know more about this site.

The same is true of a third Early Ceramic settlement near the mouth of the Belham River, midway along the island's leeward coast. It too occupied flat and fertile ground close to the sea, bisected by what used to be one of Montserrat's few perennial watercourses. Unfortunately, it was discovered only in the course of its destruction during the building of a golf course, and it has now disappeared forever beneath the devastating pyroclastic flows that have coursed down the Belham, most recently in 2010, with several laharic mudflows and destructive floods since then

[8] For Huecoid pottery at Trants, Watters and Petersen 1999; on the "Huecoid problem", Oliver 1999; Keegan and Hofman 2017: 209–210.

[9] Watters 1994a: 292. The dates are 2390±60 BP (Beta-18491), 2210±70 BP (Beta-18490), and 2120±60 BP (Beta-10582). No dates are available from the Belham River site discussed below (Watters 2015).

Fig. 28. Volcanic pyroclastic flow in the Belham River valley, February 2010. AIR Studios is the white structure at the lower right. (Photo: Montserrat Volcano Observatory, by permission.)

(Fig. 28; see also Fig. 52). All we can say is that this site too was probably large, to judge from the widely dispersed spots at which finds were collected or excavated, and that the pottery is quite clearly Saladoid, with both WOR and ZIC sherds—but no radiocarbon dates exist to pin things down more securely.

Sketchier evidence of Early Ceramic Age sites comes from three locations discovered by the *SLAM* project. One (Trants Road) is beside the former road leading northwards from Trants, and not far from that site; another is next to the ocean at Woodlands Beach; the third—surprisingly—is in the very middle of the Glendon Hospital grounds and, unlike all the other sites, not coastal (but test pits excavated here in 2011 suggest at least the possibility that this material is not in its original context of deposition).[10] Although the finds from each of these places are few in number, each contains potsherds that are diagnostic of the Early Ceramic period.

At one time, it used to be supposed that the first pottery-making horticulturalists to settle in the eastern Caribbean preferred to live in places that replicated the tropical forest environments of the South American mainland from whence they or their ancestors had originally come, and thus chose locations surrounded by neotropical jungle and near watercourses, avoiding more open areas near the coast. With far more information now at our disposal, we can see that this characterization is incorrect and locational choices were in fact far more varied. Many sites are actually on or near the coast, but often in places that maximize proximity to specialized environments and the resources

[10] For illustrations of very fragmentary material from Woodlands Beach and the Glendon Hospital site, see Cherry *et al.* 2014.

they afforded—coral reefs, for instance, salt-marshes, lagoons, stands of mangrove, or beaches. In the case of Montserrat, it is hard to generalize from a mere handful of sites and, in any case, some of these settings were never or rarely available there, because of the steep cliffs that border much of the island.[11] Nevertheless, most of the sites are coastal and seem to reflect the desire for a balance between several types of environment—flat, well-watered arable land needed for horticulture, access to the faunal and floral resources of the forests inland, and proximity to offshore reefs for fishing. Living near the shore would also, of course, have facilitated essential interactions by canoe with other communities both on Montserrat itself and on other islands.[12]

The Late Ceramic Age

The site at Trants was unoccupied by the end of the Early Ceramic Age, which archaeologists set rather loosely at ca. AD 500–600. Certainly, no finds have been made there that are classifiable as "post-Saladoid" (or, better, of Late Ceramic Age, a term that covers the entire period from about AD 600 until European contact). On the other hand, people continued to live in this same general location, albeit not at the former site of Trants itself (Fig. 14). Intensive exploration of this area in connection with planned enhancements to the then-called Blackburne Airport in 1995 (as described in Chapter 2) discovered Late Ceramic sites just to the north of Trants (Trants Bay Hill), and immediately south of the Farm River that runs on the south side of the site (the Farm Bay and Goat Trail sites). David Watters had already in 1979 located distinctive ceramics at a significant site on the coast nearby to the southeast (Windward Bluff), where subsequent visits in 1990, 1992, and 1995 resulted in the collection of more material and the excavation of three elongated trenches. Since none of these sites has produced radiocarbon dates, and because the Late Ceramic Age is protracted and difficult to subdivide with greater precision, we cannot be sure whether these various sites were all occupied simultaneously or not. We also do not know whether the people who lived there were the same as those who lived at Trants, or related to them, or represented newcomers. But it is clear that this favored area continued to support settlements for centuries after the demise of Early Ceramic-Period Trants.

In fact, the impression given by the evidence now available for the later prehistory of Montserrat is one of population growth and expansion.[13] This is in keeping with what is known about the Antilles as a whole. Starting about 1,500 years ago, the number of sites on almost every island increased; places not previously inhabited (such as Jamaica and the Bahamas) were colonized: and there was a general trend towards greater territoriality, regionalization in styles of pottery and other artifacts, and—mainly in the Greater Antilles—increased social complexity.[14] In the northern islands, these developments are associated with the dispersion of peoples and their associated material cultures that archaeologists refer to overall as Ostionoid (after the type-site of Punta Ostiones in Puerto Rico). Local developments on individual islands, along with increased diffusion, integration, and population movements over many centuries, resulted in the Taíno culture that greeted Columbus when he arrived in the Greater Antilles in the late 15th century. These developments are characterized by elaborate

---

[11] The only surviving mangrove stand in the north of Montserrat was located at Piper's Pond on the north edge of Carr's Bay; this was destroyed by infilling in 2014–2015 to facilitate development of the Carrs Bay/Little Bay capital town.

[12] For earlier views on strategies of settlement location, Haviser 1997; more recent views are summarized by Keegan and Hofman 2017: 210.

[13] Cherry *et al.* 2014.

[14] For recent summaries of these developments, see Fitzpatrick 2015: 315–324; Keegan and Hofman 2017: 83–195.

ceremonialism, ritual practices, and political complexity, supported by a very wide range of intricately designed objects of wood, shell, stone, bone, and ceramic.[15] Islands such as Montserrat and those to its south seem not to have been much affected by these sociopolitical changes in the Greater Antilles. In terms of material culture, the most marked shift is towards the making of pottery that (also like Ostionoid) is decidedly plainer and cruder than the earlier Saladoid-type ceramics, with a reduction in the use of pattern-painting using colored slips, and a preference for decoration involving only scratching, incision, or impressions on vessels that are plain, burnished, or covered with a plain red or black slip. These styles are generally referred to as Troumassoid (after the site of Troumassée on St Lucia), with local variants in different parts of the Lesser Antilles.

About a dozen sites in this Late Ceramic Troumassoid tradition are known on Montserrat. All of them are coastal, on both the windward and leeward sides of the island, and even in its remote and arid northern region (Fig. 21), at sites such as Indian Creek and Valentine Ghaut. Two points are worth emphasizing here. One is that Late Ceramic Age pottery—since it is rather simply made, thick-walled, and less commonly decorated—is more difficult to recognize in the field or identify in the lab; and yet we know of twice as many sites of this period on Montserrat as of the Early Ceramic Age. The second is that the relatively intensive survey procedures of the recent *SLAM* project led to the identification of hundreds of "features" in the field, including small scatters of pottery, often sherds of handmade, undecorated, coarse earthenware. Some of these (perhaps the majority) are probably historic-era Afro-Caribbean pottery; but others, to judge from their forms, clearly are not, and are instead of prehistoric Amerindian production. These traces of prehistoric activity out in the landscape, away from the main residential settlements, are other sources of evidence suggesting more thorough engagement with the environment on the part of a larger and growing island population.

More than half of these Late Ceramic sites have now been destroyed, either by the volcano or by modern development, and most are known only from surface collections or from brief and unpublished test excavations (*e.g.* at the Dagenham Beach and Little Bay sites). So we focus here on two locations where the *SLAM* project has undertaken detailed landscape survey and test excavations over the past several years—the Valentine Ghaut and Indian Creek sites. Both lie in the extreme north of the island, and they both date to the last centuries before European arrivals in the Caribbean.

Fig. 29. View down over the Late Ceramic Valentine Ghaut site, seen from the south. (Photo: John Cherry.)

Valentine Ghaut is a watercourse that flows down from the Silver Hills to the east, forming a steep-sided and rugged valley that today, as probably also in Amerindian times, is arid and full of unwelcoming scrubby vegetation.[16] This,

[15] For a well-illustrated introduction to Taíno culture, Bercht 1997; see also Rouse 1992.

[16] For more details of the Valentine Ghaut site, see Cherry *et al.* 2014; *UPR* 14. The intensive survey of the entirety of Valentine Ghaut in 2016 is documented in *UPR* 20.

however, was the location of a Late Ceramic Age settlement next to the ocean and at the mouth of the ghaut, on a fairly level bluff fronted by a low cliff and stony beach, with steeper ground rising immediately behind it (Fig. 29). Repeated visits to this site over the last few years show that storm activity is rapidly eroding the site and, at the time of its first occupation about 1,000 years ago, it may have been considerably larger than at present. When first examined in 2010, the site produced abundant sherds of rather abraded Late Ceramic pottery, together with flakes and débitage of Long Island chert, shells, and mammal and fish bones. Two circular stone arrangements, one close to the ghaut and another on the flat area of the site, are of unknown function, but could have been related to structures built of organic materials that have not, of course, survived.

Fig. 30. Valentine Ghaut midden 1, exposed in profile by erosion of the beach scarp, prior to its excavation in 2010. (Photo: John Cherry.)

Of special interest were several small, shallow midden-pits that had been dug into the ground, but exposed in cross-section by marine erosion (for a plan, see Fig. 41). The richest of these was Midden 1, roughly 2 × 3 m and 60 cm deep (Fig. 30). It was full of charred organic material and, although distinct layers of deposition could be seen in the pit during its excavation, several radiocarbon samples taken from its top to bottom provided dates that are essentially identical (ca. AD 1020±20). This is confirmed by many large fragments of pottery vessels, with joins between examples in the lowest and topmost levels, indicating rapid filling of the midden. Characteristic of the Mamoran Troumassoid subseries (which shows influences from the Virgin Islands and Greater Antilles), this pottery comprises small plates, deep and shallow bowls (some very large), and plain, footless griddles of various sizes, two of them larger than 50 cm in diameter (Fig. 31).[17] The size of these vessels strongly suggests communal cooking, serving, and dining. Most are without decoration other than plain painting with red, brown, or black slips, burnishing, and, in some cases scratching or scoring; the slips are sometimes applied both to the exterior and interior, but in other cases to the interior only as a band near the lip. One vessel alone, a steep-sided bowl, displays white-on-red painting in the form of white chevrons on its exterior (Fig. 32), a type of decoration that finds exact parallels in the Late Ceramic Mill Reef style defined some years ago at stratified contexts in various sites on Antigua, such as Indian Creek; whether this pot was brought from Antigua or made locally can be investigated only through analysis of its clay fabric.[18] Other contents of this midden included conch-shell adzes, a shell spoon bowl, chert flakes, grinding stones, many marine shells (including both inter-tidal and coastal molluscs), and bones of both reef and open-sea fishes

[17] Bright 2011: 239.

[18] Rouse and Morse 1999: fig. 17, A and B. The well-known site of Indian Creek on Antigua is not to be confused with the site of the same name in the Thatch Valley area of far northern Montserrat, discussed below.

(such as Scombridae). Overall, the evidence points to a settled community with links to nearby islands, subsisting on a variety of maritime and terrestrial resources, including locally cultivated crops such as manioc and maize that were cooked on large griddles.

Two more midden deposits along the cliff edge were excavated in 2011–2013, as they were progressively exposed by coastal erosion. They are of exceptional interest, since they reveal the commingling of both Late Ceramic Age sherds and materials of European origin over 600 years later, in the 17th century. These midden deposits at Valentine Ghaut indicate both that the site had a very long history of use and that it witnessed entanglements of Amerindian and European material culture and lifeways during the early years of the colonial era. We return to this evidence in the next chapter.

Fig. 31. Fragmentary Late Ceramic pottery vessels from Valentine Ghaut midden 1. (Photo: Krysta Ryzewski.)

Fig. 32. Large fragment of a white-on-red decorated bowl in the Late Ceramic Mill Reef style, from Valentine Ghaut midden 1. (Photo: Krysta Ryzewski.)

Our survey of Ceramic Age evidence from Montserrat ends, appropriately, with a site that is both the most recent to have been excavated on the island and also the latest in date. The Indian Creek site occupies a seemingly inhospitable location at the extreme northern tip of Montserrat, in a rugged landscape that is today (and probably also in Amerindian times) both remote and difficult to access either on foot or by sea. Its setting is a large flat area, fronted by a tall, crumbling sea-cliff to the north, and by land that rises on all other sides, especially the steep slopes of Silver Hills to the south (Fig. 33). The place, though extremely arid today, may have been well-watered by run-off from these slopes, as well as by the small ghaut that defines the eastern edge of the site.

Indian Creek was first noted in the 1980s, when it was added to the Montserrat National Trust's inventory of archaeological sites; but detailed examination of this place did not begin until 2011, in the course of survey by the *SLAM* project of the Thatch Valley area (the setting of a rather poor colonial-era estate that appears frequently in the archival documents and whose artifactual evidence reaches back to the late 17th century). Over the years, the site has often been visited by

Fig. 33. View over the Indian Creek site looking west; the main archaeological deposits lie in the areas bare of vegetation in the center of the image. (Photo: John Cherry.)

local hikers, resulting in the collection of a few notable artifacts including groundstone tools, a *zemi* (a three-point stone amulet housing the spirit of an ancestor or deity), and an *adorno*, currently in private hands (Box C, Fig. 24). The site's surface is liberally strewn with items such as conch shell tools, chert flakes, shells and fishbones, and large pottery sherds—the latter, unfortunately, very abraded by wind and water erosion. Several small excavation units were dug in 2017, in order to ascertain whether intact deposits existed beneath the colluvial soil-wash that covers the site, to collect samples of better preserved pottery and other artifacts, and to date the site by radiocarbon analysis. No doubt because of the severe geomorphological conditions at this site, most of these test units were "dry holes," but one, at its center, revealed good intact stratigraphy, well-preserved artifacts (mostly pottery), and charcoal samples for dating.[19]

The pottery from Indian Creek is of special interest, because it differs from, and is clearly later than, all the other Late Ceramic sites known on Montserrat, and it demonstrates different regional connections than the pottery deposited at Valentine Ghaut a couple of centuries earlier (Fig. 34). The 2017 excavations and survey at Indian Creek produced mostly pottery—189 sherds, among which were identified 45 different vessels. Of these, 31 were shapes such as bowls and jars, three were flat plates, and eight were circular griddles (the other forms were indeterminate). As at Valentine Ghaut,

[19] On the geomorphology of Indian Creek and Valentine Ghaut, see *UPR* 32 and *UPR* 33.

Fig. 34. Examples of pottery, shell tools, and chert flakes from survey and excavation at the Indian Creek site. (Photo: Krysta Ryzewski.)

the Indian Creek pottery was thick, coarse-tempered, coil- or slab-made, and manufactured using low temperatures and variable firing conditions. But at Indian Creek the fabric (or fired clay and inclusions) of the pottery vessels was more homogeneous; 94% of the pottery sherds had buff-colored bodies—a general term that encompasses various shades of light brown and tan.

As we already discussed, the Valentine Ghaut pottery was decorated in styles characteristic of the Mamoran Troumassoid subseries, indicating the existence of networks linking the site's inhabitants with islands in the northern Lesser Antilles and even the Greater Antilles. By contrast, the pottery from Indian Creek was more closely aligned with styles seen farther south, in the Windward Islands. Except for the occasional use of a red slip, most of it was unpainted, but several of the bowls and all of the griddles from Indian Creek had unusual surface treatments, particularly scoring or scratching on the interior or exterior, and some also had simple incisions and burnishing. Shapes included large open and restricted bowls, jars, griddles, and thick, poorly-made utilitarian vessels. These types of vessels and the crude surface treatments applied to them fit well within the Suazan Troumassoid pottery subseries, which appears after AD 1100 and continues until around 1450.[20] One interesting difference between the pottery at Indian Creek and its counterparts in the Windwards is that the griddles on Montserrat were apparently not made with legs. Nevertheless, prior to the excavations at Indian Creek, Suazan-style pottery were thought to occur largely on islands lying between Tobago in the south and Guadeloupe and La Désirade in the north, with only minor influences present at Late Ceramic period sites on other Lesser Antillean islands (such as Nevis).[21] The style of the Indian Creek pottery suggests that, in the century or more before Europeans arrived in the region, the networks of interaction between islands were shifting and contacts now extended to Montserrat from the Windward Islands.

This identification of the Suazan pottery style at Indian Creek is strongly confirmed by the date range of the single radiocarbon sample: cal AD 1296–1409 (at 95% confidence). This, of course, is not long before the date of Columbus's second voyage in 1493, when—being told the island was uninhabited—he merely named it and sailed on by. Had he chosen instead to land, the people and material culture of a site such as Indian Creek might have been what he would have encountered—as we consider further in the next chapter.

We end this overview of the prehistory of Montserrat by mentioning the exciting discovery in 2016 of the first known petroglyphs. They were found, by chance, in Soldier Ghaut in the island's northwest (see Box D). Although few people have seen them for themselves, since a difficult hike

[20] Bright 2011: 73–77.
[21] Wilson 1989: 436.

Box D: Petroglyphs on Montserrat

Petroglyphs—images carved, scratched, incised, or pecked onto rock surfaces—are a world-wide phenomenon, and in some places they have dates of great antiquity. Amerindian petroglyphs in the Caribbean date back to at least 4,000 BC in the Greater Antilles, although most of them were probably created later, during the Ceramic Age. Examples have been recorded in the eastern Caribbean on about half the islands, but their distribution and density vary enormously and are hard to explain. For instance, on islands close to Montserrat, none are (yet) known on the nearby islands of Antigua, Nevis, St Eustatius, and Saba, while Guadeloupe—an island equally close to the south—boasts 26 petroglyph sites containing some 1,200 separate images.[i]

Montserrat was one of those islands without any known petroglyphs—until 2016. In January of that year, the then Speaker of the Montserrat Legislative Assembly, Shirley Osborne, while hiking came across a group of nine petroglyphs on a rock face in Soldier Ghaut, a deeply incised watercourse (*ghaut*) in the northwest of the island. They were visited and documented by archaeologists between 2016 and 2019. Another petroglyph image of a square head came to light at the same location in Spring 2018, when a large slab of rock was dislodged by heavy rains and slid down into the ghaut bottom. There may well exist more to be found, currently hidden beneath the dense vegetation that festoons the steep walls of the ghaut. Plans are being formulated by the Montserrat National Trust to develop the Soldier Ghaut petroglyph site as a significant heritage resource for the island.

As is most often the case, the images are mainly anthropomorphic (human faces and bodies), but there is also a bat and several purely geometric forms. One of the human figures may be what has been termed a "wrapped ancestor"—that is, a dead elder shown enveloped in his hammock (see Fig. 35).[ii] There is no way to know whether these representations of human figures denote actual people (whether living or dead), or supernatural spirits, or mythological beings, although we can be confident that they relate to ritual and spiritual practices. The setting of the Soldier Ghaut petroglyphs—a secluded, dank, and shady spot amidst luxuriant jungle vegetation, with standing pools of water where bats flit at twilight—is certainly the kind of place where shamanistic encounters with the spirit world might well have taken place.

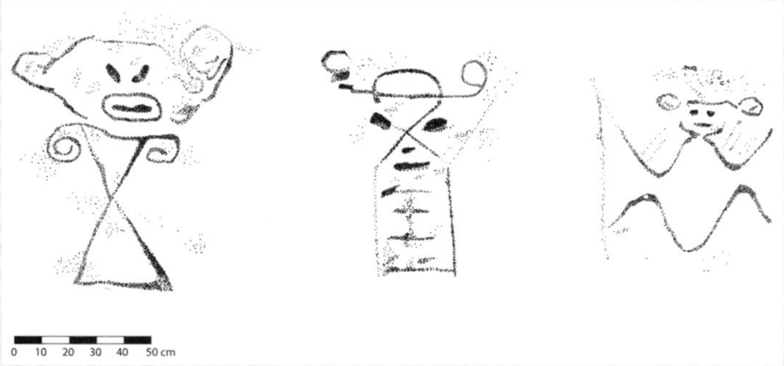

Fig. 35. Petroglyphs at Soldier Ghaut. (Drawings by Samantha Ellens.)

[i] For up-to-date overviews of Lesser Antillean petroglyphs, see Hayward *et al.* 2013; 2017. Dubelaar 1995 and Jönsson Marquet 2002 provide comprehensive syntheses.
[ii] This suggestion was made to us by Peter Roe.

Fig. 36. Petroglyphs at Soldier Ghaut: a deeply carved human head. (Photo: John Cherry).

Fig. 37. Petroglyphs at Soldier Ghaut: an unusual square-shaped head, discovered in 2018. (Photo: John Cherry.)

is required to reach the location, knowledge of them has spread quickly, both on the island and beyond (with coverage, for example, in international newspapers such as *The Guardian*), and—perhaps inevitably—t-shirts bearing the designs of these petroglyphs are now for sale. Petroglyphs are notoriously difficult to date, except by rather imprecise stylistic and comparative studies. All we can be fairly certain about is that they are Amerindian, and in all probability were created at some point during the Ceramic Age. Despite such vagueness, it is encouraging that this intriguing new find has elicited interest among the island's population and a resolve to ensure its adequate preservation as a part of Montserrat's cultural heritage.

5. The colonial period begins: European encounters and Amerindian persistence

On 11 November 1493, Christopher Columbus's Spanish fleet sailed past Montserrat during its second trans-Atlantic voyage.[1] Columbus did not stop to explore the island, but in passing, he named it *Santa Maria de Montserrat* in homage to the mountain and monastery of that name in Catalonia. But like all other Caribbean islands at the time, Montserrat already had a well-known designation in the Amerindians' Arawakan language: Alliouagana (Fig. 39).[2]

One of the still-unresolved questions of Montserratian archaeology is the extent to which Amerindians utilized Alliouagana and its resources during the first centuries of the European presence in the region, specifically between 1493 and the 1630s. European accounts written by Spanish, Dutch, French, and English voyagers depict the island as devoid of Amerindians, both in 1493 and during the following decades.

Abundant archaeological evidence from islands that include Dominica, Guadeloupe, St Kitts, St Vincent, and Trinidad clearly shows that Amerindian peoples were indeed living throughout the Lesser Antilles at the time of the first European voyages in the 15th century.[3] These people, called Caribs by European chroniclers, were skilled seafarers and horticulturalists who lived in villages and traveled frequently to other islands in dugout canoes. Early European travelers wrote down their impressions of the Caribs in chronicles of their journeys. These writings convey their own awe, fear, and often gross misconceptions of the unfamiliar natural environment and indigenous Amerindian cultures they encountered in the Caribbean. A prevalent, but exaggerated, theme is the brutality of the Carib peoples, who are depicted by Europeans as an angry and disorderly society, frequently engaged in acts of war, murder, and even cannibalism. By drawing contrasts between the Christian values of the Europeans and the foreign cultural practices of the Amerindians, chroniclers constructed the basis for legitimizing the violent displacement of Carib populations across the Lesser Antilles in the centuries to come.

Archaeologists are critical of the colonial motivations behind these European accounts, and they do not take at face value the assertions that Montserrat was neither inhabited nor utilized by Amerindians during the early colonial period. It is preferable, instead, to view the island during this time period in

[1] Major 2017: 33.
[2] Fergus 1975.
[3] Honychurch 1997.

the context of what is known about the broader networks linking the Lesser Antillean islands. This perspective is useful for considering how Carib peoples, who were highly mobile, may have continued to use smaller islands such as Montserrat as strategic bases for resource extraction and intermittent settlement during the poorly documented period of the 16th and early 17th centuries.

Fig. 38. The Landing of Columbus, *unknown artist, Frankfurt am Mein, 1594.*[5] *Columbus is depicted trading brass bells and other portable objects with Amerindian people on the Caribbean island of Hispaniola. Courtesy of the John Carter Brown Library, under a Creative Commons License.*

Were there Amerindians on Montserrat when Europeans arrived?

Almost 140 years passed between the time that Columbus sighted Montserrat and the English established the first permanent European settlement on the island in 1632. Was Montserrat in fact totally unoccupied during this period, as suggested in most historical accounts—and popular histories too?

Little is known archaeologically about the customs, social structures, and histories of the Amerindian peoples who lived on (or near) Montserrat during the first decades of European arrivals in the region (Fig. 38). They are referred to by many names that tend to be used with varying degrees of accuracy—Caribs, Island Caribs, Kalinago, and Arawak (Box E).[4] Historical records of the time refer to them simply as either Caribs or Indians, but it is certain that these Amerindians did not self-identify as "Caribs": that is a term assigned to them by the European chroniclers, one that has since been adopted by historians and archaeologists. From archaeological evidence, we can see that there was great cultural diversity within Amerindian groups throughout the Lesser and Greater Antilles, but much more research is needed to fully understand the complexities of the region's contact-period cultural mosaic.

What we do know about Montserrat in 1493 is based entirely on hearsay. The Spaniards did not disembark here during Columbus's journey. So their understanding of the island was instead informed by a Carib woman who had come aboard his ship in Guadeloupe, ostensibly to serve as a guide and interpreter. According to Dr Diego Álvarez Chanca, the voyage's chronicler, "… the Indian woman whom we brought with us said that it [Montserrat] was not inhabited, but had been dispeopled by the Carribbees".[6] To date there are no archaeological indications that large, permanent Carib settlements

[4] Honychurch 2011; Lenik 2012.
[5] *PS JCB* 43.
[6] Major 2017: 33.

existed on Montserrat during the 15th or 16th centuries. In other words, archaeological evidence (or, rather, the lack of it) seems to corroborate Chanca's and other early chroniclers' accounts. By contrast, as already noted, at the time of Columbus' second voyage, substantial Amerindian villages thrived on several islands in the Lesser Antilles; their remains have been excavated at sites such as Plage de Roseau, Capesterre-Belle-Eau (on Guadeloupe) and Argyle (on St Vincent).[7] Chanca's accounts describe the Carib villages on Guadeloupe as composed of "20 to 30 houses arranged around a public square…[with a] common house. The houses are wooden, round, their roof covered with palm ends in tip, the various elements of wood of which they are composed are very well sized and fit perfectly".[8]

Yet while Montserrat was allegedly uninhabited at the time of the first European arrivals in the Leeward Islands, the account given to Columbus by the Guadeloupean woman also suggests that it had in fact been populated by Amerindians ("the Carribbees") within living memory. Conceivably, contingents of rival Caribs from neighboring islands forcibly removed or eliminated Montserrat's inhabitants at some point in the preceding century—a possibility on which future archaeological research might shed light.

Cursory references to Montserrat's occupational history also appear in later writings by French, Dutch, and English voyagers during the 16th and early 17th centuries. These accounts continue to depict Montserrat as unoccupied or only sparsely populated, and they uniformly portray Caribs as savage heathens at best, and war-obsessed cannibals at worst. But they also hint at continuing Amerindian settlement, undocumented early European settlements, and the ongoing use of Montserrat by Caribs during the early colonial period. Recent archaeological finds now help clarify the persistence of Amerindians and their influences on the island after Europeans arrived in the region.

Following Chanca's 1493 account, the next known references to Montserrat appear in a French chronicler's descriptions from 1560 and 1566. In 1560, a ship traveling past Montserrat reported seeing "signals made by Christians", referring to Europeans who were stranded on the island, likely following a shipwreck.[9] Six years later, a Spanish *zabra* (a type of small frigate) commanded by Pedro Menendez and destined for Florida wrecked along the coast of Montserrat, stranding its crew of forty men.[10] Both instances of shipwreck were reported to the Governor of Puerto Rico, who in turn instructed Spanish fleets to travel to Montserrat to rescue the marooned passengers. But these expeditions were fruitless: the stranded crews were reportedly "caught" and "recovered" by the Caribs by the time the Spanish rescuers arrived.[11] The fate of the Spanish mariners and their treatment by the Caribs after they rescued them is unknown, and no underwater archaeological remains of their ships or their rescue site have been discovered. Nevertheless, these two chronicle accounts are particularly revealing because they confirm that the Caribs continued to be in regular maritime contact with Montserrat during the 16th century.

Four decades later, in 1607, Englishman George Percy sailed past Montserrat on his first expedition to Virginia. From his vantage point out at sea, Percy observed the island to be "uninhabited".[12] Later that afternoon, he anchored at Nevis and his crew went ashore for six days to replenish their food

---

[7] Honychurch 1997; Hofman *et al.* 2014: 86; Hofman *et al.* 2015.
[8] Jane 1930–1931, vol. 1: 23, 25, 35.
[9] *PS AGI* 16.
[10] *PS AGI* 17.
[11] *ibid.*
[12] Purchas 1906 [1625]: 7.

Box E: Arawaks, Caribs, Taínos, and other such confusions

Some of the most common questions asked by people interested in Montserrat's history are: Who were the native people who lived on the island before European contact? What were they called? And where did they come from? These are reasonable and interesting questions, but the answers are complex and sometimes confusing. In part, this is because no written records are available prior to the arrival of the Spanish and the chroniclers that accompanied them. And in part it is because so few Amerindian descendant communities have survived. It is also regrettably the case that both historical and archaeological writings have sown confusion by their use of a welter of names—Arawak, Carib, Island Carib, Kalinago, Cayo, Taíno, Ciboney (not to mention strictly archaeological terms for Amerindian cultural traditions, such as Saladoid or Ostionoid)—often in ways that are anachronistic, geographically incorrect, or that conflate linguistic and ethnic groupings.[i]

In many popular accounts, the Caribbean at the time of Columbus is said to have been occupied by two major groups of indigenous peoples: Arawaks and Caribs. The Spanish did not describe the Amerindians they first encountered in the Greater Antilles as Arawaks, but as *indios* (Columbus, remember, at first supposed he was meeting followers of the Great Khan of China in the East Indies). These *indios* appeared to the Spanish—initially, at least—to be co-operative, gentle people who could be easily subjugated. The Spanish contrasted their demeanor with the aggressive and (allegedly) man-eating Indians, much feared by those who lived on Cuba and Hispaniola, who were said to occupy islands not yet known to Columbus to the east and southeast (*i.e.* the northern Lesser Antilles). These Lesser Antillean Amerindians were known by a variety of names, including *caniba*, later modified to *canibales* and *caribes* (hence the modern Caribbean).

None of these Greater or Lesser Amerindian people would have referred to themselves as Arawaks or Caribs. Ethnic identity is generally self-ascribed and rather localized, reinforced by the use of a common name, particular codes of dress and ornamentation, and shared ideologies and origin-stories. The term *Arawak* actually came into use only in the 19th century. Linguists discovered that the language generally spoken in the Greater Antilles at the time of contact is related to that of a tribal ethnic group (the "Lokóno" or "Aruac") that occupied the Lower Orinoco Valley, part of Trinidad, and (still today) the coastal Guianas. It is part of a linguistic family, Northern Arawakan, that is in fact widespread throughout much of South America. So "Arawak" is a linguistic designation of very broad applicability and does not refer to a specific "people," any more than all those who today speak English can be regarded as a single group.

The word *Taíno*, applied to the indigenous Arawak-speakers of the Greater Antilles in late prehistoric times, also has its roots in 19th-century linguistic research. As Arie Boomert has written: "*taíno* is a native adjective meaning 'good, noble', forming the root of the noun *nítainos* which was used to indicate the aristocracy in the hierarchical (chiefdom-type) indigenous societies of at least Hispaniola and Puerto Rico."[ii] We have no evidence that Taínos—referred to in earlier writings as "Island Arawaks"—ever settled on Montserrat, although it is very likely that the late prehistoric occupants of the island were in contact with the Taíno area via travel and trade networks. ("Ciboney", another often-misused term, refers specifically to a western Taíno group living in central Cuba at the time of contact in the 15th and 16th centuries.)

Finally, the word "Carib". For the Spanish, this never denoted a specific ethnicity or a clearly-defined people, but rather was a catch-all descriptive term for any fierce, war-like Amerindians whom they had difficulty subjugating. It was, in fact, deliberately applied as widely as possible after the 1503 decree of the Spanish Crown declaring that Caribs (on account of their supposed cannibalism) could—unlike other Amerindians—legitimately be enslaved. By the Late Ceramic Age, peoples known in the historical sources as "Island Caribs" had spread northwards from source areas in coastal areas of northeastern South America to occupy all of the Windward Islands and some of the more southerly of the Leewards, including Guadeloupe, Montserrat, and St. Kitts. The present-day Caribs who live in Venezuela and coastal Guiana call themselves Kali'na and are speakers of Cariban languages. The Island Caribs, in contrast, were Arawak-speakers, but with the interesting feature of female and male linguistic registers: both women and men spoke a version of Northern Arawak, while men—when by themselves, in the forest building canoes, or on trading and raiding trips—also spoke a different version of the Arawak language, infused with large numbers of Cariban lexical borrowings. Even in the 17th century, they felt sufficient ethnic affinity with mainland Caribs to use the name Kali'nago. These, certainly, were the Caribs whose raids so terrified the early European settlers of Montserrat throughout the 17th century.

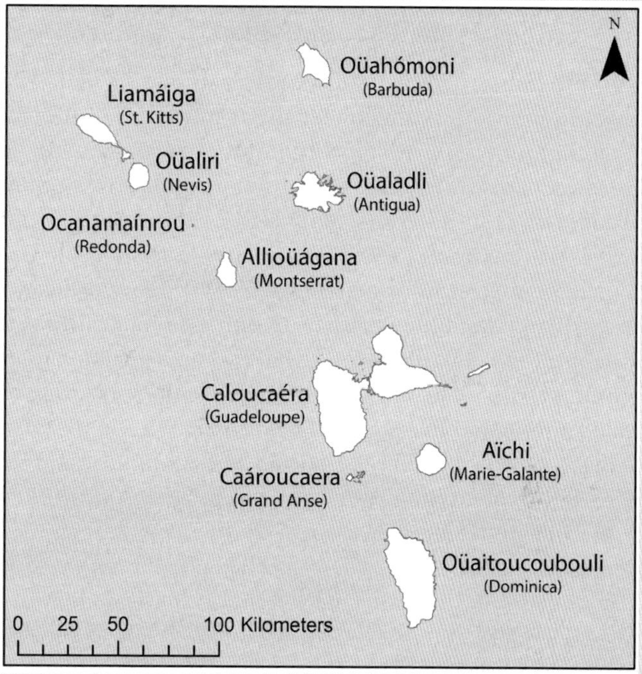

Fig. 39. Kalinago (Carib Indian) names for islands of the central Lesser Antilles. (Map: Miriam Rothenberg.)

We can continue to use the terms "Arawak" and "Carib" as a convenient shorthand— in fact, we have little choice in the matter, since we simply do not know the names by which pre-Columbian peoples living on Montserrat and elsewhere referred to themselves. But we should also be aware that these terms are relatively modern, and ones that carry the risk of significant confusion.

[i] This is true even in the few pages devoted to Amerindian cultures in the standard work on Montserratian history (Fergus 1994: 10–16), in which, for example, Montserrat is said to have been settled by Taíno Indians originally from Asia, via Venezuela; the Ciboneys are described as a "less culturally advanced" people who preceded the Taíno; and credence is given to the notion that Africans were in the Caribbean before either Arawak or Carib people
[ii] Boomert 2016: 7.

stocks. In the course of a hunting trip, the crew encountered a few Indians who "ran swiftly through the Woods to the Mountaine tops" when they saw the Englishmen. In the "thickest of the Woods", Percy's crew then discovered a "most pleasant [Carib] Garden, being a hundred paces square on every side, having many Cotton-trees growing in it with abundance of Cotton-wooll, and many Guiacum trees".[13] Like Montserrat, Nevis does not have any known Carib village settlements that date to this time. But Percy's account is important for understanding how the Caribs were highly mobile and how they routinely utilized small, mountainous islands as important resource bases for food and raw materials during the early colonial period. Given that Nevis' mountain gardens and Amerindian hunters would not have been visible to Percy or other mariners from the sea, it is conceivable that similar activities took place, unobserved, on Montserrat. Both islands probably remained important locations for Amerindians to collect and cultivate natural resources—wood for canoes, hunting, fishing, agriculture—even during the early colonial period.

The first historical descriptions of colonial-period settlements on Montserrat appear in chronicles written during the 1620s and early 1630s. In 1631, Englishman Henri Colt visited Montserrat for four days, observing that the island was uninhabited, but that he had seen the footsteps of "naked men".[14] His account suggests that Amerindians were present on Montserrat in some capacity at the time the first settlements were established by the English the very next year. Indeed, just four years before Colt's visit to Montserrat, in 1627, Dutch voyagers reported seeing Amerindian dwellings on the north side of the island, where shallow reefs made it impossible for European ships to dock. A Dutch chronicler noted that "… if one wants to speak to the inhabitants one has to cross the land on foot oneself" after anchoring on the island's south side.[15] Two years later, in 1629, the French chronicler Coppier also observed dwellings on Montserrat. The French appear to have visited the settlement, where they found the houses empty, but recently occupied. He inferred that the village's Amerindian residents had quickly fled upon hearing of the European's arrival, because they left behind "lots of manioc and sweet potato".[16] Coppier does not provide any clues about this settlement's location: was it the same village as the one mentioned by the Dutch chronicler in the island's north, or a different one elsewhere? Whatever the case, it is clear from these historical sources that Amerindians were living on Montserrat in the 1620s, at the same time that the English were establishing their first Caribbean colony nearby on St Kitts.

Where were the Amerindians living on Montserrat in the early colonial period?

These Dutch and French accounts, then, report Amerindians living in a remote, northern coastal location that was difficult to access by sea and land. Given the slight clues contained in these descriptions and newly discovered archaeological evidence, is it possible that one candidate for such an Amerindian settlement is the site of Valentine Ghaut that we have already described in Chapter 4? Its location certainly fits—in the most northwesterly tip of the island, at the northern end of the exposed and rocky beach of Rendezvous Bay, and backed by a rugged valley framed by steep ridges that extend down from Silver Hills (Fig. 40). The area is difficult to negotiate on

[13] *ibid.*
[14] Quoted in Harlow 2017: 83.
[15] van den Bel 2015.
[16] Coppier 1645; see also Hunt 2013: 281.

Fig. 40. View of Valentine Ghaut from Rendezvous Bay. (a) Location of Late Ceramic Age Amerindian settlement; (b) 18th-century British cannon battery. (Photo: John Cherry.)

foot and an extensive shallow reef complex just offshore would certainly have prevented European vessels from anchoring safely or coming ashore at this point on the coast.

Archaeological finds from Valentine Ghaut provide clear evidence of interactions between Amerindians and Europeans in the 17th century. Between 2010 and 2013, the *SLAM* project excavated a series of three trash deposits (midden-pits) along the coastal edge of the site and just to the south of the ghaut (Fig. 41).[17] Each of them contained remnants of artifacts typically associated with Amerindian food preparation and tool-making. The richest midden in artifactual terms (Midden 1, discussed in Chapter 4) is closely datable, both from the shapes and decorative styles of a series of restorable pottery vessels and by six radiocarbon dates, to the early 11th century AD, in the Late Ceramic period. But close by, and no more than 10 m apart, are two other middens (Midden 3, excavated in Unit 5, and Midden 2 from Units 4 and 6). These two deposits contain European trade goods that place them six centuries later, in the 17th century.

In total, some 439 finds were recovered from these two 17th-century midden deposits (85% of these items were either faunal or shell, the remains of consumed food). Portable objects from the middens included low-fired coarse earthenware bowls of various sizes and shapes. Most (29) of the pottery sherds from these bowls had a buff-colored ceramic body and were undecorated,

[17] *UPR* 14.

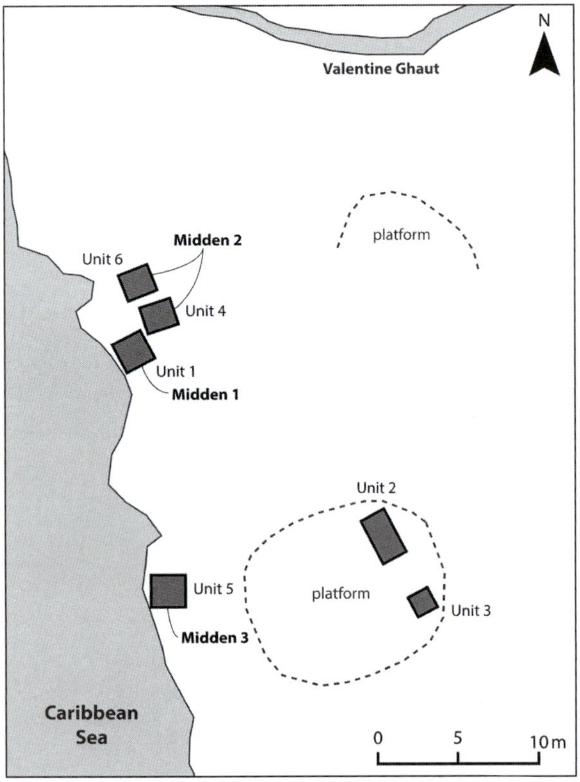

Fig. 41. Plan of the Valentine Ghaut site and the locations of excavation units, middens, and possible structural platforms. (Map: Miriam Rothenberg.)

Fig. 42. Low-fired coarse earthenware pottery recovered from excavation of Midden 2 (Unit 4) at Valentine Ghaut includes vessels with red-slipped decoration, scoring marks, basketry impressions, and a black clay fabric. (Photo: Krysta Ryzewski.)

indicating that the vessels were probably used for utilitarian purposes, such as food preparation or storage. Other fragments were finished with a red slip, scored to create a cross-hatched surface, or burnished (smoothed) during manufacture to create a sheen on the vessel's exterior (Fig. 42). The decoration of some of these bowls may indicate that they were used for special purposes.[18] In addition to the bowl sherds, one fragment of a circular griddle was recovered, of the kind used for cooking cassava (manioc) or other tuber-based breads, staples of the Amerindian diet. The find of such a griddle in Midden 1 alongside abundant quantities of food remains confirms that the site's inhabitants were spending enough time at Valentine Ghaut to process, prepare, and consume food.

None of the decorations on these coarse earthenware pottery fragments are sufficiently diagnostic to date their manufacture or identify their geographic origin. But one unusual pottery type recovered from excavation of Midden 2 may be similar to vessels manufactured by Carib peoples during the early colonial period. This pottery is black-bodied, with walls somewhat thinner than those of the

[18] Archaeologists would characterize the style of this pottery and its decoration as generally in the late Troumassoid tradition (*i.e.* late in the Late Ceramic age).

other vessels. Notably, this black-bodied pottery type does not appear in earlier Amerindian assemblages on Montserrat. At Valentine Ghaut, three sherds of black-bodied pottery were recovered, all of them burnished (smoothed) on the vessel's exterior surface (see Fig. 42). The discovery of this pottery style seems to confirm the presence and continued influence of Caribs on the island at the time of the first English settlements.

At first sight, these finds from the midden deposits appeared to be mainly of Late Ceramic Age date. Typical of pre-colonial assemblages, they contained a range of low-fired pottery, bones of fish and small mammals, large quantities of West Indian topshell, chert flakes, and a shell adze probably used for cutting plants and wood. But buried deep within each midden there were also discovered European-manufactured objects (Fig. 43).

Fig. 43. European-made pottery, iron nail, fragments of a tobacco pipe, local fauna, coral, and chert recovered from Midden 3 (Unit 5) at Valentine Ghaut. (Photo: Krysta Ryzewski.)

A white clay pipe-stem for smoking tobacco was recovered from Midden 2; although undecorated, it is possible to estimate a mid-17th-century date of manufacture, based on the diameter of the bore-hole in its stem. In Midden 3, three different types of European-made goods came to light: a decorated white clay tobacco-pipe stem, fragments of a mug or jug, and an iron nail. The pipe-stem fragment was decorated with multiple molded fleur-de-lis grouped together in a diamond shape, a design utilized uniquely by a pipe-maker in the city of Gouda in the Netherlands between 1625 and 1660 (Fig. 44). The presence of tobacco pipes in Middens 2 and 3 suggests that the site's inhabitants either had access to the tobacco that we know European planters on the island were growing at this time, or were perhaps cultivating it themselves for trade with Europeans, as did their Carib counterparts on Dominica.[19]

In Midden 3, near the decorated pipe stem, we also recovered fragments of a brown and gray stoneware mug or jug made in England in the mid- to late 17th century and a lone iron nail (Fig. 43). Since iron was not manufactured in the Caribbean, this nail would have been imported from Europe or North America. Iron, in fact, was one of the most highly desired European trade goods among Amerindians. During Columbus' journeys, Caribs offered Spanish traders gold and other luxury items in exchange for nails and tools with which to make their canoes.[20] Utilitarian metal objects remained sought after by Caribs on Dominica into the 18th century, where they

---

[19] Honychurch 1997: 299.
[20] Major 2017: 36.

Fig. 44. Clay tobacco pipe stem fragment with molded fleur-de-lis decoration, recovered from Midden 3 (Unit 5), manufactured in Gouda in the Netherlands between 1625 and 1660. (Photo: Krysta Ryzewski.)

modified them into tools for processing cassava on griddles and as items of personal adornment.[21]

Although it is intriguing to think of Valentine Ghaut as a site of Carib habitation in the early colonial period, where they continued to practice longstanding traditions of cultivation, feasting, and canoe-making, the archaeological evidence is not entirely definitive. We do know, from historical records well into the 18th century, of a lasting memory of Amerindian occupation in the island's extreme north. For example, on the northern side of the ridge that bounds Valentine Ghaut and within the area that Europeans named Thatch (or sometimes "Thatched") Valley, is a location called Indian Creek. As described in Chapter 4, recent archaeological excavations there have identified a settlement that dates to the 14th century (in ^{14}C terms, between AD 1296 and 1409).[22] But even though the archaeological evidence suggests that Indian Creek was no longer occupied by the 17th century, early European settlers continued to associate it with a historical Amerindian presence. The toponym Indian Creek was carried over into place-names used by Europeans: it first appears in a 1678 land grant and is then repeatedly referenced in legal documents throughout the 18th century.[23]

While the artifacts from Valentine Ghaut confirm that Amerindian and Europeans interacted with each other on Montserrat in the earliest years of its colonial settlement, the mixtures of local and foreign materials recovered from the site raise more questions than answers. Were people living in a small settlement at Valentine Ghaut? If so, were these people Caribs who incorporated European goods into their daily lives? Or were the inhabitants Europeans who adopted Amerindian food, tools, and pottery into their new environment? Or was this a site where both populations met to trade, interact, or even live side-by-side? We might arrive at more conclusive answers to such questions as archaeologists in the Lesser Antilles, and on Montserrat, continue to expand their research focus on the early colonial period and uncover more comparative artifact assemblages in the process.

The myth of Carib disappearance on Montserrat

Archaeological evidence and historical documents both show that Caribs had not disappeared from Montserrat by the time the English established settlements on the island in the 1630s. In fact, these sources of information illustrate how Caribs and their cultural practices remained strong influences on the island well into the 18th century.

Written accounts portray a climate of distrust, fear, and animosity between early English settlers on Montserrat and the Carib inhabitants of the region. In the early 1630s, for example, the French Jesuit priest Father Du Tertre wrote an account describing how Montserrat's governor, Anthony

[21] Honychurch 1997: 297.

[22] *UPR* 25. The ^{14}C date from the site (Beta-469143) is 600±30 BP.

[23] *PS MNT* 63. This Stapleton land grant involves 90 acres near Indian Creek, also described as three parcels of "waste or King's land".

Brisket, tried to enslave Caribs from Dominica on his Montserrat estate.[24] It was a disastrous plan, with lasting consequences. The enslaved Caribs fled Brisket's estate and attempted to escape from Montserrat, but they were caught by the Governor, who then reportedly poked out their eyes and left them to starve. Whether or not this account has any historical accuracy or rather is an instance of French propaganda at the time, the retelling of this story throughout the Lesser Antilles certainly gave Carib peoples in the region just cause to direct their anger against the English on Montserrat over the course of the next several decades.[25]

For the early years of English settlement on Montserrat, government records provide vivid evidence of the extent to which settlers lived in constant fear of attacks by Caribs from neighboring islands. The first of four recorded raids on Montserrat occurred in 1650, when Caribs from Dominica launched a surprise attack on the island, burning properties, killing settlers, and taking cattle, provisions, and warehouse stock in the process.[26] Similar raids continued intermittently until 1682.[27]

Most of the official accounts in the 17th century that mention Caribs describe conflicts with Amerindians who invaded Montserrat from elsewhere. But—surprisingly, given this grim record of mutual hostility—there are also passing references, in records from the 1670s, to Caribs who apparently resided on the island and worked cooperatively in the service of the government.[28] Moreover, although specific mentions of Caribs disappear from Montserrat's records in the early 18th century, their lasting cultural influences on the lifestyles, technologies, and foodways of early European and African settlers on Montserrat clearly continued. For example, inventories of personal estates belonging to wealthy 18th-century planters routinely list, among luxury imported goods, hammocks and canoes, two Amerindian technologies that European settlers readily adopted to suit the local environmental conditions.[29] Similarly, archaeological evidence from laborers' villages at Galways and elsewhere draws a clear line of continuity—from Amerindian to enslaved African inhabitants—in the use of griddles for the making of cassava bread.

Today there are no identifiable biological descendants of Montserrat's contact-period Carib population living on the island. The last major concentration of Amerindian descendants in the Lesser Antilles lives within the protected Carib/Kalinago Territory on Dominica.[30]

---

[24] du Tertre 1667; see also *PS MNT* 60 (Somerville Papers).
[25] Southey 1827, vol. 2: 485.
[26] Gwynn 1932: 209; see also Fergus 1994: 14.
[27] Crandall 2000.
[28] *PS RLM* 82.
[29] *PS LLA* 45, a long five-part inventory of Thomas Duberry's holdings at the Grove Estate; his total estate value was £12,879.8.5. In *PS MNT* 55, Widow Jane Liddell's estate is appraised at 81,420 pounds of sugar and £3,190.01.05; the inventory includes three old hammocks valued at £2.5 and two canoes valued at £15 (these values are ambiguous in their formatting, and are reported here as they appear in the original source).
[30] Honychurch 2011.

6. Establishing the English colony: new arrivals transform Montserrat

Montserrat's first permanent colonial settlement was established by England in 1632, when Sir Thomas Warner, Governor of St Kitts, sent Captain Anthony Brisket and a contingent of 800 Irish indentured and other laborers to the island.[1] Their first village was probably situated by the Belham River, in present-day Old Towne. Four years later, in 1636, Don Luis de Valdes, Governor of St Martin, observed that "Montserrat is occupied by the English, more precisely, Irish people who make tobacco there".[2] In the 1630s colonists quickly established small-scale agricultural industries on Montserrat, initially based on cultivating indigo and tobacco.

The period from the establishment of the first English settlements on Montserrat until the devastating French invasion of 1712 was a tumultuous time for the island's inhabitants. Despite early agricultural successes, the new colonial society was deeply apprehensive; its unstable plantation-based economy faced constant threats from its enemies and weather-related disasters. Montserrat's own local government Assembly summarized the 17th century as a time of disruption caused by "several Hurricanes, Fires, Invasions, by French and Indians, Insurrections of Negroes, and other unforeseen Accidents".[3]

It is perhaps no surprise that life in 17th-century Montserrat was so challenging. For the first time in Caribbean history, peoples from vastly different cultural and geographic backgrounds—Amerindian, European, and African—were compelled to live alongside each other and to compete for access to space, sustenance, and economic resources. Unfamiliar with each others' cultures and motivated by very different priorities, Montserrat's early colonial society existed in a fragile state of uneasiness, punctuated by frequent violent conflicts. These circumstances were exacerbated by the environmental difficulties of living on a mountainous island prone to natural disaster, water shortages, and disease.[4]

This chapter combines historical sources and archaeological evidence to recount how European settlers in the 17th century established permanent settlements, strategic military installations, plantation-based agriculture, and compulsory labor systems on the island. It was this infrastructure that

[1] Dunn 2012 [1972].
[2] *PS AGI* 15.
[3] *PS MPL* 66.
[4] Wheeler 1988 lists fourteen disasters impacting Montserrat between 1638 and 1707, including ten hurricanes, three earthquakes, at least one major flood, and impacts from the eruption of Mt Misery on St Kitts in 1692.

Fig. 45. Map of Montserrat, showing places mentioned in Chapter 6. (Map by Miriam Rothenberg; base map from Wadge 1988, provided by the Montserrat Volcano Observatory.)

laid the foundation for the island's wholesale transformation into a sugar- and slave-based society in the 18th century, as discussed in Chapter 7.

The first European settlements

The first generations of European settlers constructed small villages along the leeward southwestern coast of Montserrat, from Old Road Bay at the mouth of the Belham River to Sugar Bay at Kinsale (Fig. 45).[5] No records survive from the 1630s that pinpoint the exact location of these earliest settlements, but the present-day area of Old Towne was certainly home to one of them. Unfortunately, this part of Montserrat has been significantly altered by 20th-century villa and hotel developments, the construction of the former Belham Valley Golf Course, and devastating volcanic deposits, so there is now little possibility of further archaeological investigations into the 17th-century settlements in the area.

Old Towne's importance to the early colony is conveyed by its different 17th-century names, both of them associated with the island's highest-ranking government officials. The settlement was initially called Brisket Town, and the adjacent inlet Brisket's Bay, after the island's first Deputy Governor (1632–1649). It was later renamed Stapletown, after Montserrat's sixth Governor, William Stapleton (1668–1672).[6]

The first English-speaking settlers lived in small thatched-roof cottages, built out of wattle and daub (woven sticks bound together with clay and/or mud). Remnants of these post-in-ground buildings are extremely difficult to detect archaeologically, and none have been recovered. Living conditions during the 1630s and 1640s were difficult, as colonists struggled to produce profitable surpluses of agricultural cash crops—indigo, cotton, and tobacco, for example—before the establishment of sugar production around 1650. As profits began to mount from the growing sugar trade, some of the island's planters, men such as Samuel Waad and Henry Blake, erected more impressive stone dwellings towards the end of the 17th century. Traces of some of these buildings survive at Blakes Estate (Fig. 46).[7]

Montserrat's early colonists relied heavily on Dutch traders in the Caribbean to supply them with basic goods, food, and other necessities, even though at the time the British Navigation Acts prohibited trade with them. Evidence of their influence in early Montserrat is apparent in the presence of landowners with Dutch surnames, as well as artifactual remains, including the Dutch-manufactured tin-glazed pottery and tobacco pipes recovered from the habitation sites at Thatch Valley, Potato Hill, and Valentine Ghaut (described in Chapter 5).[8]

The Emerald Isle of the Caribbean: Montserrat's multi-cultural society develops

As elsewhere in the Caribbean, Montserrat's society during the first generation of English colonization gradually developed into what is sometimes called a "plantocracy"—that is, a society in which the majority of wealth and land ownership was controlled by a small, elite stratum of plantation estate owners. Although economic stratification on Montserrat was similar to that on other islands,

[5] *PS MPL* 67; Fergus 1994: 18.
[6] Wheeler 1988: 9.
[7] *UPR* 7; *UPR* 9.
[8] *UPR* 12; *UPR* 14.

Fig. 46. Blakes Estate warehouse and outbuilding in 2010, prior to its recent renovation. (Photo: Krysta Ryzewski.)

its cultural context was nonetheless quite distinct. By the time of the first census in 1678, nearly 70% of the island's population self-identified as Irish.[9] This meant that Montserrat's population was more Irish than any other island in the Caribbean, a fact that has inspired its modern nickname, "The Emerald Isle of the Caribbean". Of the self-identifying Irish population, the majority were Roman Catholics of Gaelic Irish ancestry, and they generally constituted the laboring class.

Who were the "Irish" settlers on Montserrat?

Today links between Montserrat and Ireland are prominently asserted through material displays of "Irish" identity (*e.g.* national dress, place-names, iconography), and the national holiday and annual festival of St Patrick's. But these modern conceptions and depictions of Irishness on Montserrat do not acknowledge the diversity and complexity of identities that were present among the earliest European settlers. Indeed, the ways in which people identified themselves with a particular homeland and culture changed throughout the course of Montserrat's modern history. Ethnic, religious and national identities of the people from England and Ireland (what is now called the British Isles), were changeable, complicated, and fluid. There are some important differences related to the entangled histories of the various islands that affect how we talk about Montserrat's colonial history. These circumstances are worth briefly clarifying here.

[9] *PS CEN* 29.

First, Great Britain did not formally come into existence until the 1707 Acts of Union, which united England, Wales, and Scotland (although the term Great Britain had been officially, but infrequently, used by King James I and King Edward IV in the centuries beforehand). The Kingdom of Ireland remained a separate entity with its own parliament until it was incorporated into Great Britain in 1801. People from England did not commonly refer to themselves as British until the 18th and 19th centuries. This is why we say that Montserrat was established as an English rather than a British colony.

Second, it is generally accepted in Ireland (and, later, on Montserrat), that the Anglo-Irish were the elite, landed ruling class from the 12th century until the time of independence. But to complicate matters, there was more than one wave of 'Anglo Irish' ruling classes in Ireland, each associated with different iterations of plantation-based settlements. The first major plantations were established in the 12th century by the Anglo-Normans in the southern provinces of Munster and Connaught. The later 16th- and 17th-century plantations were associated with the Tudor and Jacobean dynasties, and they focused on Munster and Ulster. The protagonists of these two waves of plantations became known after the 16th century as the 'Old English' and 'New English' respectively. The 'New English' supplemented the pre-existing plantations by evicting Gaelic Irish clans in Ulster for the first time, and also by replacing many of the long-standing Hiberno-Norman plantations in Munster.

As a result of these earlier settlement processes, by the time the 'Irish' started to move to Montserrat they could be divided into three, at times overlapping groups: the Gaelic Irish, the Old English and the New English. The Gaelic Irish and Old English in many ways had most in common; they tended to be Catholic, and many of the Old English had been in Ireland so long that they were considered 'suspect' by the English authorities—politically and culturally—but they were still elite and powerful members of Irish society. Outside of Ulster and parts of Connaught the Gaelic Irish had not been major landholders for many centuries. By contrast, the New English were primarily young adventurers who gained land, wealth, and prestige through their conquests. They tended to embrace the new Protestant religion established by Henry VIII.

These socio-cultural differences matter when they are translated to Montserrat. Primarily because of their Roman Catholic affiliations, Montserrat's Gaelic Irish and those Old English who did not convert to Protestantism were intermittently subjected to the restrictive Penal Laws enacted by English authorities between the 17th and 19th centuries. At their height, in the 18th century, the Penal Laws stripped Catholics of the ability to occupy positions of power, inherit land, or participate in certain professions. These restrictions were periodically but inconsistently extended to Montserrat.

Montserratian society and cultural identity in the 17th century

In general, Montserrat's 17th-century social hierarchy was structured by English and Anglo-Irish (New and Old English) gentlemen in the top echelons of planters and merchants, with lower-class Gaelic Irish indentured laborers and farmers at the bottom.[10] The quest for profits apparently overshadowed divisive cultural and religious differences, at least initially, and there were exceptions made to the membership of the island elite, with the inclusion of planters such as the Blakes, Kirwins, Galways, and Lynches—descendants of the Tribes of Galway and Norman or Gaelic-descended Irish

[10] Hiberno-English refers to a version of the English language that was introduced to Ireland when it was conquered by the Normans in the 12th century.

Box F: Were there Irish Slaves on Montserrat?

Some have recently tried to claim that the experiences of Montserrat's 17th-century Irish laborers were comparable to those of the African slaves who were forced to work on the island's sugar plantations.[i] These conceptions are misinformed and, if allowed to perpetuate, have the potential to distort history and bolster harmful political agendas. Indentured servitude and chattel slavery are two very different circumstances of bondage, and there is absolutely no evidence that Irish laborers were ever enslaved on Montserrat. Nor is there any basis for the suggestion that Irish indentured servants were treated with the same degree of perpetual inhumanity and exploitation as were enslaved Africans in the Caribbean.[ii]

In 1678, at least two-thirds of Montserrat's white population were poor farmers, laborers, or indentured servants who self-identified as Irish.[iii] Most of the Irish Montserratians lived in the inhospitable environment of St Patrick's Parish. Beginning around 1650, Africans were forcibly imported to Montserrat to labor on sugar plantations and in other settings, where they sometimes worked alongside Irish indentured servants. Unlike the Irish, plantation-based slaves were always required to live in villages on the estates where they worked, under the constant watchful eye of the resident owner or overseer.

Slaves and indentured laborers shared the experiences of being unfree and bound to a master who held absolute authority over them. But there are some key distinctions between their circumstances.

Indentured laborers were bound to serve their masters on a temporary basis, usually a set term of between three and seven years. Once the term expired, they were free citizens. Their bondage was not hereditary, meaning that their offspring were not born into servitude. They also retained legal rights as servants. Nevertheless, indentured laborers on Montserrat were certainly impoverished, with limited material resources and spartan accommodations. Records show that they were cruelly punished when they broke rules.

By contrast, African slaves were held as chattel—literally the property—of their masters for the duration of their lifetimes. Slavery, moreover, was hereditary. Slaves had no legal recourse, and they routinely experienced brutal, inhumane treatment at the hands of their owners, other planters, and government officials. Enslaved Africans were typically held in bondage for their entire lives. They had no contractual agreements with their masters, and no end date to their servitude. Like indentured servants, they had limited resources and lived in inhospitable settings.

Fig. 47. Iron shackles used on African slaves during their journey across the Middle Passage and in trade transactions are powerful artifacts of the lifelong experiences of bondage and depravity that accompanied chattel slavery. (From the collections of the International Slavery Museum, Liverpool (UK). Photo: John Hay Library, Brown University, by permission.)

Both groups of laborers undoubtedly suffered from the

poor quality of life they experienced while working on Montserrat. Much can be learned about the lives of these two laboring populations both by accurately acknowledging the distinctions between them and by recognizing the similarities in their daily lives—factors that might be evident in archaeological remains and historical accounts.

[i] Grenham 2015; McCormack 2017.
[ii] Hogan *et al.* 2016; Graham 2017.
[iii] *PS CEN* 29.

Catholic families—who operated some of Montserrat's most profitable estates.[11] By 1650, African laborers were increasingly being brought by force to the island and sold to estate owners. It needs to be emphasized, however, that there is no evidence whatsoever that Irish-descended laborers—no matter how harsh their daily lives may have been—were ever enslaved, as some popular revisionist histories have suggested (see Box F).[12] Nonetheless, the multifaceted Irish presence and its lasting cultural legacy on Montserrat is undeniable.

The majority of 17th-century settlers were Roman Catholics from Ireland; those who arrived with Brisket in the 1630s had recently been freed from indentures to English planters on St Kitts and Nevis.[13] Throughout the remainder of the 17th century, Montserrat attracted multiple groups of Gaelic Irish and Anglo-Irish settlers, adventurers, skilled laborers, indentured servants, and exiled political prisoners.[14] As early as 1634, Montserrat was described as a "noble plantation" of Irish Catholic settlers.[15] While Roman Catholicism was not openly sanctioned by the Crown (English Penal Laws were not regularly enforced), government officials recognized the need for cooperation among the population and the early Governors it appointed were men who had connections to Ireland through family or property.

Within their own communities, Gaelic Irish planters took care to preserve their Catholicism in the face of an increasingly Anglican island. One fascinating example appears in the 1685 will of Edmond Murphy, a local surgeon. In his instructions to his executors he insists that his three sons and daughters must remain Catholic in order to inherit benefits from his estate. If any of his sons renounced the church, he instructed that "his part [is to be] taken away from him & given to the rest". Likewise, he promised his daughters Catherine, Elizabeth, and Jemima 20,000 pounds of sugar when they reached age 15, but only on the condition that they married Roman Catholic husbands. He added the explicit warning: "…if any or either of them should marry a Protestant her portion to be taken away and given to the rest".[16]

English settlers who arrived during the first generations of the colony promptly established institutions that reinforced their colonial authority. One such example was the construction of

[11] The Tribes of Galway was a group of fourteen families who dominated mercantile and political activities in western Ireland (centering on the maritime city of Galway) between the mid-13th and late 19th centuries. All but two of these families traced their ancestry to the Normans, who conquered Ireland in the 12th century; the Kirwin and D'Arcy families were Gaelic Irish.
[12] Hogan *et al.* 2016.
[13] Dunn 2012 [1972].
[14] Fergus 1994: 19.
[15] Father Andrew White, quoted in Akenson 1997: 30–35. See also Gwynn 1932: 184.
[16] *PS MNT* 61.

St Anthony's Church by Governor Brisket in 1636. This church, destroyed and rebuilt on the original site several times over the course of its long history, is today a standing ruin within the volcanic Exclusion Zone, where it has been heavily damaged by the effects of recent volcanic episodes (see Box L).

Amerindian and African peoples living on Montserrat during the 17th century were not taught (or permitted) to read or write, and therefore left behind no primary documents detailing their families, social groups, religious practices, dwellings, or personal property. As a result, we must rely exclusively on secondhand accounts (written by Europeans) and archaeological remains to interpret the extent to which they continued or adapted long-standing practices within the new island environment during this early colonial period.

In general, few records exist from these earliest years of colonization, and so it is challenging for archaeologists to identify exactly where settlements were located or to provide details of what life was like for the people who lived within them. Owing to the impermanent architecture of the early settlements and the frequency with which such flimsy structures were destroyed during raids and storms, very few archaeological sites survive from the 17th century. Those that do are limited to the remains of remote, isolated European settlements atop Potato Hill in Little Bay and at Thatch Valley, both in the island's northernmost region of St Peter's Parish, a region that has escaped the worst of the recent volcanic devastation.

Fear and fortifications

Montserratians lived in constant fear of violent, catastrophic foreign invasions throughout the early colonial period. Between 1650 and 1712, Montserrat was attacked 15 times by various groups of French, Dutch, Carib, and other privateers.[17] The most devastating of these raids happened in February 1666 when the French, assisted by Caribs from Dominica, invaded the island, causing widespread damage and leading to the island falling briefly under French control. According to DuTertre, as the French landed on Montserrat, the English retreated to a natural place of refuge high in the mountains in the South Soufrière Hills in the extreme southeast. This is the location labeled as the *dos d'âne* on the 1734 map of Montserrat; although the map is not detailed, this place is north of Dry Ghaut and probably near Roches Bluff (Fig. 45).[18] During the 1666 siege French and Carib invaders took prisoner Governor Nathaniel Reade and 200 other islanders. They then burned English dwellings, looted warehouses, destroyed sugar mills, and took from the island cannon, enslaved Africans, horses, and cattle. Irish laborers who pledged an oath of allegiance to the French were the only residents left unscathed. The French continued to occupy Montserrat until the English regained it in June 1667.[19]

Ruins of military fortifications, cannon, and other strategic installations from the 17th and 18th centuries survive along the leeward coast of the island, at such places as Bransby Point, Carr's Bay, St George's Hill, Valentine Ghaut, and Woodlands. These stone-built gun platforms, enclosures,

---

[17] Wheeler 1988; see also Crandall 2000. Raids and invasions of different magnitudes, involving various combinations of people (French, Dutch, Carib, buccaneers) occurred in 1650, 1665, 1666/67, 1672, 1674, 1676, 1682, 1693, 1697, 1702, 1707, 1710, 1711 (twice), and 1712.

[18] *PS TNA* 94. The term *dos d'âne* (donkey's back) refers to a flat-topped ridge used for protection; locations of this name existed on several other islands of the Lesser Antilles.

[19] Jean-Baptiste Du Tertre 1667–1671, vol. 4: 199–205; *PS MPL* 65.

and lookout points convey the anxieties of the early English settlers about securing the colony and eliminating external threats from other Europeans and Caribs.

Efforts to fortify and defend Montserrat began in the immediate aftermath of the 1666 invasion. Lord Willoughby appointed William Stapleton as Governor in 1668 and, in his letter of appointment, granted him authority to maintain order and enlist militia in instances of "foreign invasions, as well as local mutineys, insurrections, or rebellions".[20] Willoughby's letter not only addressed the colonists' concern about losing the island to other European imperial powers, but it also signaled that threats to order existed from home-grown sources. In the case of Montserrat, the local Irish laboring population, who had readily assisted the French and Caribs in 1666, were viewed as problematic and disorderly. This sentiment may have also carried over, to a lesser degree, to any resident Amerindians and foreign traders who may have still been living on the island.

Upon his appointment in 1668 Governor Stapleton's first order of business was to take stock of the island's defenses. The resulting 1672 inventory of military supplies shows how ill-equipped Montserrat was to survive another attack: the island only had seven guns (cannon) and 12 barrels of powder to protect its able-bodied male population of 1,171 European colonists and 523 enslaved Africans.[21] Both written records and archaeological remains suggest that Montserrat's government moved rapidly to fortify the island after this inventory was completed. In 1674, there were already four fortifications on the island: Kinsale (then called Kingsale), Old Road, Bransby's and St George's Hill. Old Road and Kinsale forts had existed since at least the 1660s, but both were burned during the 1666 invasion. Government account records from 1674 detail concerted efforts to rebuild, expand and strengthen them—for example, new flooring for gun platforms was added to the forts at Old Road and Bransby's.[22]

By 1678, fortification efforts had expanded northward, and Carr's Bay was protected by at least one cannon.[23] Secondary monitoring stations were also added in other parts of the island, including a guard house at Windward.[24] Signal beacon stations, positioned to surveil maritime traffic and to serve as early warning systems for approaching enemies, were erected around the entire coastline of the island. The government required that these lighthouses were built of stone or solid wood with walls 8 to 10 feet high. They were to be set up on hilltops in each of the island's four parish divisions.[25] According to an Act passed by the Montserrat Assembly in 1668, the lighthouses were not to be lit except for a "just cause", such as "upon appearance of a fleet of shipping or pireaugues (canoes) of Indians".[26]

To man the defenses, Governor Stapleton established a militia of 11 companies, comprised of 868 armed and 42 unarmed men. Each company of the militia was headed by a sergeant, usually a reputable landowner, and it was comprised of six men, typically from the laboring class. Militia rolls from 1681 list all company members, and they include the names of many of the Irish laboring class of small farmers, indentured servants, and other settlers who otherwise rarely appear in official records. For example, the membership of Company 4 was characteristic of the militia regiments;

[20] *PS RLM* 87.
[21] *PS MNT* 60, File 42.
[22] *ibid.*
[23] *PS RLM* 90.
[24] *PS RLM* 89.
[25] In the 17th and 18th centuries Montserrat was divided into four administrative divisions, called parishes: St Anthony, St Peter, St Patrick, and St George.
[26] *PS MPL* 68.

it included Teige Collines, Owen Carby, Cornelis Callahan, Mortogh Kery, Cornelis Sullivan, and William Mullane.[27] In addition to the militia, Governor Stapleton mandated enslaved Africans to assist in the building of all fortification structures. Interestingly, despite considerable angst about invasions by Caribs from other islands, Stapleton's accounts also show that the Montserratian government provided provisions for both soldiers and Amerindians during the 1670s. These provisions were likely granted in exchange for assistance or information locally-based Caribs provided during infrastructure building or defense planning.[28]

In the following decades, during the 1680s and 1690s, the government erected new fortifications and expanded existing defenses around the island. Guards were stationed in the north at Bunkum Bay, Carr's Bay, and Soldier Ghaut.[29] Carr's Bay, on the remote northwest coast of Montserrat, was the best landing spot in the northern region of St Peter's Parish during the colonial period, and it was frequented by traders, invaders, and smugglers. Nestled between two hilltops and at the base of the Collins River, it occupied a strategic vantage point for monitoring maritime traffic headed for Montserrat from the directions of Nevis, St Kitts, and Antigua. Carr's Bay was bounded to its southern side by Gun Hill, a low promontory headland bounded by vertical sea-cliffs to the south and west, and on its northern side by Potato Hill, a steep scrub-covered bluff.

In 1693 the Montserrat Council and Assembly ordered for "2 great Guns be sent to Carr's Bay for the defense of that place".[30] The guns were placed within a stone-built battery, positioned on the coast by the beach. Later, in 1756, archival documents indicate that the Carr's Bay battery was upgraded with four additional cannon and the construction of a small powder magazine, measuring 10 × 8 ft. The battery itself consists of a stone parapet ca. 100 ft in length, running parallel to the beach, with shorter parapets running inland to the north and south, and a flat stone paving on the interior to provide a platform for the cannon.[31] In 1985 and again in 1995, the battery was restored by the Montserrat National Trust (Fig. 48). Today the site is under threat from coastal erosion and corrosion from the salty air, as well as by plans to develop a marina in Carr's Bay.

Archaeologists from the *SLAM* project first examined the Carr's Bay gun battery and the surrounding landscape in 2010. Careful, systematic survey revealed additional architectural components of the military installation that are not mentioned in existing historical accounts, and that have been forgotten over time, since they were obscured by dense vegetation. On top of Gun Hill, which flanked the south side of Carr's Bay, there was discovered a line of four flat-faced, cut stones peeking out from the tall grass. These stones were typical of the ashlar masonry used to erect substantial buildings or other architectural features during the colonial period, and they indicated that a durable, man-made structure once existed atop Gun Hill. Along the hillside, archaeologists documented a rockshelter measuring 6 m long, 3 m deep, and 1.5 m tall, and a massive boulder with a 2 × 3 m depression along its base, showing signs of having been used for fires, perhaps as a makeshift oven. Next to these features were collected European-made pottery fragments whose manufacture dates ranged from the 17th to late 18th century. The most interesting find was a fragment of a 17th-century English plate (Staffordshire slipware) that had

---

27 *PS RLM* 88.
28 *PS RLM* 82.
29 *PS ABNA* 10.
30 *PS ABNA* 9.
31 Crandall 2000.

Fig. 48. Carr's Bay gun battery, reconstructed 17th- and 18th-century fortification in St Peter's Parish. (Photo: John Cherry, 2014.)

been whittled into a circular disk so that it could be used as a gaming piece or token, possibly by the guards who manned the installation on Gun Hill.[32] In 2013, in response to the imminent threat of the removal of its entire northern part, archaeologists from the *SLAM* project peeled back the thick vegetation atop the hill and excavated the area, revealing an unexpectedly massive and well-constructed platform that would have been used as a cannon battery—as the hilltop's local name already intimated (see Box M).[33]

Roots of the sugar plantation economy

Montserrat's sugar industry began by 1650 and quickly developed into the profitable backbone of the island's economy.[34] At the time of the French and Carib invasion of 1666, there were already more than 40 sugar mills on the island.[35] Sugar was such a valuable commodity in these early years that it became the standard currency for business transactions, both local and foreign.

---

[32] *UPR* 7.
[33] *UPR* 11.
[34] Bridenbaugh and Bridenbaugh 1972: 82, cited in Fergus 1994: 38.
[35] Jean-Baptiste Du Tertre, quoted in *PS MNT* 60, File 35.

Fig. 49. "Map of Mountserrat Island", 1673, Blathwayt Atlas. Courtesy of the John Carter Brown Library, under a Creative Commons License.

Global demands for sugar initiated massive transformations to Montserrat's natural environment and its society. Geographer Lydia Pulsipher has estimated that, in response to the profitability of sugar on the international market, more than two-thirds of Montserrat's landscape was deforested and sub-divided into estates by the 1680s.[36] The scale of land clearance is well illustrated by the Blathwayt Map of 1673, now in the John Carter Brown Library at Brown University (Fig. 49; Box G).[37] Drawn from the vantage point of a ship out at sea, this unusual and fascinating map depicts a series of coastal profiles of the island as seen from several viewpoints offshore. The unknown cartographer painstakingly noted the plantations, major village

[36] Pulsipher 1977; 1986.
[37] Pulsipher 1987.

settlements, and other landmarks that were visible from offshore. Pulsipher identified a total of nine sugar grinding mills (five cattle, two wind, two water-powered), but also noted that there were more sugar works in existence on the island than are depicted on the map.[38] Already by 1673 the island landscape would probably have been unrecognizable to the settlers who first arrived with Anthony Brisket in 1632.

Social and economic status in early colonial Montserrat was largely dependent upon the position one occupied in the plantation-based society. An elite class of wealthy planters emerged in tandem with the development of the sugar industry. They included the Blake, Galway, and Stapleton families, each of whom operated and lived on large, profitable estates by the 1670s. Other influential sugar planters of the 17th century included Captain Andrew Booth, Nicholas Meade, Thomas Nugent, Nicholas Lynch, Captain William Carr, William Bramly, and John Daly, among others. These English, Anglo-Irish, and Irish planters accumulated wealth based on the output of their sugar crops. The success of sugar production depended, in large part, on the laborers who cultivated and processed sugar on their estates. Beginning in the early 1650s, these laborers were enslaved Africans, who were purchased by the planters and forced to spend their entire lives working in bondage on local estates.

Remains of some of the earliest sugar plantations have survived in the northern portion of Montserrat outside the Exclusion Zone, and several have been the focus of archaeological documentation. Prior to the French invasion of 1712, the Belham River valley was home to the island's oldest and largest sugar estates, including Waterworks, Old Road, and Weekes, as well as defensive structures and guns at the Old Road Fort. Archaeological and architectural remains of three of these sugar estates still exist.[39] Two plantations, once owned or operated by Governor William Stapleton, survive along the Belham Valley: Old Road and Waterworks. Buildings from another, Blakes Estate, survive in St Peters Parish, the island's northernmost division.

Ruins from the Old Road Estate can be seen in Old Town among the dense vegetation along the northern edge of the Belham River. This estate dates to the 1660s and was operated through the 19th century.[40] An 1866 description of the estate lists at least seven buildings, which were probably similar in location and function to those that existed in prior centuries. All but one of the buildings were then listed as being in considerable disrepair; they included a dwelling house (in good order), kitchen, servants' room, "negro huts", curing house, still house, and cattle mill.[41] By the 21st century, the best-preserved surviving building was the estate's former boiling and curing house, constructed with mortared, ashlar stone masonry. Although it was later converted for use as the Club House of the Belham Valley Golf Club in the 1960s, its three-story high chimney remained intact. The chimney would have released the steam from the succession of boiling kettles (the so-called "Jamaica train") that once lined the inside of the processing facility. A large stone-built cattle mill, used to crush sugar cane, measuring over 3.5 m in diameter also survived into the 2010s.[42] Unfortunately, between 2010 and 2018 pyroclastic flows, lahars, the spread of invasive plant species, and development of mining

[38] Pulsipher 1977, 142–143; Du Tertre reported that Montserrat had 40 sugar estates in 1666; see Box G [Blathwayt Atlas map of Montserrat].
[39] *UPR* 7; *UPR* 26.
[40] *PS LLA* 46.
[41] *PS MPL* 71.
[42] *UPR* 7.

Box G: The 1673 map of Montserrat in the Blathwayt Atlas

There is only one surviving map of Montserrat from the 17th century and it is part of the Blathwayt Atlas.[i] The 1673 map of "Mountserrat Island" was produced for William Blathwayt, clerk to the Committee of the Lords of Trades and Plantations, for his atlas of the British Empire. The map is considered a cartographic curiosity because of its unusual orientation and ring-shaped appearance (Fig. 49). So rather than adopting the usual Cartesian map-making view of land as "seen from above", the Blathwayt map is drawn from the perspective of someone on a boat anchored offshore in various positions around the island.[ii] Montserrat's perimeter appears in a series of seven adjoining profiles, which, connected to one another, create the outline of the island as if viewed from above and to the side. We do not know who made the map, since the cartographer left it unsigned, but scholars believe that it was commissioned, and perhaps also informed, by William Stapleton, Montserrat's Governor at the time.

The Blathwayt map is an indispensable resource for understanding 17th-century Montserrat at a time when sugar cultivation had only very recently been introduced yet was already rapidly transforming the island's landscape, environment, and society. The map identifies significant

Fig. 50. Portion of the 1673 "Map of Mountserrat Island" in the Blathwayt Atlas showing Captain William Carr's Plantation (K) and Thomas Caines' Plantation (I), and, along the coast, the locations of Soldier's Ghaut (10), Carr's Bay (11), Little Bay (12), and Rendezvous Bay (13). Courtesy of the John Carter Brown Library, under a Creative Commons License.

landmarks, plantation estates, towns, signal towers, windmills, waterways, fortifications, and a single church (St Anthony's in Plymouth: see Box L). These features are shown as tiny not-to-scale drawings. The mapmaker included keys in the map's corners that provide additional information about the labeled properties and features. One note, for example, references the place south of Kinsale village where the French landed during their invasion of the island in 1666–1667. Two other symbols indicate the ruins of Stapletown and of Kinsale fort, also destroyed during the French and Carib siege. These markers indicate that the damage from, and memory of, the catastrophic invasion was still fresh in the minds of the English map-makers half a dozen years afterwards.

The Blathwayt map is full of fascinating small details. For example (Fig. 50), the extreme northwestern portion of the island identifies various bays and ghauts, as well as two planter's estates (those of Thomas Caines and William Carr); but it is difficult to say whether the Carr plantation is in the same place as the 18th-century plantation at Little Bay owned by various members of the Piper and Allen families. What is most striking is the extent to which the slopes of the mountains had already been cleared for sugar-cane production, as can be seen in the detail of the land behind the capital town of Plymouth (Fig. 51).

The original map is in the possession of the John Carter Brown Library at Brown University in Providence, Rhode Island.

Fig. 51. Detail of the area around Plymouth (G) and the cleared agricultural lands surrounding it. Courtesy of the John Carter Brown Library, under a Creative Commons License.

[i] *PS JCB* 44.
[ii] Pulsipher 1987.

Fig. 52. Remains of the Old Road Estate warehouse buried in pyroclastic material in 2010, and covered by further volcanic deposits and vegetation in 2018. (Photos: Elizabeth Murphy and Krysta Ryzewski.)

in the Belham Valley have buried or damaged both of these ruins (Fig. 52). The animal mill, clear to see in 2010, was by 2018 no longer visible above ground; and the one-storey boiling house and former Club House is now engulfed in ash to within a meter of its ceilings. These deep ash deposits at Old Road Estate unfortunately make archaeological excavations impossible.

Further up the Belham Valley and east of Old Road Estate are the well-preserved remains of the Waterworks Estate, part of which is still inhabited by descendants of the historic families associated with the plantation. Waterworks was owned and operated by Governor William Stapleton during the 1670s and 1680s, and remained in continuous operation as a sugar- and then cotton-producing operation until the 20th century.[43] Industrial operations at Waterworks were supplied with water power from the Killiecrankie spring in the Centre Hills. The major industrial works on the estate, including the boiling house, were water-powered. Two windmills also assisted in processing sugar cane; one was located within the domestic compound on the estate's hilltop, and a second located above the Belham River, well to the south of the processing building, which still stands today and is well-preserved (Fig. 53).

In the northernmost region of the island are the remains of Blake's Estate. Blake's was purchased in 1675 by Henry and John Blake, two brothers from Galway, Ireland, and it operated as a sugar plantation from the last quarter of the 17th century until the 19th century, at which time it was converted for cotton production. John Blake resided at the Estate and died there in 1692.[44] Blake and his successors erected a stone dwelling house, windmill tower, boiling house, and curing house, remains of which are still visible (Fig. 46). The planter's dwelling and industrial complex are located adjacent to each other. As was generally the case, this deliberately close proximity allowed the Blakes to keep a watchful eye over the sugar production process and their laborers. Numerous historical artifacts,

[43] *PS RLM* 91.
[44] *PS MNT* 60, File 50.

Fig. 53. Industrial processing building at Waterworks Estate, 2012. During the 17th through 19th centuries a water-powered sugar mill operated inside of this building; it was later converted for cotton production. (Photo: Krysta Ryzewski.)

including pottery, glass bottle fragments, and tobacco pipes, have been recovered by archaeologists from the area of the planter's house. The diversity and high quality of imported goods reflect the Blake family's global connections, wealth, and prestige within Montserrat's early sugar-producing period.[45]

The agricultural fields that produced the cane for Blake's sugar works extended uphill south of the estate, along the ridge between Sweetwater and Cat ghauts. Archaeological survey between 2012 and 2017 in the fields of Upper Blakes—still agricultural lands today, and also the setting of the Amerindian Archaic site discussed in Chapter 3—revealed historical artifact assemblages deposited by the laborers who once lived and worked at Blakes Estate. These included locally-made coarse earthenware pottery (13 vessels), and European-made pottery (24 vessels) manufactured during the 17th and 18th century, mainly in England.[46] The varieties of pottery include a white salt-glazed stoneware plate, a porcelain platter, an agateware bowl, creamware bowls and plates, and a large tin-glazed serving bowl (Fig. 54).

---

[45] *UPR* 9; *UPR* 23.
[46] *ibid.*

Fig. 54. Early colonial-period pottery sherds recovered from the Upper Blakes area of Blakes Estate include decorated English- and Dutch-made vessels that date to the 17th and 18th centuries. (Photo: Krysta Ryzewski.)

The pottery from the fields at Upper Blakes suggest that this area of the estate was used for domestic as well as agricultural purposes during the sugar plantation era. Unfortunately, as is the case for most of the island's 17th- and 18th-century sugar works, few property plans or plat maps of individual estates are known to have survived. So we must rely on the patterns that emerge from distributions of artifacts on historic landscapes to determine where certain activities most likely took place. In the case of Upper Blakes, the artifact concentrations in the upper agricultural fields suggest that the area may have been the site of an overseer's house and/or slave laborers' village.

Labor, ethnicity, and inequality

In 1678 when the first census was taken for Montserrat, 69% of the total population of 3,674 identified as Irish.[47] Because residents of Irish descent occupied all ranks of Montserrat's early plantation society and came from very different historical and cultural backgrounds in Ireland, there was no singular experience common to the island's inhabitants who had ancestral Irish connections. Nevertheless, Irish place-names and family names have been in use since the 17th century to identify landmarks, property and lineages. By 1700, 18 of the island's 48 estates had Irish names, as did nearly half of the island's villages. Some of these place-names, such as Cork Hill, Fogarty, and Sweeneys still exist today.[48]

Historical records indicate that by the 1680s, sharp distinctions existed between an Anglo-Irish plantocracy and poor Gaelic Irish farmers and laborers.[49] These laborers were part of an indentured workforce, contractually bound to particular masters and estates for a period of three to seven years. Prior to the introduction of sugar agriculture in the 1650s, indentured laborers cultivated indigo, cotton, and tobacco, the island's primary cash crops.[50] The British colonial government viewed the Irish laboring class as a troublesome, "dissident majority", and they limited their influence by allocating them parcels of land on the margins of Plymouth, in the town of Kinsale and other nearby villages in St Patrick's Parish. This southwest region of the island was unattractive for agricultural development because of its poor soil, steep terrain, and dry land.[51] Regrettably, Kinsale and other parts of St Patrick's Parish have been destroyed by volcanic eruptions since 1995; and since no

---

47 *PS CEN* 29.
48 Zacek 2010.
49 Ryzewski and Cherry 2015.
50 *PS RLM* 86.
51 Akenson 1997: 12; Ryzewski and Cherry 2015.

surveys or excavations had previously been conducted within these communities, the archaeology of this part of Montserrat in the 17th century is now lost forever.

Fractures between planters and laborers of Irish descent also occurred. Following the invasion of 1666, David Galway, planter of Galway's sugar estate, formally condemned the servants and laborers from St Patrick's Parish for aiding the enemies during the conflict.[52] In these instances, profits from sugar production held priority over loyalty to fellow countrymen.

Irish laborers were not enslaved; but they nonetheless received brutal treatment, especially from the local English government. In September 1698 the Montserrat Council and Assembly issued punishments for two "servant women" who were caught taking off with a canoe. The women, who were most likely of Irish descent, were sentenced to be whipped on the bare back, with no more than thirty-nine lashes. Greater quantities of lashes were reserved for more serious crimes, and for offenses committed by African slaves. The second part of their punishment confirms their identity as indentured servants; the women were required by the government to serve their master until the end of their indentures, including for time lost during the incident, and then they were to be "sold for 4 more years' service".[53]

With the introduction of widespread sugar cultivation in the mid-17th century, indentured servants were increasingly replaced by enslaved African laborers. In 1672, there were 288 African slaves and 44 slave owners on the island. The largest slaveholding estate was Bransby Plantation, with 28 laborers. Initially, it was more common for planters to own between four and ten enslaved laborers. But many of the men who started out owning a handful of slaves would go on to develop the island's largest and most profitable plantations in the 18th century, including Thomas Roach (Roche's Estate), George Wykes (Weekes' Estate) and Captain David Galway (Galway's Estate). These men launched their efforts with one, three, and eight slaves, respectively.[54]

Astonishingly, within just six years between 1672 and 1678, Montserrat's slave population more than tripled. The 1678 census records 992 slaves, comprising 26% of the island's total population.[55] At Blake's Estate in the north of the island, the census lists John Blake, Sr as the owner of 38 slaves, representing 24% of the entire slave population of St Peter's Parish. John Davies, an Irish planter whose impressive tombstone with a bilingual Latin-English inscription is still preserved in the Rocklands burial ground above Bunkum Bay, is listed in the same census as being the island's largest slave-owner, with 64 laborers.

Slaves most often lived in small villages on the plantation estates where they worked.[56] Since family members were often separated from one another during slave sales, these villages became tight-knit communities whose residents shared in the efforts to raise children, cultivate provisions, and maintain personal lives in an otherwise oppressive environment. The houses in enslaved laborer villages were constructed from wood, thatch, and daub. They had well-maintained yard spaces, where cooking and leisure activities took place, and often kept small house gardens, where medicinal plants, herbs, and produce were grown. Archaeologists have excavated enslaved laborer villages at the estates of Galways, Delvins, and Little Bay. Although these three estates were certainly home

52 Pulsipher 1982; Zacek 2010: 80–83.

53 *PS ABNA* 11.

54 *PS RLM* 84.

55 Berleant-Schiller 1989: 540; *PS CEN* 29; *PS CEN* 30; Ryzewski and Cherry 2015.

56 Smaller quantities of slaves were bound to households in Plymouth and other ports, where they assisted their masters with mercantile, trade, service, and maritime industries. These slaves are more difficult to locate in the archaeological record.

to enslaved laborers during the 17th century, the excavated remains at these sites date to the 18th and 19th century (see Chapter 8).

With the introduction of African slaves to Montserrat, the local government quickly established policies that enforced stark distinctions between the island's white and black residents. Restrictive laws were put into place that forbade commercial and other interactions between them.[57] Slaves who committed offenses were subjected to brutal treatments intended to instill fear and command obedience among the wider enslaved population. One such instance from 1672 involved a slave named Gregory Billy, who ran away from his master. After he was caught, Billy was publicly executed: his master was reimbursed by the government for the loss of his property.[58]

The French invasion of 1712 and the destruction of 17th-century Montserrat

Most buildings associated with the first generations of settlement and the island's emergent plantation economy were totally destroyed by the French invasion of Montserrat in 1712. Armed with a force of 3,500 men, the French burned properties and sugar estates, captured 1,200 slaves, and removed portable equipment, livestock, and provisions from the island.[59] One local resident recounted the attack as follows:

> [The French] burnt our town, destroyed our houses in the country, sugar works and plantations, carried away sundry of our slaves, killed and took with them most of our horses, cattle and small stock, broke burnt and carried with them our household stuff, cloathing and merchandizes, insomuch that they left many destitute of the very necessaries of subsistence, food and raiment.[60]

Stapletown, one of the island's first English settlements, was destroyed by the French and never rebuilt. In 1963, when bulldozers were clearing the Belham Valley in Old Town to build the Golf Course, they encountered a midden with early historic materials in the area where Stapletown may once have stood.[61]

The widespread devastation caused by the French invasion of 1712 created a blank slate for the English to re-develop, strengthen, and expand industrial-scale sugar production across the island during the following decades of the 18th century.

---

[57] *PS MPL* 69.
[58] *PS RLM* 85.
[59] Sheridan 1974; Fergus 1994; Akenson 1997.
[60] *PS TNA* 92, quoted in Sheridan 1974: 172.
[61] *PS MNT* 60, File 42; archaeologists were unable to further investigate the area before it was deeply buried by pyroclastic flows in the early 2000s.

7. Montserrat's sugar era, 1712–1834

Montserrat's plantation-based sugar industry thrived in the decades after the 1712 French invasion. In the wake of the attackers' widespread destruction, the island's government and planters combined forces and converted the local economy into one based almost entirely on sugar. Indigo and cotton cultivation continued on a modest scale in the more remote parishes of St Peter's in the north and St Patrick's in the south. But these exports were of secondary importance in the sugar era—the period between the French invasion in 1712 and emancipation in 1834.[1]

Montserrat's sugar production peaked in 1735, a century before emancipation. At its height, planters exported 3,150 tons of sugar.[2] Production then remained relatively steady until the 1780s, with annual exports averaging 2,136 tons (Fig. 55).[3] In comparison with other sugar-producing islands in the Lesser Antilles, Montserrat's 18th-century industry ranked among the lowest in terms of output.[4] But given the island's small size, steep terrain, lack of permanent freshwater sources, and chronic labor shortages, the ability of Montserrat's enslaved laborers and estate managers to maintain a profitable sugar industry for much of the 18th century should be recognized as an impressive feat.

This chapter integrates primary historical accounts from archival documents with archaeological information to illustrate the effects that industrial-scale sugar production and forced labor had on Montserrat's economy, society, and landscape during its sugar era. All across Montserrat, there exist dozens of archaeological remains of sugar production facilities, residential areas, and agricultural lands (Fig. 56). As described in Chapter 2, these have now been documented and studied by two generations of archaeologists. Archaeological findings from these sites are detailed below.

---

[1] In 1732 Nicholas Skerrett deeded to John Blake several small parcels, indigo works, and 27 associated slaves (*PS MNT* 58). The 1729 census lists 18 plantations where indigo was grown, 9 in St Patrick's and 7 in St Peter's. Indigo cultivation covered 36 ¼ acres island-wide. Cotton was only cultivated in St Peter's Parish at the time; there, a total of 18 acres was under cultivation on 11 different estates (*PS CEN 30).*

[2] Akenson 1997: 154–170; Fergus 1994: 259.

[3] This figure is for the period between 1756 and 1780: Berleant-Schiller 1996: 256.

[4] Zacek 2010.

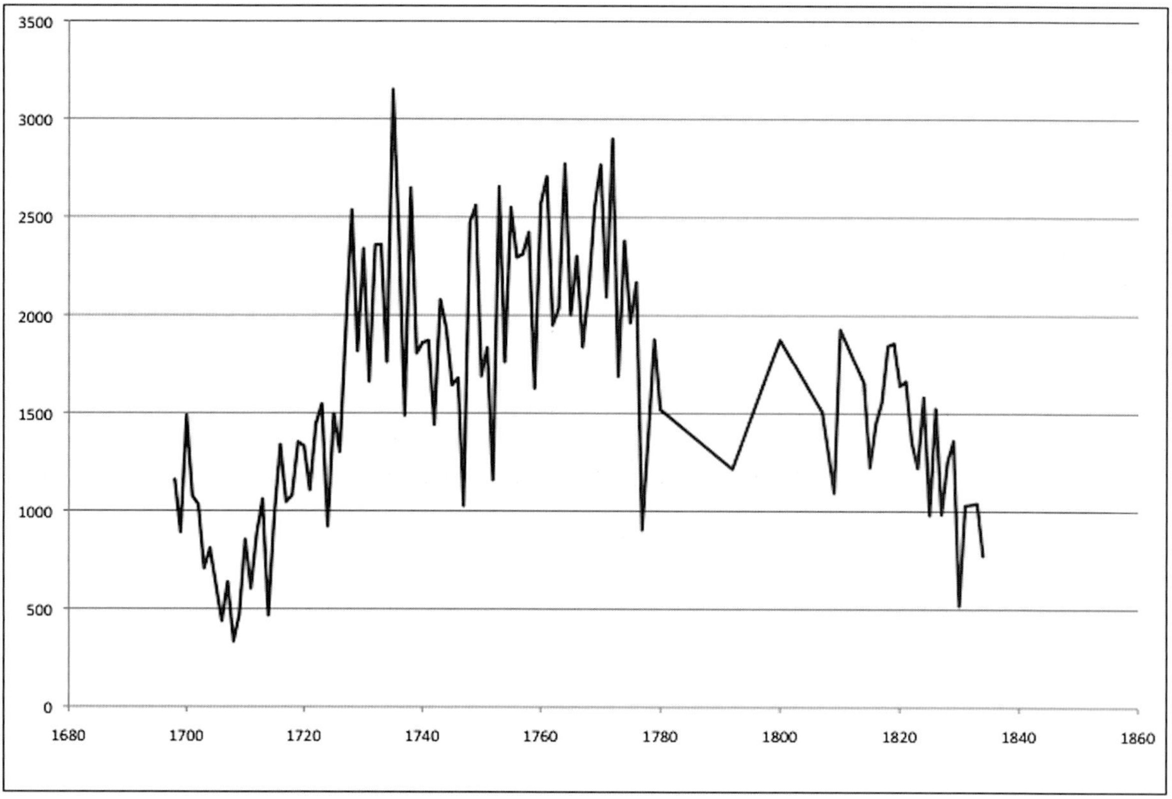

Fig. 55. Annual sugar production (in tons) on Montserrat, 1697–1834. (Sources: Deerr 1949: 196; Fergus 1994: 44, table 2.2.)

A sugar society

Montserrat experienced a major demographic shift between 1678 and 1729, the years in which two colonial censuses were taken. In just over 50 years, its population nearly doubled, from 3,674 to 7,219 inhabitants, and Irish Montserrat became a majority black island: in 1729, African-descended slaves made up 84% of the population. Slaveholding continued to increase steadily throughout the 18th century, and in 1768 the island's slave population peaked at 10,177 (of a total population of 11,497 individuals).[5]

This increase in chattel slavery was directly stimulated by the profitability of sugar. The more planters expanded their landholdings and sugar production, the greater the number of laborers they required. During the first half of the 18th century, a powerful network of planters, from English, Anglo-Irish, and Irish backgrounds, became extremely wealthy from the sugar plantations they owned. Some were affiliated with families which had been part of the first generation of European settlers on Montserrat, while others were relative newcomers who took advantage of the disorder following the 1712 French invasion by consolidating landholdings for sugar production. These

[5] Population figures are compiled from the following sources: *PS CEN* 29; *PS CEN* 30; English 1930: 224–225; Sheridan 1974: 171–172; Wheeler 1988; Berleant-Schiller 1989; 1996; Akenson 1997: 155; Zacek 2010.

Fig. 56. Map showing estates, military installations, and certain other historic-era sites mentioned in Chapters 7 and 8. (Map by Miriam Rothenberg; base map from Wadge 1988, provided by the Montserrat Volcano Observatory.)

elite 18th-century planters included men with the surnames of Allen, Blake, Farrell, Trant, Galway, Roach, Lynch, White, and Tuite, among others. Most of them, by 1729, owned upwards of 150 slaves, an estate of at least 500 acres, and two or more types of mills for crushing sugar cane.[6]

In 1729, sugar was under cultivation on 59 different estates, and cane fields covered 5,294 acres of fertile land across the island. The census of the same year listed all the owners of sugar estates and the different types of mills used for sugar processing on estate properties. Other surviving legal records from the 18th and 19th century, such as wills, probate inventories, and deeds of sale, itemize their buildings, equipment, and other property, including slaves, sometimes in great detail. Coupled with archaeological traces of ruined buildings, landscape modifications, and artifact finds, it is possible to reconstruct a clear picture of how sugar production worked on Montserrat, and how all segments of the island's plantation-based society were impacted by it.

How did sugar plantations operate?

During the 18th and 19th centuries, it was common on Montserrat for each individual sugar plantation to contain agricultural lands for growing sugar, an industrial complex where the sugar cane was processed, and dwellings where the laborers and plantation managers lived. Laborers' daily work routines and living conditions were dictated by an estate's manager. He could be the planter—the actual estate owner—or a managerial agent appointed on behalf of an absentee planter, or an overseer, who was typically a trusted slave from the estate.

The industrial center of sugar plantations contained buildings and other features necessary for the processing of sugar cane into liquid molasses and crystallized sugar (see Box H for the steps involved in sugar production). Many estates also included facilities for distilling rum. By the 18th century, sugar works' industrial buildings were almost always constructed with durable faced stone and mortar so that they could withstand the burden of constant use, as well as the natural disasters that frequently impacted the island. The mill and boiling house were the two most important industrial buildings on sugar estates. Mills crushed the juice from the cane stalks, and it then traveled through a trough downslope to a boiling house for processing into other products (Fig. 57).

The boiling house tended to be the largest sugar works building. As we clearly see in the boiling houses at the Galways and Weekes Estates, this single building could be the site of many different steps of sugar processing, such as refining, distilling, and storage. Or, as with the facilities at the Blakes or Little Bay Estates, it could be used solely for the initial processing of cane juice into molasses and sugar, with other processing steps taking place elsewhere. Reliable sources of water, too, were needed for sugar production: so, in addition to the industrial buildings, it is also common to find irrigation channels, clay-lined man-made ponds, and lime- or plaster-lined stone cisterns within the industrial areas of sugar works.

The stone bases of former windmill towers, which are typically two- to three-stories high, are still prominent fixtures on Montserrat's landscape. It is striking, in fact, that—whether one circumnavigates the devastated Exclusion Zone of Montserrat by boat, or flies over it in a helicopter (Fig. 57)—the most prominent landscape features remain these stone towers, so sturdily built that they seem virtually impervious to destruction. The majority of those that have survived into the 21st century (even through the eruptions of 1995 and later) were constructed after the hurricane of 1751. At that time, builders began to use more durable masonry for the towers, and intentionally designed the thick walls

[6] *PS CEN* 30.

Fig. 57. Ruins of Bethel Estate windmill tower and boiling house, still standing despite the devastating pyroclastic flows that overran this area in 2010. (Photo: John Cherry, 2018.)

and mortared stones to withstand wind damage and flooding from hurricanes. Previous windmills had been no match for the hurricanes of the first half of the 18th century. In June 1733 a hurricane destroyed three-quarters of the structures on Montserrat, including 36 sugar mills; four years later the island's rebuilt or new windmills were destroyed again in another hurricane, along with the island's sugar crop; and a third hurricane in 1751 also leveled many mills, houses, and sugar works.[7]

In 1729, 48 of the island's 59 sugar estates had mills for crushing the sugar cane. Fifty-two of these were animal-powered cattle mills, 23 were windmills, and 3 were water-powered mills.[8] Windmills were expensive to construct and maintain, but they were powerful and energy-efficient mechanisms for crushing cane relatively quickly: the fastest windmills could crush up to 200 tons of cane per week, producing 5,500 gallons of juice in the process.[9] Windmills typically appeared on the wealthiest and largest sugar estates on Montserrat. Nineteen of the 23 windmills listed in the 1729 census belonged to the largest and most profitable 30 plantations.[10] And in half of those instances, as at Galways Estate, the windmills were operated alongside a second animal- or water-powered mill.[11] At other estates, such as Old Road and Little Bay, cane was only crushed with

[7] Diderot 1758: 126; Southey 1827, vol. 1: 265, cited in Zacek 2010: 21–22.
[8] Southey 1827, vol. 1: 265.
[9] Goodwin 1987.
[10] Miles and Munby 2006: 64.
[11] Goodwin 1987.

Box H: Sugar processing: a step-by-step guide

Montserrat's plantations had sugar works of many different sizes and configurations. But the process of making sugar and its byproducts, such as molasses and rum, involved the same six general steps: planting, harvesting, crushing, boiling, drying, and distilling. The most detailed information we have about sugar-processing during the heyday of 18th-century production on Montserrat comes to us from the archaeological excavations of Galways Estate (see Box I). The following descriptions are based on archaeological finds there.[i]

Steps 1 and 2. Planting and harvesting: These steps took place from January to late June. Cane was harvested 15 months after it was planted. Enslaved laborers used cutlasses (machetes) to cut the cane six inches above the ground.

Step 3. Grinding: Freshly cut sugar cane stalks had to be ground within 24–36 hours of harvest in order to avoid spoilage. Grinding involved loading the stalks between iron rollers, which crushed the juice from them. Iron rollers could be propelled by animal, wind, water, or steam power. Animal mills had a central post and flanking gears that helped turn them. Cattle or other animals walked around the circular mill, propelling the gears, which, in turn, operated an upright iron roller. Laborers fed stalks of sugar cane back and forth through the rollers. The juice produced from the crushed cane gathered in a pan under the rollers, and then traveled in a wooden trough to the boiling house downhill. The leftover stalks, called *bagasse*, were dried and used later as fuel for the boiling house furnace. The crushing mechanisms inside wind mills worked similarly (although the rollers were often positioned horizontally rather than vertically).[ii] Windmills consisted of a stone base tower, on top of which sat a wooden shed and sails. A long pole was attached to the shed's exterior, and a wheel at the bottom of the pole allowed laborers to orient the sails according to the wind direction. As the windmill's sails spun, the gears and rollers inside the tower base rotated.

Step 4. Boiling: When sugar juice arrived at the boiling house from the mill, it was sent to a large vat, where it was allowed to settle. After laborers skimmed impurities from the settled juice, the liquid was transferred to a clarifier. This was the first step in the so-called "Jamaica train" process of evaporating the liquid and crystalizing the sugar. In the Jamaica train configuration, several open-topped copper kettles of various sizes (known simply as "coppers") were used in succession (Figs 58 and 59).[iii] The first and largest copper was farthest away from the fire. The juice boiled slowly there until it reached the required temperature. Then the impurities were strained and laborers ladled the contents into the second copper. Eventually, by the time the contents reached the hottest copper, closest to the furnace, a thick mass of sugar crystals formed.

Step 5. Cooling: The mass of crystallized sugar was removed from the smallest copper by the boiler and positioned in cooling trays, where it sat for up to 24 hours. Then the sugar would be packed into barrels (called hogsheads) and moved into a curing room. Holes in the bottom of the barrels allowed molasses to drip out. Hogsheads could hold 100–120 pounds of sugar.[iv] After the sugar was cooled, it was ready for sale or shipment.

Step 6. Distilling: The byproducts of sugar processing, including molasses and other remnants of the boiling process, were often converted into rum. In the still house, laborers rotated mixtures of molasses, skimmings from the boiling process, and water through a series of cisterns and barrels. After a week, the fermented liquid would be boiled in a still to produce the finished product—rum.

Fig. 58. Sketch by Diderot of sugar processing inside a Boiling House in the French West Indies, 1762. The sugar juice traveled down a sluiceway from the crushing mill and settled in a large vat (B); it was then transferred, using ladles (D), by enslaved laborers into a succession of boiling cauldrons (C). (Diderot 1958[1758]: Pl. IV.)

[i] Goodwin 1987: 48, 50, 115–117.
[ii] Animal mills could reportedly process about 1¼ tons of cane per hour (equal to 1/12 of an acre of cane), producing 125 gallons of cane juice per hour.
[iii] Diderot 1958 [1758].
[iv] Goodwin 1987: 115–117.

Fig. 59. Remnants of the Jamaica train system in the boiling house at Waterworks Estate. (Photo: John Cherry.)

animal mills. Today, the remains of windmill tower bases and animal mills are useful indicators of where the central industrial areas of historic sugar estates once existed.

Tuite's Estate: a profitable 18th-century enterprise

During the 1760s, Tuite's Estate was one of the largest sugar plantations on the island.[12] In 1766 the estate's owners, Richard Tuite, Nicholas Tuite, and their relative Robert Skerrett, appointed Charles O'Garra to act as the manager of the estate on their behalf. A copy of the original agreement (or indentureship, in 18th-century terms) survives today in the Lamont Library Archives at Harvard University. At the time it was made, the Irish-descended Tuites were in the process of establishing new sugar estates on St Croix, and they were increasingly absent from Montserrat. This indenture includes a detailed account of all of the buildings and property on Tuite's Estate. It provides an excellent illustration for archaeologists of the spatial layout and dimensions of buildings that we might expect to find on other less well-documented estates. An inventory appended to the end of the agreement enumerates 75 buildings, but it does not include a map.[13]

[12] In 1766 the estate was also spelled as Tuitte's. In modern times, it has been written as Tuitts.
[13] *PS LLA* 50.

In 1766 Tuite's was so large that it was divided into two parts: an upper and lower estate. The sugar-processing buildings in both the lower and upper estates are described as being built of lime and stone, with wooden roofs. All of the industrial buildings were reportedly in good condition. The lower estate contained 18 structures:

- One windmill, in good order, [with] everything new
- One boiling house [66 feet long, 26 broad, and 20 high] with a roof of hard wood
- Inside the boiling house, 9 coppers [boiling kettles] hung and not hung
- One curing house [54 feet long, 20 broad, and 22 high] with a roof of hard wood
- One still house [54 feet long, 20 broad, and 22 high] with a roof of hard wood
- One cattle mill
- One dwelling house [48 feet long, 26 feet 9 inches broad, and 12 feet high]
    - Inside the dwelling house there were 4 chambers, a hall, piazza, and porch, most of it built of hard wood, and a little out of repair
    - A kitchen and steward room are listed separately; they would have been detached from, but near, the dwelling house
- One manager's house
- Nine "Negro" houses (for enslaved laborers)

The upper estate contained 57 buildings:

- One stone windmill
- One boiling house
- One curing house
- One still house
    - Two cellars under the still house with 8 coppers hung
- A manager's house
- Forty-seven "Negro" houses
- One large cistern of lime and stone that will hold about 500 hogshead of water [plus] 40 buckets
- One large dwelling house of lime and stone [63 feet long, 21 broad, and 35 feet high]
    - Inside the dwelling house there were 3 large rooms and 3 cellars
    - Two outbuildings contained a kitchen and a steward room
- One sick house [30 feet long and 16 broad], built of lime and stone
- One horse stable [40 feet long and 13 broad]

The productive capacity of Tuite's Estate was impressive. The lower estate's curing house had two stills for distilling rum, each able to produce 300 gallons, and a third smaller one with a capacity of 120 gallons. The upper estate's curing house also had two stills, one with a capacity of 300 gallons, and one that could hold 120 gallons. In addition, the building held 31 liquor casks of 300 gallons each for storing finished rum.

Tuite's generated spectacular wealth for its owners and their families. In 1763, three years before the indenture with O'Garra, upon the death of Robert Tuite, officials inventoried his personal possessions, creating an itemized list and valuation in the process. This probate inventory affords a fascinating glimpse into the material world of an elite planter family on Montserrat.

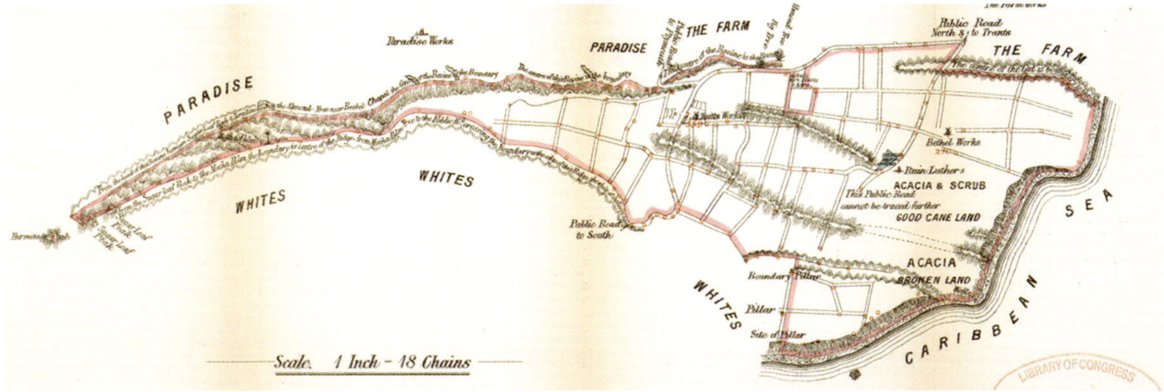

Fig. 60. Map of Tuite's estate, 1886; the sugar works, including a windmill tower, are identified in the center of the estate. (Source: PS LOC 52.)

Robert Tuite was the brother of Richard and relative of Nicholas; the latter was one of the owners of the family plantation in 1766, when the indentureship listing the estate's buildings was written. Robert's profits from the sugar industry evidently afforded him a life of luxury on Montserrat. His personal estate inventory of 1763 displayed a world of refinement, excess, and global connections.[14] He had a substantial wardrobe of gentleman's clothing, including 23 pairs of breeches, 51 pairs of slacks, 113 pairs of stockings made of various fabrics, 61 shirts, 44 caps, 15 neck scarves, 15 gingham jackets, 5 formal waistcoats, 3 dozen linen waistcoats, and 25 colored handkerchiefs. Tuite's outfits would have been accessorized by one of 17 wigs, a gold watch with chain, and perhaps one of the two swords that are also listed. In addition to garments, his inventory itemizes the furnishings, portable objects, and liquor stocks in his dwelling. They included mahogany furniture, china tableware, glassware, books, and a pistol, as well as 15 gallons of old rum, and cases of sour claret and brandy. The Tuite planters' material world and personal appearances undoubtedly stood in stark contrast to the enslaved laborers who occupied the 56 houses on the estate.

The first map of Tuite's Estate appears a century later, in 1868, when the then-bankrupt property was up for auction as part of the Encumbered Estates Act (Fig. 60).[15] Interestingly, only the industrial complex appears on the 1868 map: the rest of the dozens of buildings listed in the 1766 inventory would have to be the work of archaeologists to relocate. But, unfortunately, Tuite's Estate was destroyed by the recent volcanic crisis before they had the opportunity to study it. Nevertheless, the information in the 1763 probate inventory and 1766 indentureship provides historians and archaeologists with a clear picture of building sizes, construction materials, portable objects, and other traces of plantation activities that might be encountered during archaeological investigations.

Not all planters on Montserrat managed such vast estates as Tuite's. In fact, during the 18th century the majority of them cultivated relatively modest parcels of between 50 and 400 acres.[16]

---

[14] *PS LLA* 51.
[15] *PS LOC* 53.
[16] Ryzewski and Cherry 2015.

These estates, if they had industrial processing facilities, typically operated with animal mills. But even on smaller estates, planters sought to maximize profit from every inch of fertile land. Records reveal how planters fiercely guarded their lands and took legal action against each other in disputes over boundaries and property ownership. Court proceedings from 1737 summarize "sundry lawsuits" between neighbors (and also cousins) Robert Piper and Hugh Allen, who squabbled over the title to 100 acres of land in the remote area of northern St Peter's Parish: Allen claimed that the land belonged within the boundaries of his Rendezvous Estate, while Piper insisted that it was part of his adjacent estate lands in Little Bay.[17] Archaeological evidence of their border disputes is materialized today by a network of thick, sometimes mortared stone walls that traverse the hillsides and once marked estate property boundaries at Little Bay, Drummonds, and Rendezvous (Fig. 61).

Fig. 61. Historic stone boundary wall running along the northern edge of Drummonds Estate. (Photo: Emanuela Bocancea, 2011.)

Archaeology on, and of, sugar estates

By the 18th century, sugar plantations were built at all elevations and in all regions of Montserrat, from the fertile farmlands of the south and southwest (Farm, Weekes), to the heights of the Centre Hills (Locust Valley, Fairy Walk), to coastal areas in the island's north and east (Little Bay, Trants). Archaeological finds from four different sugar estates that were active during the height of sugar production in the 18th century—Galways, Weekes, Little Bay, and Locust Valley/Trants—illustrate the diversity in the types of sugar estates that were operating at this time.

Galways

Galways Estate was established in the 1660s by Captain David Galway, the estate's founder and namesake. Captain Galway was already an active planter in St Patrick's village at the time of the 1678 census, and by 1729 his was the largest sugar plantation on the island. Covering an area of 1320 acres, the estate then had 100 acres of land in cultivation or producing sugar cane, and a force of 62 enslaved laborers to work it.[18] The archaeological research at Galways, conducted over the course of two decades by Lydia Pulsipher and Conrad Mac Goodwin, was the first project on Montserrat to focus on the physical layout and operations of a sugar plantation, and how these processes changed over time in response to particular environmental, social, and political situations (see Box 1).

---

[17] *PS MNT* 59.

[18] Pulsipher 1986; 1987; Goodwin 1987; Pulsipher and Goodwin 2001.

Box I: Galways Estate: Archaeology reveals the workings of a historic sugar plantation

Perched at 350 m above sea level on a steep slope on the southwest flanks of Soufrière Hills, Galways Estate operated as a sugar plantation for over 200 years, from the 1660s until the late 19th century, when a new sugar works was constructed farther downhill, in Lower Galways. The Upper Galways sugar works and surrounding landscape were the focus of an interdisciplinary research project, directed by geographer Lydia Pulsipher and archaeologist Conrad Mac Goodwin. Their work combined approaches from archaeology, anthropology, and geography to understand how the plantation and the different classes of people who lived there functioned within the surrounding mountainous environment. Excavations and ethnographic research began in 1981 with the help of volunteers, students, and the Montserrat National Trust; many Montserratians also participated in the excavations and laboratory analysis of artifacts.[i] Fieldwork continued until volcanic eruptions made the site inaccessible.[ii] The project produced a comprehensive understanding of how sugar production worked on Montserrat, including industrial operations, water management, landscape modification, and laborers' living and working conditions. This is the sugar estate on Montserrat that we perhaps understand the best—even though, sadly, it no longer exists.

At the height of its sugar production in the mid-18th century, Galways covered 1300 acres. The plantation's industrial facilities and dwellings were clustered in a central area spanning just 3 acres along the ridge. When investigations began in 1981, the buildings were in ruins and covered by vegetation. Goodwin's subsequent doctoral dissertation research examined the spatial organization of over a dozen buildings and other human-made features in this central area. His excavations of these buildings provided detailed information about how they were used as part of the sugar-production process between about 1750 and 1850.

Goodwin determined that, in the 1770s, Galways' owners organized the buildings on the estate to reflect the aesthetically pleasing, orderly Georgian architecture that was in vogue in Europe and North America at the time. The placement of buildings conveyed Galway's prestige and global connections as a sugar planter. He positioned his buildings in ways that took advantage of the estate's natural topography. At the top of the complex, upwind of the sugar works, he built the L-shaped manor house. Two substantial mills—one animal-powered, one wind-powered—were positioned 75 and 100 feet uphill from the boiling house (Fig. 62). As these two mills crushed cane, the resulting juice flowed downhill through troughs and into the boiling house (Fig. 63). Excavations in the boiling house revealed a multi-room, two-storey structure. Evidence was also found that the boiling-house infrastructure was renovated in the 18th century to accommodate state-of-the art "Jamaica train" sugar-boiling technology. Downslope from the boiling house were documented a large warehouse and a still house, where a series of four massive cisterns were once used to distill rum from the sugar that was being processed further uphill. At the lowest level of the site were found the remains of the enslaved laborers' village, including at least twelve houses.

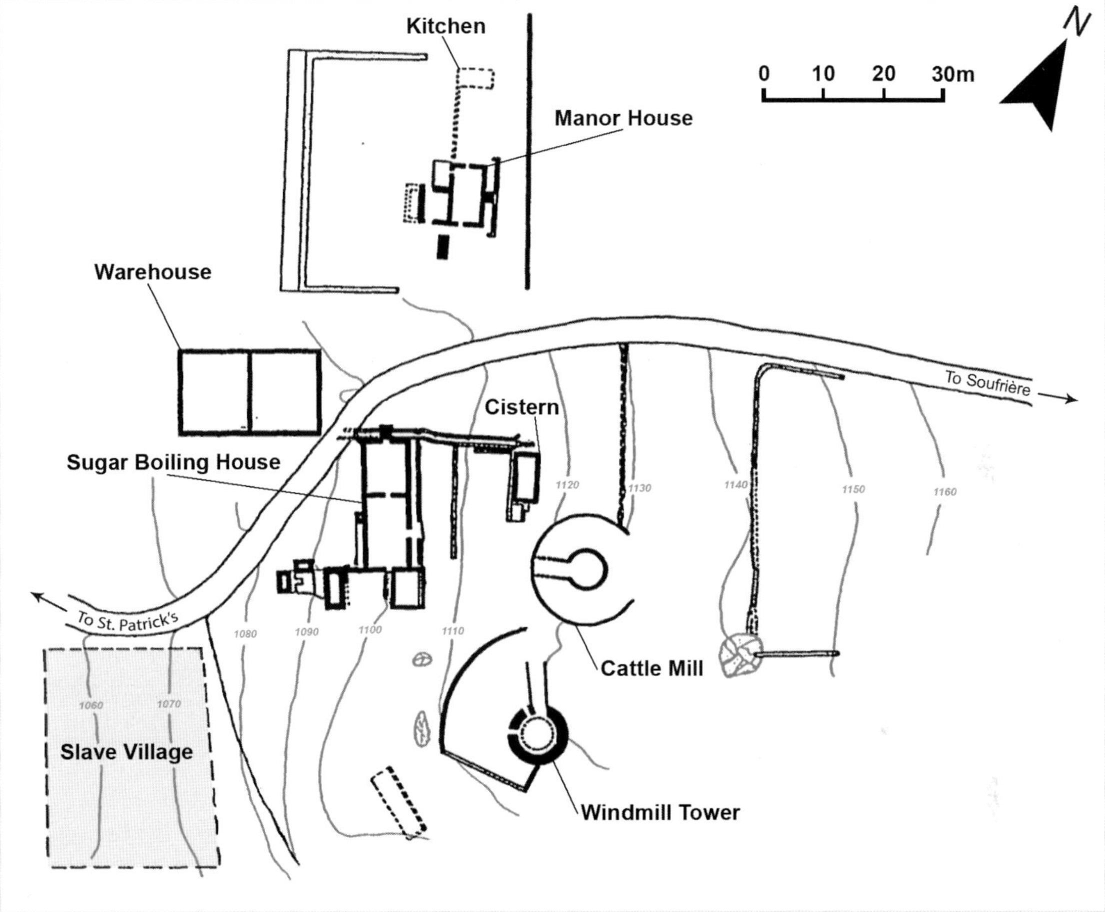

Fig. 62. Plan of Galways Estate. (Original plan in Goodwin 1987: 91, fig. 5.2; redrawn by Miriam Rothenberg.)

[i] Numerous publications report on the excavations and ethnographic research on Galways, and they provide the basis for the information presented here. These include: Goodwin 1982; 1987; Pulsipher and Goodwin 1989; 2001; Pulsipher 1982; 1986; 1987; 1990; 1994; Howson 1990; 1995.

[ii] The site now lies deep in the Exclusion Zone and is inaccessible. Pyroclastic flows overran the site in the early stages of the current volcanic crisis, and none of the standing buildings have survived. In June 2018 John Cherry and Miriam Rothenberg conducted a helicopter fly-over of the site to ascertain whether any structural remains had survived; the whole area is now heavily overgrown with vegetation, but no signs were seen of any part of the former site.

Fig. 63. Galways Estate boiling house, viewed from the windmill tower entrance, 1991. (Photo: Jan Bester.)

Weekes

Like Galways, Weekes was one of the island's largest and wealthiest estates by the 18th century.[19] Weekes is located south of the Belham River, about 2 km southeast of Old Road Bay, and along the northern flank of St George's Hill; some of its ruins survive in good condition and have been investigated archaeologically. Along with Waterworks and Old Road Estate, it was also one of the first plantations established on the island. Upon his death in 1649, Anthony Brisket, Montserrat's first Governor, bequeathed Weekes and Waterworks estates to his wife and son. At that time, Weekes was simply referred to as "Ye Southe Side of the Riverier [*sic*]", and sugar production had not yet begun on the island.

This estate has had several different names over the course of its existence, including River Head, Wykes, Week's, and its present-day version, Weekes. By the time the island-wide census was taken in 1729, Weekes was owned by Captain George Wyke, and it was the third largest estate on the island. Compared to Galways, Weekes was smaller in area (700 acres). But it had three times more sugar under cultivation (300 vs 100 acres), and its industrial complex and labor force were both considerably larger. In 1729 Weekes processed sugar with the assistance of two stone-built

[19] *PS MNT* 60, File 12.

Fig. 64. Weekes Estate windmill tower base. (Photo: Beau Kromberg, 2017.)

windmills, one water mill, and 223 enslaved laborers. In 1817 the estate, then called River Head, was under the ownership of William Irish, who held 369 slaves there.[20] By the time the estate was listed for auction in the aftermath of the Encumbered Estates Act, its acreage had been reduced to 212 acres. The inventory accompanying the 1870 auction indicates that sugar production continued at Weekes into the 1860s. It lists "a Dwelling House in tenantable order, Wind Mill in working order, Boiling House, Curing House…Still House [with] Still out of order", and a variety of sugar processing equipment, including copper kettles, boiling tubs, ladles, skimmers, vats, a clarifier, and a sundial.[21]

In 2016 and 2017 archaeologists recorded seven historic stone building remains at Weekes.[22] Remnants of the estate's sugar processing complex are still well preserved, as are other outbuildings, boundary walls, cisterns, pillars marking the historic road approaching the property, and a vaulted tunnel.

The most prominent surviving architectural feature is a ca. 10 m-tall stone-built windmill tower (Fig. 64). Its interior diameter measures 5.65 m, and the mortared, faced stone walls are 1.2 m thick. The main entry is through a 2 m-wide archway, with two additional, narrower archways serving as windows. The windmill is built roughly 2.5 m above the present ground level, and from this elevated

[20] *PS TNA* 96; *PS CEN* 30.
[21] *PS LOC* 54.
[22] *UPR* 26.

Fig. 65. Pottery recovered from the SLAM *survey of Weekes Estate include 18th and 19th-century varieties manufactured in Europe (tin-glazed earthenware, white salt-glazed stoneware, creamware, pearlware, and whiteware with painted, slipped, and transfer-printed decorations, porcelain, redware, and stoneware). (Photo: Krysta Ryzewski.)*

position cane juice would have flowed downhill to the sugar works, about 16 m to the northeast. This sugar-works complex is a large (13.5 × 15 m), two-storey, multi-room building built against the slope of the hill, similar to the placement of the boiling house at Galways. It contains three large rooms, each of which would have been utilized during a different step in the sugar production process—boiling, curing, and storage. A series of three lime-plastered cisterns are nestled between two of the rooms and run from the upper to lower storey of the structure.

In 2015 the banks of a newly-cut road leading to a geothermal drilling facility exposed artifacts associated with the estate's dwelling house, which may have initially been the "Great House" residence of the planter and then of a local overseer, once the owners moved off the island. Its location matches that of a T-shaped structure on the 1870 map of the property, labeled "Site of Old Dwelling".[23] Archaeologists recovered 177 artifacts during a surface survey of the area near this house. The majority were European-made, decorated pottery from the mid- to late 18th century, including pearlware, creamware, porcelain, British brown stoneware, and tin-glazed earthenware (Fig. 65). Laboratory analysis identified 41 different vessels among the individual sherds. This variety implies

[23] *PS LOC 54.*

that the occupants of the dwelling house had a wide assortment of imported wares with which to entertain and display wealth and global connections.

In addition to pottery, there were also recovered fragments of white clay tobacco-pipes, dark green alcohol bottles, and a characteristic 18th-century French blue-green rum bottle; only one piece of locally-manufactured coarse earthenware pottery was recovered. The prevalence of decorated and refined European pottery at Weekes' dwelling house reinforces the ways in which planters aspired to set themselves apart, with material distinctions, from the laboring class.

Little Bay

The Little Bay estate was one of the northernmost plantations on the island. Located a little inland and slightly uphill from the shore at Little Bay (behind the present-day cricket pitch), this estate was modest by comparison with Galways and Weekes. In 1729 the entire plantation comprised an area of 100 acres, of which 36 acres were under cultivation for sugar and four for cotton. At that time, Robert Piper, Sr owned the estate, along with its labor force of 39 slaves.[24] Archaeological remains here were first located in 1981.[25] Remnants of five stone structures are now visible on the surface of this heritage site: a cattle mill, a boiling house, a domestic structure, a curing house or barn, and a large rectangular structure whose function is unknown. As already described in Chapter 2, over the course of several years archaeologists excavated the enslaved laborers' village on the estate's periphery (discussed in Chapter 8) and the manor house, the remains of which sit on a hilltop above the site's industrial buildings.[26]

From 2010 to 2012 Jessica Striebel MacLean led the excavation of the manor house as part of her doctoral dissertation research (see Fig. 13).[27] Even though Little Bay was a modest-sized plantation, the finds reveal that Piper and his family nevertheless amassed considerable wealth and influence during the years when they resided in the home. Excavations produced an array of household and luxury items, which provide intriguing insights into what life was like for the planter's family on the estate. Elaborate dining vessels, manufactured in Europe during the mid-18th century, included porcelain plates, a porcelain punch bowl, a creamware sauceboat, soup plates and dinner plates with feather-edged decoration, a creamware teapot, and a mustard pot. Remains of animal bones excavated from trash deposits near the house document a diverse range of dining options: beef, pork, mutton, goat, fowl, and fish. Accompanying their formal, multi-course dinners, the excavated artifacts show that the Pipers used glass drinking-vessels, including wine glasses with decorative stems, and knives and forks (the latter a utensil that was just coming into usage at elite dining tables in Europe and America at this time). In addition to imported wares for eating and drinking, there were found brass components of an English long-case clock (dated to ca. 1765), a flintlock pistol shank (manufactured ca. 1760–1775), a fob seal (Fig. 66) decorated with the figure of a cupid and inscribed "Au Plus Adroit" ("to the most skillful"), red and blue glass beads, and gaming tokens made of broken pottery.[28] The Little Bay Estate, and its association with the Piper family, disappears from historical records after the

[24] *PS CEN 30.*
[25] Pulsipher 1982; 1986.
[26] *UPR* 6.
[27] MacLean 2015.
[28] MacLean 2015: 286, 307.

early 1780s. The manufacturing date-ranges of the artifacts, together with soil evidence of a structural fire, confirm that the manor house was quite possibly burned by the French when they occupied the island between 1782 and 1784.

Fig. 66. A gentleman's watch fob seal dating to the mid-18th century, recovered during the manor house excavations at Little Bay Estate in 2010. Its intaglio design includes Cupid piercing a heart atop a column with his arrow and the words "Au Plus Adroit" (to the most skillful). (Photo: Mary Beaudry.)

Trants and Locust Valley

By the mid-18th century, the Trants Estate was among the most profitable on the island. Located on the windward coast, adjacent to the former Bramble Airport and just north of the major prehistoric site of Trants (see Chapter 4), the buildings of this sugar and cotton estate were still well-preserved at the time the volcanic eruptions began in 1995. In 2010, the site, by then already badly damaged, was finally buried altogether by pyroclastic flows.

The Trant family was part of Montserrat's Irish-descended plantocracy and they arrived on the island with the first generation of 17th-century settlers. The family's involvement with sugar production intensified in the 1720s under Dominick Trant. During the 1720s and 1730s, records show that Trant became one of the island's largest landowners by purchasing sections of smaller estates and consolidating them into one massive estate.[29] At the time of the 1729 census, when he was just beginning to annex smaller estate lands, he owned 350 acres, with 250 under sugar cultivation, and 225 slaves.

The center of Trants 18th-century estate was located near the coast at Trants Bay. It contained an industrial processing facility and dwelling houses for the planter and managerial staff. These facilities remained active into the 20th century, when a steam-powered mill was introduced for processing sugar and cotton. Archaeologists David Miles and Julian Munby recorded the standing ruins and cultural landscape features of Trants Estate in May of 1995, just before the first volcanic eruption that took place a few weeks later (Fig. 67).[30] The complex contained standing ruins from the 18th and 19th centuries, including the planter's dwelling.

The surviving Great House at Trants consisted of a 20th-century timber-framed dwelling built on top of what appeared to be an 18th-century stone basement foundation (Fig. 68). There was evidence that the first house had been constructed of mortared stone, and likely included stone

[29] Akenson 1997: 152.
[30] Miles and Munby 2006: 58–62.

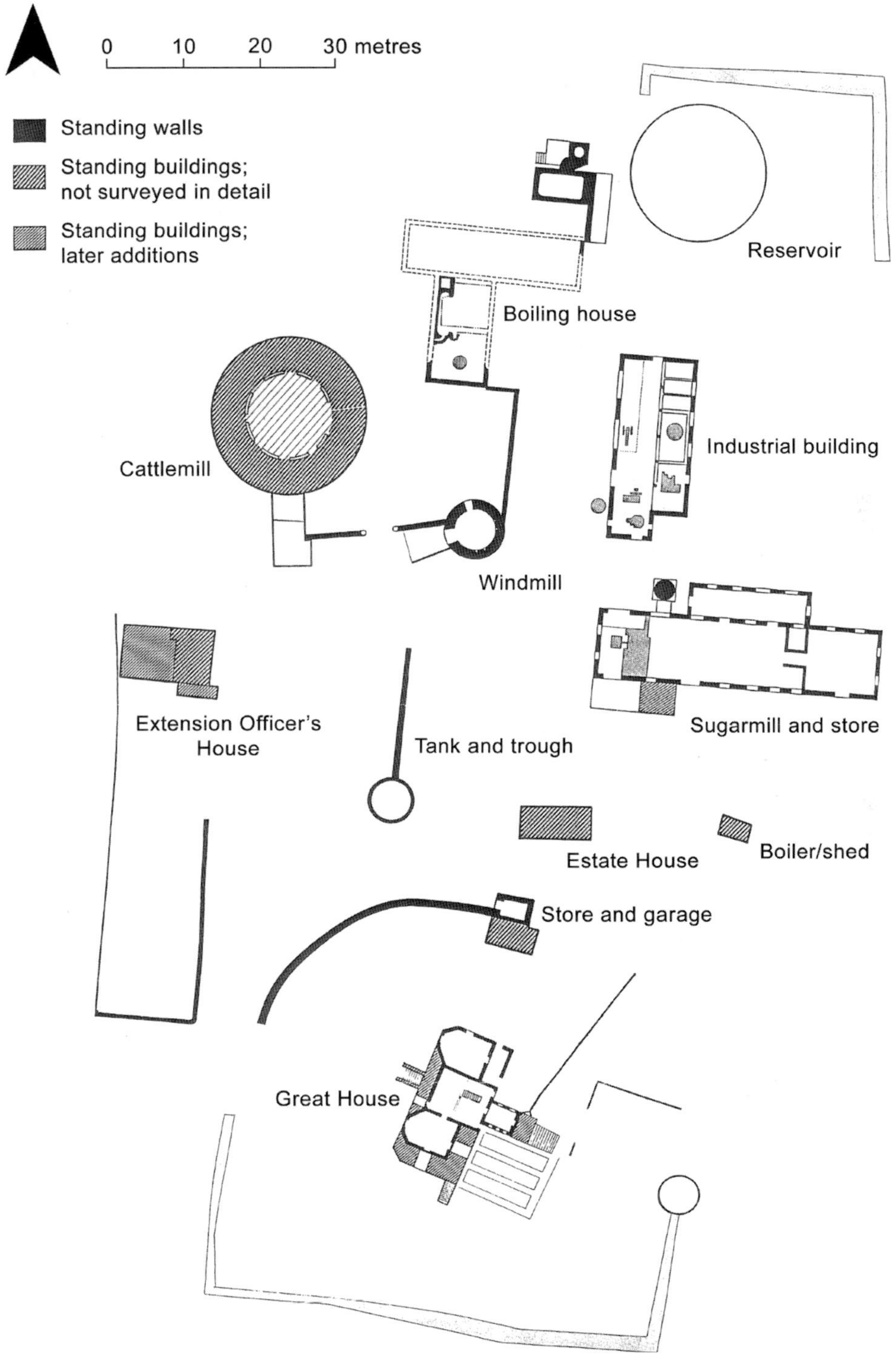

Fig. 67. Archaeological plan of the central industrial and domestic area of Trants Estate. (Plan redrawn by Miriam Rothenberg, after UPR 30: 14.)

verandahs, arched windows, and hipped roofs. It was surrounded by stone walls, which would have enclosed an ornamental garden and separated the dwelling from the industrial processing facilities to the north.

Fig. 68. Trants Great House in the 1980s. (Photo: Bob Bell.)

The sugar works complex included two mills (a windmill and cattle mill), near a substantial boiling house. Two additional industrial buildings were located south of the boiling house. At either end of this complex were two water catchment features: a man-made reservoir measuring ca. 15 m in diameter, and a smaller cistern and trough. Two other dwellings also stood between the industrial complex and the Great House; at the time of the 1995 survey they were called the "Estate House" and known as the "Extension Officer's House". These dwellings would have likely housed overseers and managers during the plantation's operations.

The ruins of the Trants Estate industrial buildings and Great House that were visible in 1995 barely convey the extent to which Trants drastically transformed the regional landscape for sugar cultivation. Archaeological landscape survey conducted by the *SLAM* project has revealed how, by the late 18th-century, Trants aggressively expanded sugar production and processing into the high elevations and steep terrain of the Centre Hills, approximately 2 km west of the central area of the estate at an elevation of 305 m above sea level, maximizing every plantable acre of land for profit. With the assistance of aerial LiDAR imagery (see Box A), archaeologists relocated and mapped the remains of a substantial secondary sugar processing complex in an area called Locust Valley, which only appears in passing references in archival sources.[31] The Locust Valley site contains the remains of two windmills, one with a keystone that reads either 1773 or 1777, and three associated sugar-processing structures, all built in a robust mortared-stone architectural technique. A two-storey boiling house is situated downhill from the uppermost windmill tower base, built into the hillside. Man-made water-retention ponds, raised earthen platforms where laborers' housing may have existed, boundary walls, trackways, and an extensive system of terracing running down the steep flanks of Mournful Ghaut were also documented, using LiDAR and survey in combination.

Informed by the results of archaeological surveys, subsequent archival research revealed a few cursory references to this Locust Valley estate. The estate apparently contained a sugar works prior to 1727, when the land and its "buildings, mill, still, and coppers" were sold by John Farrill to his cousin, Dominick Trant.[32] Other references indicate that Trant and his heirs continued to expand and utilize the Locust Valley sugar works into the 1780s.[33] By the mid-1780s, Trants Estate and its secondary, upland sugar production site at Locust Valley were generating enough profit that the family moved away from the island, leaving the estate's management in the hands of local attorneys

[31] Opitz *et al.* 2015; *UPR* 15; *UPR* 16.
[32] *PS MNT* 56.
[33] Locust Valley Estate is mentioned in a trespassing lawsuit in 1780 (*PS MPL* 70).

and overseers.[34] Their departure from Montserrat was part of a growing trend of absenteeism among the island's plantation elite. By the turn of the 19th century, many of the owners who had been the most financially successful operated their estates on Montserrat remotely from the comfort of their stately homes in England or on other Caribbean islands.

Smaller estates

Smaller plantations proliferated on Montserrat in the 18th century, often nestled in remote or inaccessible parts of the island's northern region, where land was less suitable for large-scale sugar cultivation. Estates such as Thatch Valley, Valentine Ghaut, Rendezvous, Drummonds, and Silver Hills in the northernmost parish of St Peter's are not well-reported in historical documents, but they are known to exist as early as the 1670s, when they appear on the map of Montserrat in the Blathwayt Atlas.[35] Diagnostic historic-period European pottery and other artifacts recovered during the *SLAM* project survey confirm that these estates continued to be occupied into the 19th century. Information about the spatial layout, age, operations, and inhabitants of these smaller plantations are known mainly from historical artifact remains, building foundations, and landscape modifications. Extensive archaeological surveys of the entirety of St Peter's Parish have documented how these less substantial estates functioned. They typically had no more than three stone-built structures. The absence of windmill or animal mill remains at the Thatch Valley and Valentine Ghaut estates, for example, suggests that their lands were used for cultivating provisions or raising livestock during the sugar era, thereby providing an important source of local sustenance for the people living on sugar estates who did not have enough space to cultivate crops for their own workers or livestock.

Archaeology beyond sugar estates

Scholars often examine sugar estates as though they were self-contained entities. But in reality sugar plantations were connected to each other and with other centers of activity across the island, including forts, markets, ports, towns, and villages. For example, in the immediate area surrounding Carr's Bay and Little Bay in the island's north, there were the sugar estates of Drummonds, Rendezvous, Geralds, and Little Bay. Military installations were situated between these estates at Carr's Bay, Gun Hill, and Valentine Ghaut. Small settlements on top of Rendezvous Bluff, along the ridge above Valentine Ghaut, and on top of Potato Hill were positioned at the margins of existing estates. These smaller settlements and the people who lived in them are almost totally absent from detailed historical records, yet archaeologists have documented artifacts and structural remains at all of the aforementioned sites. The most intriguing of these "in-between" settlements is located on top of Potato Hill.[36]

Potato Hill is an elongated low hilltop that divides Little Bay from Carr's Bay, covering an area of 19 acres (Fig. 69). It is isolated from the surrounding inlets and sugar estates by its steep slopes, a feature that made the hilltop defensively advantageous and suitable for settlement.

[34] Akenson 1997: 152.
[35] *UPR* 7; *UPR* 9; *UPR* 12; Ryzewski and Cherry 2016; *PS JCB* 44.
[36] Ryzewski and Cherry 2016.

Fig. 69. Potato Hill and its steep sea-cliffs, between Carr's Bay (foreground) and Little Bay. (Photo: John Cherry.)

No known maps or detailed records provide information about the inhabitants of Potato Hill or the structures that were once occupied there; a passing reference to it, in a description of Geralds Estate, mentions only that Potato Piece (as it was then called) was under sugar cultivation by the plantation's managers. The systematic gridded survey of the hilltop conducted by the *SLAM* project in 2013 (see Chapter 2) identified the location of four dwellings and located over 2,000 artifacts on the surface, the majority of which had manufacturing dates from the 18th century. Follow-up excavations focused on a small (3 × 2.2 m) dwelling on the south slope, and a modest dwelling with a mortared stone foundation situated on top of the hill, measuring 6 × 4 m. (A 19th-century schoolhouse structure, unrelated to these earlier 18th-century dwellings, was also excavated on the hilltop and is discussed in Chapter 9.)[37]

Excavations of the smaller of these structures recovered nearly 140 artifacts. The majority were fragments of locally-made, Afro-Caribbean, coarse earthenware pottery, as well as a few fragments of European-made creamware and salt-glazed stoneware vessels, bottle glass, and white clay tobacco pipes. Chert flakes utilized as gunflints or expedient tools, and building materials such as plaster, were also recovered. The most interesting find was a musket ball lodged in the structure's

[37] Excavation and artifact analysis data appears in *UPR* 17; *UPR* 22; *UPR* 27.

Fig. 70. Artifacts excavated from the 18th-century dwelling on Potato Hill include pottery (locally-made coarse earthenware, European-made porcelain, creamware, Whieldon ware, and tin-glazed earthenware), glass bottles, tobacco pipe fragments, iron nails, an iron horseshoe, brick, and a token modified from a broken piece of a tin-glazed plate. (Photo: Krysta Ryzewski.)

foundation wall, possibly after having been fired from nearby. The diagnostic artifacts from the dwelling date its occupation to the last half of the 18th century.

Located 40 m uphill from this small dwelling, the larger domestic structure was the focus of excavations in 2015 and 2016. Over 1,400 artifacts were recovered, 61% of them pottery, representing 81 identifiable individual vessels; of these, one-quarter were locally-made, low-fired, coarse earthenware vessels (mostly pots and bowls), and the remainder were European-manufactured plates, bowls, and serving vessels (Fig. 70). These European varieties included Staffordshire slipware, creamware, pearlware, and agateware—all with mid- to late 18th-century manufacturing dates.

Also recovered were bottle glass, chert flakes, lead musketballs, and architectural materials (including brick, plaster and iron nails) that indicate a well-constructed, wood-framed house, built by someone who obviously had the resources to obtain imported building materials. The dwelling was carefully built on top of 40 cm-thick walls with mortared faces of flat stones and a rubble fill; they stood two courses tall and were set into a layer of thick brown clay which the builders had spread over the bedrock (Fig. 71). Two circular postholes at the building's corners imply large wooden posts supporting the wooden structure that probably sat on these durable stone walls, a reconstruction also made plausible by the quantity of iron nail fragments recovered from the excavations.

We don't know who lived in these houses on Potato Hill in the 18th century. But artifacts from the larger structure's excavation hint at the residents' activities, perhaps even their beliefs. Lead fishing-net weights imply the harvesting of local resources, whether for subsistence or the market. Various intriguing artifacts may suggest connections with African-based spiritual

Fig. 71. Aerial view of the 18th-century rectangular structure on the east side of Potato Hill at the conclusion of excavations in 2016 shows the stone foundation walls and stone rubble in the structure's interior (partly removed by excavation). (Drone photo: Matthew Pihokker.)

practices, such as blue and red glass beads, broken pottery fragments with single holes drilled in them (for hanging or wearing as a pendant), small lead scraps cut into triangles, and a coin cut in half. Other unusual finds include pottery fragments whittled into circular tokens or gaming pieces, and a cut gemstone that would have been set into a ring or pendant.[38] Overall, this

[38] Stine *et al.* 1996.

group of finds suggests that the residents lived a life of modest means, played out locally. It might have involved informal economic activities, perhaps using makeshift objects for exchange, and the conversion of everyday items into objects with special meaning (such as drilled broken plate fragments). We can only speculate, but the diversity of the finds and the dimensions of the structure both suggest that Potato Hill's residents were not enslaved laborers who worked on the nearby sugar plantations, but free people and—based on the ways in which they modified and selected personalized objects in line with documented African spiritual practices—quite possibly of African descent.

The decline of sugar and continued threats

Montserrat's sugar industry began to unravel during the second half of the 18th century on account of various economic, political, and purely accidental factors. In 1755, for example, a Yellow Fever epidemic struck the island, affecting the entire population, especially the enslaved laborers. The most devastating interruption to the sugar industry, without doubt, came in 1782, when the French invaded Montserrat and occupied it for the following 24 months. During the initial onslaught, the French burned crops and buildings on sugar estates, including, probably, the Great House at the Little Bay Estate.[39]

After the French evacuated Montserrat in 1784, local authorities took measures to increase the island's security. Archaeological evidence of these defensive efforts is visible in the construction of a gun battery above Valentine Ghaut, the expansion of the Carr's Bay battery, and the enlargement of Fort St George on the hilltop above Plymouth (Fig. 72). By the end of the 18th century there were nine strategic batteries with cannon placed around the island, mostly in coastal areas: Valentine Ghaut, Carr's Bay, Bransby Point, Power's Battery, Daniel's Battery, Swana Ghaut, St Patrick's, Woodlands, and Gun Hill in Streatham Village.[40] These defenses apparently proved to be effective deterrents during later, continued attempts by the French to take Montserrat in 1805 and 1806.

Fig. 72. The 18th-century gun battery above Valentine Ghaut held three cannon, two of which remain on the platform, and one that has fallen downhill to the north. (Drone photo: Matthew Pihokker, 2016.)

Following the French occupation of Montserrat, the value of sugar declined steadily. The rise of more competitive sugar industries outside the Caribbean, together with various trade wars in which England was involved, diminished the profitability of local

[39] Wheeler 1988; Crandall 2000; Ryzewski and Cherry 2015; MacLean 2015.

[40] Crandall 2000.

sugar. In a predictable response to these changing economic conditions, Montserrat's planters started to diversify their crops, as the export records indicate clearly. By 1789 planters had converted 2,000 acres of former sugar fields to cotton cultivation.[41]

In the decades leading up to the abolition of slavery in 1834, Montserrat's slave population remained around 6,000.[42] The profitable family-run sugar estates of the 18th century and their slave labor forces were increasingly grouped into large corporate-run enterprises managed by overseas agents. As a result of this consolidation, the island's remaining sugar estates in the early 19th century were larger and operated with more slaves than ever before. In 1810 there had been 245 slaveholders on Montserrat, but on the eve of abolition in 1834 there were only 166.[43] Between them, they owned all of the island's 6,218 slaves; Queely Shiell was the island's largest slave-owner, with 370 individuals listed as his personal property.[44] These individual laborers, many of whom are absent from archival accounts, were the hands that built the sugar industry and sustained it through Montserrat's most profitable decades of monocrop agriculture. The conditions in which they lived, the creativity they exhibited with limited resources, and the ways in which they coped with the oppressive structures of the plantation-based society of the 18th and 19th century are apparent in the archaeological remains to which we turn in the next chapter.

[41] Ryzewski and Cherry 2015.
[42] *PS BOA* 18:114.
[43] Howson 1995: 322–323.
[44] English 1930: 271.

8. Slavery and the slave experience

In plantation-era Montserrat slaves were the property of their owners. They were not allowed to participate in the island's government, they had limited legal rights, they were routinely separated from their families and sent away to other estates, and they were often illiterate. Planters had little regard for their health, safety, or longevity, and subjected them to brutal corporal punishment for seemingly negligible offenses. They also designed the spatial layout of their estates so that their Great Houses were optimally positioned to surveil the laborers' villages and whatever activities residents participated in during their leisure time; as a result, slaves had limited privacy.

Slaves built the infrastructure of the plantation system—the mills, great houses, and processing complexes. They erected the defensive structures that protected the island against enemy invasions. They maintained the roads between villages. They constructed docks for ships, and even some of the vessels that anchored there. Their works of skilled masonry, carpentry, and engineering survive today in all of the extant traces of plantation-era buildings and landscapes.

The oppressive conditions that planters and government officials implemented during the plantation era were designed to command obedience and strip agency from the slave population. These conditions were undeniably hostile. But, while freedom was non-existent, enslaved laborers were not altogether powerless. Archaeological evidence and historical accounts detail some of the ways in which the African-descended individuals coerced into chattel slavery coped with the oppressive structures of plantation-based society in the 18th and 19th centuries by developing and maintaining their own Afro-Caribbean culture from the limited resources at their disposal. This chapter examines aspects of the slave experience on Montserrat based on archaeological and historical sources of information.

Who were Montserrat's enslaved laborers?

From 1724 until emancipation in 1834, Montserrat's slaves comprised no less than 80% of the island population.[1] In 1811, three years after the passage of the Slave Trade Act, Montserrat's enslaved laborers comprised a staggering 91% of the total population. In reality, this Act made no noticeable impact on Montserrat, partly because slave trading vessels rarely stopped in Montserrat after 1780.[2]

[1] See Chapter 7, n. 5.
[2] Fergus 1994: 42–45.

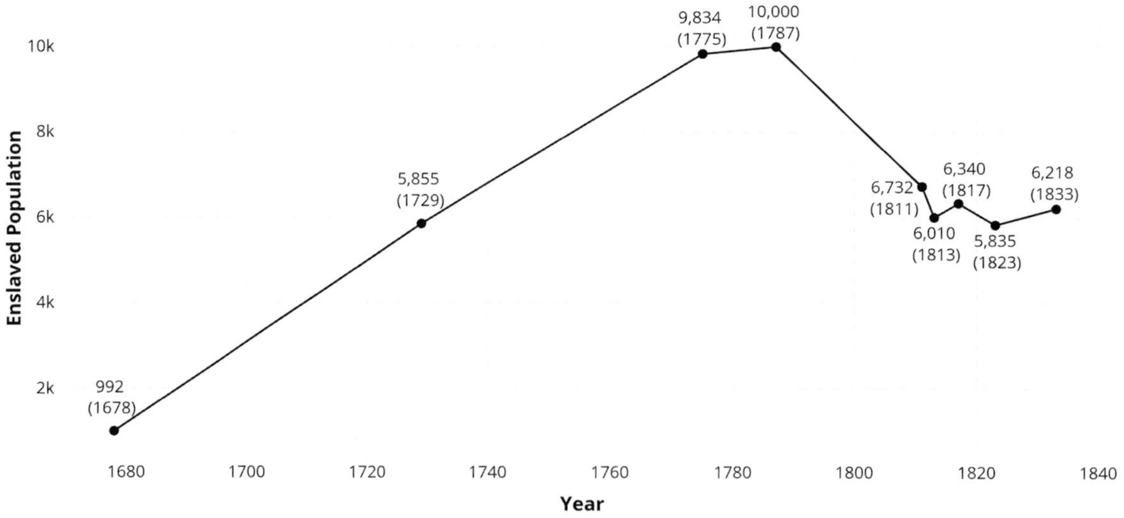

Fig. 73. Montserrat's slave population over the course of the plantation era, 1678–1833; data from Akenson (1997) and Wheeler (1988).[3] (Diagram by Miriam Rothenberg.)

Instead, local planters relied on the "natural increase", or offspring, of their slaves to expand and strengthen their labor force. Montserrat's 19th-century slave population ranged between 6,000 and 6,700 individuals. The decline in the population from its peak of 10,177 in 1768 reflected the fact that slaves were sold to estates on other islands after 1807 (Fig. 73).

Despite the enormous quantity of enslaved laborers living on Montserrat during the plantation era, we know very little about what life was like for them on a day-to-day basis. There is but one known firsthand account written by a former slave on the island, Olaudah Equiano (he is discussed later in this chapter). The documents that do survive from this period, and provide some detail about the names of individuals and the conditions of slavery, were authored by free planters and government officials. The names of enslaved laborers appear most commonly in estate inventories, slave registries, and other legal documents. This information typically includes individuals' first names and, in estate records, is often accompanied with their sex, age, and an associated monetary value indicating their potential worth as a worker. Sometimes the individuals are grouped according to whether they were assigned to hard labor tasks, such as field work, or domestic jobs, such as cooking. Other individuals are associated with a particular task, skillset, or occupation. In addition to the demographic information, this sort of detail conveys how internal differentiations existed among slaves, who had various identities and statuses within the settings of particular estates, and within Montserrat's slave society more generally.

One example of such distinctions between slaves and their duties appears in the 1766 inventory of Tuite's Estate. Tuite held 271 slaves in bondage. The estate inventory divides them into two categories, "House Negroes" (80 individuals) and "Negro Slaves" (191).[4] Grouped within the latter

[3] Population figures compiled from Census records; Wheeler 1988; Akenson 1997.
[4] *PS LLA* 50.

category are the individuals who performed hard labor in the sugar fields, and those who worked in the industrial sugar-processing complex. Several individuals are listed in association with a trade or occupation. The most valuable individuals were the drivers: Johnny, Andrew, and Limerick. These men managed and enforced discipline on those who performed hard labor in the fields. Other skilled and highly-valued individuals included Ned (blacksmith), Dick (cooper), Nick Skerrett (distiller and carpenter), Long Tom (head mule man), Tom (mule keeper), Billy (boiler and boatman), Mercury and Caesar (boilers), Nero, Alexander, and Anthony (masons), and Frank (boatswain). These men each had expertise in one step of the sugar refining process, whether making barrels for the finished rum, controlling the temperature of the fires in the boiling house, nurturing the mules who crushed cane in the animal mill, or ensuring that cargo was safely transported aboard small vessels to local ports for shipping abroad. Within the listing of house slaves, female cooks Robin, Cupid, and Punch are assigned the highest value, followed by house boys Joe, Mile, and Matty.

The names listed in slave inventories also provide a lens for detecting the continuity of lasting cultural influences on Montserrat. For instance, planters in the mid-18th century connected with their Irish roots by naming enslaved individuals after places in Ireland. In 1766 Tuite's estate had slaves named Galway, Tipperary, and Kilkenny, and two men named Limerick.[5] Similarly, in 1764, Thomas Duberry, owner of the Grove Estate, held men named Cork Harry, Cromarty Cudjoe, and Limerick.[6] Another kind of connection to European homelands across the Atlantic, and the education at least some of the planters would have received there, is evident in the frequency with which slaves were given Classical names—Alexander, Anthony, Caesar Mercury, and Nero (among the names just mentioned on Tuite's Estate). Both on Montserrat and elsewhere a wide range of other similarly ostentatious Greek and Roman names, such as Achilles, Plato, Scipio, Pompey, Aurelia, and Myrtilla, were commonly used. One has the sense that estate-owners took a perverse delight in demonstrating their intellectual superiority by assigning to slaves, whom they regarded as property little different from a cow or a windmill, the ridiculously inappropriate names of Classical gods, Greek philosophers, and Roman politicians.[7]

Daily life and death in slave village settlements

Unlike historical records, archaeological sources of information only very occasionally furnish information at the individual level. Except in the rarest of circumstances, excavated artifacts cannot be proven to be possessions of a single, identifiable person. Instead, archaeological data informs us about broader group behaviors and social practices—for example, how enslaved communities organized their villages, how they cultivated personal provisions grounds, what types of material objects they brought into their living spaces, how they recycled and refashioned objects to suit their needs, and how they treated deceased members of their community. Specific details about these practices are largely absent from historical records, but this is precisely where archaeological remains come into their own. Indeed, much of what scholars know about slave experiences during the plantation era on Montserrat, and indeed much more widely, comes from *archaeological* information. In what follows, we discuss evidence from Galways, Delvins, Little Bay Estate, and the Harney Site—four of the most extensively-researched archaeological sites associated with enslaved laborers on Montserrat.

---

[5] *ibid.*

[6] *PS LLA* 45.

[7] Kolchin 1993 offers a useful account of choices of slave names.

Galways village

Fig. 74. A 20th-century house, built into the slope of St George's Hill, rests on wooden poles or "nogs". Although using different materials for roofs and siding, the slave houses at Galways probably had similar dimensions and architectural elements. (Photo: Lydia Pulsipher, 1986 on file in the Montserrat National Trust.)

The most comprehensive insights about life within a Montserratian enslaved laborers' village comes from the excavations at Galways Estate. During the 18th and 19th centuries, the enslaved laborers' village at Galways consisted of at least 12 individual houses, clustered together along the hillside immediately below the main sugar-processing area of the estate.[8] Archaeological excavations at Galways during the 1980s and 1990s collected detailed information about the spatial layout and construction of these houses, as well as the types of portable objects that residents used in their homes, and how they utilized their adjacent outdoor spaces. Archaeologist Jean Howson suggests that during the 19th century, the Galways village would have needed more than the twelve houses that archaeologists identified to accommodate the estate's 150 laborers. But additional houses were not located during archaeological survey, mainly because they left behind no trace of stone groundsills or foundation platforms on the hillside. It is likely, Howson says, that any additional houses were invisible on the modern landscape of Galways, because they were constructed of wattle and daub walls and wooden posts (or nogs), ephemeral materials that do not leave traces on the ground surface after they decay.

Some indication of what life was like in enslaved laborers' villages comes to us from the 1794 autobiography of Olaudah Equiano, who lived on Montserrat in the early 1760s. He recounts how many estate owners paid:

> the least attention to the lodging of the field-negroes. Their huts, which ought to be well covered, and the place dry where they take their little repose, are often open sheds, built in damp places; so that, when the poor creatures return tired from the toils of the field, they contract many disorders, from being exposed to the damp air in this uncomfortable state, while they are heated, and their pores are open.[9]

The houses identified by archaeologists in the Galways village were apparently not "open sheds", but they were still less than ideally situated in a location where they were subjected to the runoff and odors from the sugar works and the other structures positioned uphill from them. The Galways slave-houses were detectable because their groundsills survived and left traces on or near the surface for archaeologists to examine. The groundsills were single-course stone walls, outlining the placement of rectangular domestic structures. Since the homes were built on a hillslope, these stone bases

[8] Howson 1990; 1995.
[9] Equiano *et al.* 1815: 135.

provided some structural stability.[10] On top of the groundsills laborers constructed their homes of wood or other organic materials (wattle, daub, palm leaves), with post-in-ground ("nog") supports set into the bedrock (Fig. 74). Excavations at seven of the house sites revealed that the dwellings ranged in size from 8 × 16 ft to 10 × 20 ft.[11] Large quantities of nails were recovered from seven of these houses, indicating that those homes had wooden floors or walls. In the soil around the house exteriors, archaeologists unearthed circular stains, remnants of wooden posts that once supported some of the structures' wooden flooring and walls.[12] At least one of the houses appears to have had a packed clay floor surface, instead of wooden planking.

Abundant fragments of household objects were found during excavations in this village, especially pottery, but also glass and white clay tobacco-pipes. Locally-made coarse earthenware pottery comprised up to 40% of the pottery rims recovered—low-fired utilitarian bowls and pots that would have been used for food storage and cooking; this pottery was probably made by enslaved or freed Afro-Caribbean Montserratians (Fig. 75).

Fig. 75. Coarse earthenware Afro-Caribbean pottery fragments recovered from Upper Blakes, similar to those excavated at Galways village. Afro-Caribbean coarseware pottery was made from local clays, hardened by firing at low temperatures, and used for utilitarian cooking, storage, and serving purposes. (Photo: Krysta Ryzewski.)

The Galways laborers also had an assortment of European-made, imported pottery within their homes. Varieties included a range of mass-produced wares popular in the late 18th and 19th centuries: industrial slipware (especially annular ware), as well as pearlware and whiteware with transfer-printed, shell-edged, and painted designs.[13] Decorated wares, in fact, were more common than undecorated pottery, suggesting that the enslaved laborers may have been able to exercise some degree of choice in selecting their wares during their weekly market day.[14] Slaves also procured their household goods from the Great House, when planters cast off items that were damaged or that had become unfashionable.

Evidence also came to light from archaeological excavations about the uses of outdoor spaces by enslaved laborers in and around the village. A defining, albeit ephemeral, feature of enslaved laborer housing on Montserrat

[10] Goodwin 1987: 106.
[11] Goodwin 1987: 102–103.
[12] Goodwin 1987: 106.
[13] Howson 1990; 1995.
[14] Pulsipher 1990.

is the house yard, a cleared ground surface outside of, but next to a dwelling that was used as an outdoor gathering and work place. Residents took care to keep their yards well-maintained, and signs of their repeated cleaning and sweeping can be visible archaeologically when heavily compacted soil deposits containing few artifacts are located next to former dwellings. The archaeologists at Galways noted that house yards were defined within the slave village in ways that may have created central points of connection between clusters of houses.[15]

Yet another section of the Galways village was apparently dedicated to cassava processing. The processing of cassava for bread and other dishes would have provided the laborers with a nutritious supplement to the meager provisions that planters allocated to them, and surplus cassava could have been sold for profit.[16] Enslaved laborers at Galways and at other plantations on Montserrat were permitted to participate in a weekend market in Plymouth where they exchanged surplus produce, manufactured pottery, and a variety of other objects with one another. Until the mid-18th century, this market was held on Sundays, but later switched to Saturdays. Slaves were also encouraged to maintain small garden plots next to their houses and larger provision gardens at higher elevations.[17] Planters encouraged the development of these provision gardens as a way to offset the costs of feeding their slaves, while the laborers embraced this opportunity to diversify their diet with produce and to gain small degrees of economic agency by growing surplus cash crops for trade.

Delvins village

Archaeologist Jean Howson also conducted a survey and excavation of the laborers' village at Delvins Estate. Her findings revealed contrasts between the types of laborer houses and living conditions at Galways and Delvins. Like Galways, Delvins had its origins in the 17th century, but it was always smaller than Galways in terms of both area and the level of slaveholding; so, for example, this estate held only 73 slaves in 1778 and 129 at its maximum in 1806.[18] Located 0.5 km southwest of Weekes Estate and 2 km northwest of Plymouth, Delvins lay close to major plantations and the island's main city and port, but its dry, low-elevation setting was never ideal for the cultivation and processing of sugar. The estate continually struggled with eroding soil and at no time became as profitable as its counterparts at Galways or Weekes. By 1778 the estate buildings were listed as dilapidated and in need of repair, but it nonetheless continued to operate through the first half of the 19th century.[19]

Unlike Galways, the laborers' housing at Delvins during the 18th and 19th centuries was positioned above the Great House and sugar works. Archaeological investigation has revealed that these dwellings were more ephemeral than their counterparts at Galways, and there is no surviving evidence to suggest that they were constructed with durable stone groundsills or wooden planking. Instead, it seems likely that their walls and roofs were constructed entirely of organic materials, and their floors were packed clay or dirt.[20] There are also no surviving indications of maintained house yards, garden plots, or other processing areas within the village. These notable absences convey the

[15] Howson 1995: 102.
[16] *ibid.*: 311; Pulsipher 1990.
[17] Goodwin 1987: 52.
[18] Howson 1995: 93–94.
[19] *ibid.*
[20] *ibid.*: 103–104.

poor quality of life, relative scarcity of resources, and limited space available to enslaved laborers at Delvins—a domestic environment noticeably less hospitable than the village at Galways.

Despite stark contrasts between the environmental settings of these two estates, it appears that enslaved laborers at Delvins nonetheless were able to obtain similar types of household goods as the Galways residents. At Delvins, Howson recovered the same variety of decorated European-imported pottery, as well as locally-made ceramics. This similarity of pottery between the two sites underscores the important role of exchange within Montserrat's internal slave economy that was facilitated, in large part, by the weekend market in Plymouth (Fig. 76).

Fig. 76. The Plymouth Market (pictured here in 1914, long after emancipation) attracted enslaved laborers from across the island on weekends during the slavery era. (Source: The National Archives, Kew, CO 152/341/25 folio 179.)

Little Bay village

In 2006 and 2007 Mary Beaudry and Lydia Pulsipher directed excavations of an enslaved laborers' village associated with the Little Bay Estate.[21] This was the first time that a laborers' village had been examined in the northernmost region of the island (St Peter's Parish), which was home to smaller-scale sugar and cotton plantations between the 17th and 19th centuries. In 1729 the Little Bay Estate covered an area of 100 acres, and 39 enslaved laborers lived and worked at its sugar and cotton works.[22]

The laborers' village was located on a sloping hillside about 40 m south of the estate's main sugar works and Great House (Fig. 77). Within this village there were identified the remains of two concentrations of houses.[23] Excavations uncovered stones that would have been used to support wooden posts on which the houses or their flooring was set. Based on a variety of evidence—the alignment of the stones, remnant postholes, stone steps still in place, and concentrations of artifacts—archaeologists determined that the laborers' houses were generally oriented along a north–south axis, a position that took advantage of the prevailing winds and also faced away from the manor house, which was perched on a low hill oriented towards the village on the other side of the sugar works. One house revealed a drainage ditch dug into the underlying bedrock along the edge of a house platform, a feature interpreted as evidence of villagers' efforts to maintain the space around their home by channeling rainwater runoff away from their dwelling.

Fragments of household goods were found only around the exterior of the house areas, typically outside their entryways, where most processing activities and leisure time seems to have taken

[21] *UPR* 6.
[22] *PS CEN* 30.
[23] Information and data from the excavations of the Little Bay Workers village are available at DAACS 2015. Digital Archaeological Archive of Comparative Slavery. https://www.daacs.org/sites/little-bay-workers-village/.

Fig. 77. Excavations of structural remains of the Little Bay workers' village (foreground), with the remains of the Little Bay estate in the background, including the animal mill (left), and the Manor House (on hilltop to the right of the tree). (Photo: Krysta Ryzewski, 2007.)

Fig. 78. Archaeologist Barbara Heath examining coarse earthenware pottery fragments and architectural remains recovered from excavations of the Little Bay Estate's slave village. (Photo: Krysta Ryzewski, 2007.)

place. Most finds from the Little Bay Estate village were locally-made coarse earthenware pots, used for storage, cooking, and serving food (Fig. 78). Lesser quantities of European-made pottery vessels were found, including varieties of English Staffordshire, pearlware, whiteware, and yellow-ware pottery. The availability of these wares to the estate's enslaved laborers indicates that they, too, were participants in the local market economy, perhaps within the same exchange networks as their counterparts at Galways and Delvins Estates. Minimal quantities of bottle glass and white clay smoking pipes were also recovered.

Harney site slave cemetery

As described in Chapter 2, in 1979 archaeologist David Watters conducted a salvage excavation of an unmarked burial ground disturbed in the course of a house construction project about 1 km east of Bransby Point, Montserrat's westernmost extension. The Harney Site was a previously undocumented cemetery that contained the remains of seventeen skeletons.[24] The burials that remained in place were carefully excavated, and several other skeletons that had already been disarticulated and damaged by construction equipment were also studied.

Archaeologists and biological anthropologists identified six males and six females (three could not be sexed), ranging in age between 7 and over 60 years old.[25] Statistical and morphological analysis of cranial elements determined the likely African ancestry of those individuals whose skulls were intact. Pathological examination of skeletal remains determined that three of the individuals suffered from osteoarthritis (in the foot and leg), and three females skeletons had indications of healed bone fractures (in their hands and leg). Further analysis revealed that 17 of the 92 teeth recovered

[24] Watters 1987.
[25] Watters 1994b: 58.

during the excavations were heavily damaged by abscesses, root hypercementosis, and thinning enamel.[26] Watters concluded that these pathological diagnoses were consistent with individuals who suffered from malnutrition, bodily trauma, and repeated physical stresses over the course of their lifetimes.[27] Based on available osteological, archaeological, and historical evidence, he concluded that the site was an unmarked cemetery for enslaved laborers.

In addition to skeletal remains from 17 individuals, Watters excavated 10 separate graves and recovered 134 artifacts (Fig. 79). The artifacts date to the late 18th century, and they illustrate the mortuary practices of enslaved laborers at the time. They include nails from coffins, pottery fragments (both locally made and imported), a metal disc, tobacco pipe fragments, and an intact glass pharmaceutical bottle of Robert Turlington's Balsam of Life, dated precisely by the patent labeled on it that read October 29, 1751.[28] Watters also surmised that the Balsam of Life phial was intentionally interred as a burial good, suggesting that it may have contained rum for the deceased or soaked medicine into the grave.[29] A smooth metal disc interred with another individual may have been payment for the spirit's return to Africa. Metal tokens and coins found in similar burial contexts, such as the African Baptist Church cemetery in Philadelphia, have been so interpreted.[30] Interestingly, the canine tooth of one of the adult males in the burial ground was worn where it would have repeatedly held a smoking pipe, remains of which were also excavated from the cemetery.

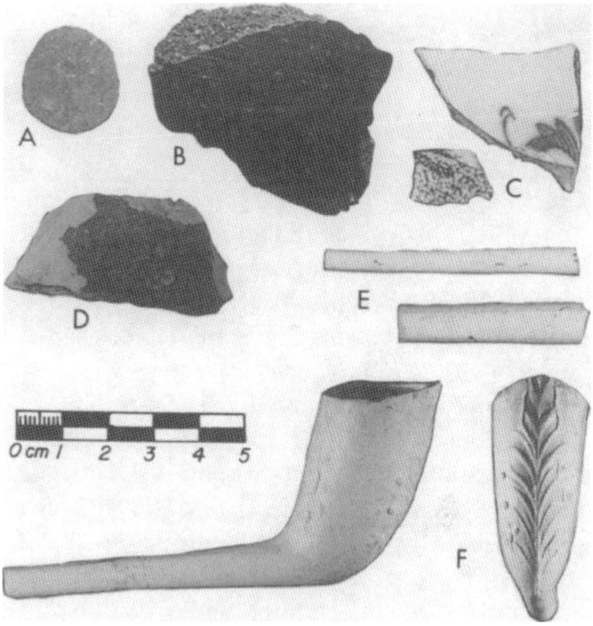

Fig. 79. Artifacts from the Harney Slave Cemetery site include: A) metal disc; B) coarseware potsherd; C) two decorated tin-glazed earthenware potsherds; D) Buckleyware potsherd; E) two white clay tobacco pipe stems; F) side and front views of a white clay (kaolin) tobacco pipe bowl with raised molded relief decoration. (Source: Watters 1994b: 65, fig. 8.)

The ingenuity of enslaved laborers

Archaeological finds from several different plantation-era village and estate sites across the island illustrate the resourcefulness and ingenuity of enslaved laborers. With limited access to the tools they required for basic daily tasks—cutting, sewing, butchering, cooking, and tilling the soil—laborers manufactured their own to satisfy these needs. For instance, slaves continued

26 Mann *et al.* 1987.
27 Watters 1994b: 60.
28 Petersen and Watters 1988.
29 Watters 1994b: 64.
30 *ibid.*: 64.

Fig. 80. A cut coin (bottom right) and pottery fragments modified into square and triangular tokens, circular discs, and drilled pendants excavated from the 18th-century dwelling on top of Potato Hill in 2015 and 2016. (Photo: Krysta Ryzewski.)

to use knapped pieces of chert, imported from Long Island, Antigua, as expedient tools for scraping and cutting, much as the island's Amerindians had done millennia before. During the plantation era, moreover, enslaved laborers employed manufacturing techniques quite similar to those used on chert to knap sherds of broken bottle-glass and transform fragments of it into tools, such as scrapers and perforators. Examples of such makeshift tools made of glass have been recovered from Blake's Estate, Upper Blakes, Underwood, Potato Hill, Thatch Valley, and Rendezvous Village.[31]

Enslaved laborers also modified everyday household items into objects that held special significance for them. Some of these special objects functioned as adornments on garments, others may have been incorporated into spiritual rituals, while some were modified for use in leisure activities. At Potato Hill, there were recovered broken 18th-century pottery fragments that had been carefully drilled so that they could be strung and possibly worn as pendants or included as decorative attachments on clothing (Fig. 80). Beads made of glass and stone have also been found at Potato Hill, Woodlands Estate, and the Little Bay Estate. Blue glass, in particular, held special significance in African-derived spiritual practices because of their perceived power to ward off evil; the vast majority of beads recovered from Potato Hill, for example, were made of blue glass.[32]

The most common type of modified objects found on plantation-era and post-emancipation sites are broken pottery fragments that have been carved into circular disks (Fig. 80). Archaeologists have recovered examples of such disks from contexts associated with enslaved laborers, as well as with planters' residences and military sites, at Little Bay Estate, Gun Hill, Potato Hill, and Upper Blakes. Although these disks may also have served utilitarian purposes (such as blanks for cloth buttons or even as trade tokens), most Caribbean archaeologists recognize them as gaming tokens.[33] Most pottery disks from Montserrat have one blank side, and one decorated side. Montserratians today recall using pottery fragments to play a game called "china money", a name that refers to pottery (china) and perhaps its use as an informal currency or token of value in the contest. In an interview with geographer Lydia Pulispher in 1987, an older Montserratian man named R. Pemberton described "chiney money" as a dice game that made use of threepenny- or

[31] Ryzewski and Cherry 2016.
[32] Stine *et al.* 1996; Ryzewski and Cherry 2016; *UPR* 27.
[33] MacLean 2015; Ryzewski and Cherry 2016. For similar examples excavated from sites in Jamaica and Cuba, see Armstrong 2010 and Singleton 2015.

nickel-sized pottery disks; it involved tossing three disks on a table and awarding either 3, 17, or 18 points based on how many of them landed with the decorated side facing upwards.[34]

Fighting for freedom

The 1768 St Patrick's Day uprising

One of the most significant events in Montserrat's history is the attempted uprising by slaves and free people of color against the island's plantocracy on 17 March 1768 (see Box J). The attempted insurrection left behind no material remains of which we are aware. But numerous accounts of the rebellion in newspapers, letters, and other historical documents reveal piecemeal information about the events leading up to St Patrick's Day and detail the unrest that consumed the island society in the aftermath of the plot's exposure. These documents contain clues that offer incomplete, sometimes contradictory, accounts of the rebellion. The application of an archaeological approach to these documents—one that places them in the context of the society at the time, considers their authors and intended audiences, and identifies common themes in the various accounts—is useful for creating an informed narrative of the attempted uprising.

On the evening of 17 March 1768, the island's planter elite were gathered at Government House to celebrate St Patrick's Day. In the weeks leading up to the event, a group of Montserratians, enslaved and free, allegedly stockpiled ammunition in the mountains. They planned to coordinate with the domestic slaves inside Government House in Plymouth, who would "secure the swords" of the gentlemen arriving for the celebration. Upon a signal, the room would be seized by the rebel party, and they would kill everyone who tried to escape. Records indicate that a woman "much in Liquor" overheard two co-conspirators discussing details of the plot and forewarned the authorities. The rebellion was thwarted and all who were allegedly involved in its planning were severely punished.[35]

Brutality breeds contempt

Montserrat's sugar industry began to fall apart during the second half of the 18th century for a number of reasons: repeated storms and floods, blight, a Yellow Fever epidemic in 1755, a number of raids, and various other conflicts.[36] As a result, in the decade leading up to the St Patrick's Day uprising, Montserrat's estates were beginning to experience widespread labor shortages, and more slaves were required to undertake hard labor, regardless of age or gender.[37] In times when the island suffered from labor shortages, droughts, and lack of provisions, it was of course the enslaved laborers who struggled the most.[38]

The organizers of the St Patrick's Day uprising were reacting against oppressive treatment by their masters (in the case of slaves) and more generally by the Montserratian government, which continued to deny basic rights to enslaved, free black, and mulatto residents. At the time of the planned uprising, there is no question that antagonistic relationships prevailed between many slaves and their masters, as is evident in the *Minutes of the Council of Montserrat 1768–1779*.[39] The

[34] Pulsipher and Goodwin 1989: 30, cited in MacLean 2015.
[35] *PS ABNA* 7.
[36] Fergus 1994: 45–59, 220–227; Wheeler 1988: 18–34; Crandall 2000: 3.
[37] Mason 1993: 120.
[38] *ibid.*: 103–131.
[39] *PS TNA* 95.

Box J: A celebration of Irish and Afro-Caribbean heritage: St Patrick's Day on Montserrat

St Patrick's Day is not only a national holiday on Montserrat, but it is also the impetus for an annual week-long festival that combines a fusion of Irish and Afro-Caribbean cultural traditions. On Montserrat, St Patrick's Day is both a celebration of the island's Irish heritage and also the recognition of an uprising planned by enslaved Afro-Caribbean and free black communities during the 18th century.

Fig. 81. Musicians perform in Little Bay during the week-long St Patrick's Festival, 2007. (Photo: Krysta Ryzewski.)

Visitors to the island during St Patrick's week are greeted with a flurry of festive, Irish-inspired symbols—shamrocks, leprechauns, Guinness, and the island's (only recently adopted) orange-white-and-green national dress. Combined with these familiar representations of Irishness are concerts featuring Montserratian music, a recreated slave village, feasts of local food, and performances by an Afro-Caribbean masquerade dance group, the Emerald Shamrocks (Fig. 81).

St. Patrick's Day has evolved over the past several decades into a multi-faceted commemoration and celebration of the island community's cultural heritage, its difficult colonial history, and its resilience in the face of contemporary natural disasters.[i]

In the 17th century, Montserrat was, by far, the most "Irish" island in the Caribbean: in 1678 nearly 70% of the population self-identified as Irish.[ii] Several Irish families became wealthy sugar-plantation owners and masters of African slaves during the 17th and 18th centuries. In response to the inhumane conditions of chattel slavery, a group of enslaved and free Montserratians planned a rebellion against the island's plantocracy on St Patrick's Day in 1768. It was to take place at Government House in the island's capital, in Plymouth, where the island elite would be gathered in celebration. The uprising's plot was discovered in advance, and all who were alleged to be involved with its planning were executed or punished in other brutal ways. Today, St Patrick's Day simultaneously commemorates Montserrat's Irish roots and the acts of bravery displayed by the people involved in the planned uprising of 1768.

During the 1970s, Montserratians began to recognize St Patrick's Day as an opportunity to reconnect the island's Irish historical roots with contemporary Montserratian identity—also, admittedly, with an eye towards boosting tourism.[iii] At that time, St Patrick's Day was mainly observed at the Roman Catholic Church in St Patrick's Village, a settlement in the southwest of the island that was home to the earliest Irish laborers in the 17th century. The push towards nationalizing the holiday began in the 1980s, and St Patrick's Day was adopted as a national holiday in 1985.

St Patrick's Day eventually gained popularity among a wider, international community, and festivities came to be extended across the whole island. Following the population displacement and damage caused by Hurricane Hugo in 1989 and the eruptions of the Soufrière Hills volcano in 1995, St Patrick's has grown into a week-long festival that draws large numbers of visitors to the island from the Montserratian diaspora and elsewhere. Although there remain divergent perspectives about how St Patrick's Day should be celebrated and whom it should commemorate, the festival has allowed Montserrat to brand itself as the "Emerald Isle of the Caribbean" and to sustain local pride in the island community's history of resiliency, especially in the aftermath of recent crises.

[i] McAtackney *et al.* 2014; Ryzewski and McAtackney 2015.
[ii] *PS CEN* 29.
[iii] *PS MPL* 71; *PS MPL* 72; *PS MPL* 73.

details of these government records show that a substantial portion of regular Council meetings was spent reviewing charges against slaves and doling out punishments to them. For example, in the months leading up to the uprising, the Council ordered the hanging at Fort Ghaut of a slave named Redmond for failing to perform work for his master, Thomas Meade, over a period of three months (6 January 1768). Numerous other slaves were tried and punished for both petty and serious offences in the period between January and March 1768.

Response to the rebellion

In the weeks and months following the betrayal of the plan for the 1768 St Patrick's Day uprising, Montserrat's population was consumed by anxiety and civil disorder. The Montserratian government responded swiftly to the news of the planned rebellion. On Friday 18 March, the morning after the incident, the Assembly was summoned to an urgent conference with the Deputy Provost Marshall to collect depositions about the "intended Insurrection among the Slaves".[40] They sent word immediately to William Woodley, Governor in Chief of the Leeward Islands, and he, in turn, dispatched Admiral Pye from St Kitts along with two ships, and a detachment of 50 men from the 68th regiment to maintain order.[41] The local Montserratian government identified between 50 and 80 alleged conspirators in the uprising plot and temporarily imprisoned them on the military ships at Plymouth, while they awaited trial.

Meanwhile, a letter from St Kitts, written on 29 August 1768 and published in numerous colonial American newspapers, reported that nearly six months after the attack Montserrat was still in a state of "terrible confusion" due to ongoing "civil discord and insurrections" in the wake of the "late conspiracy of the Negroes". The letter reports delays in bringing the accused conspirators to

[40] *ibid*, entries for 18–21 March 1768.
[41] *PS ABNA* 7.

trial, because of disagreements between the Governor and the Assembly about how to handle the situation. This delay triggered waves of violence against both enslaved and free black communities on Montserrat, as well as against government officials. A body of enraged residents apparently "destroyed all the habitations of the free Negroes, threatened to burn the jail with all the Negroes in it unless immediately brought to trial", and they also threatened the commissioners.[42]

Eventually, most of the alleged ringleaders of the uprising were brutally punished. An account appearing in the *Pennsylvania Gazette* for 26 May 1768, reported that three of the convicted conspirators had suffered the rack, two were burnt, one gibbetted, and one was hanged. Others apparently committed suicide.[43]

In the months and years following 17 March 1768, brutal punishments against slaves appear even more frequently in Government records. The Montserrat Assembly routinely enacted severe punishments that were designed to publicly humiliate and demean slaves, even in cases where their guilt could not be proven. This was the situation on 12 January 1771 when:

> A Negro man slave named Nal the property of the Honourable Michael White brought before this Board and charged with feloniously Stealing a Board from his said Master the value of five shillings current money the Fact not being fully proved, he was Ordered to be whipped thro the town of Kinsale this day.[44]

In other words, Nal was accused of stealing a single wooden board and, although not found guilty, was publicly whipped through the town of Kinsale anyway. Such an unfair punishment, presumably, was ordered by the Council to serve as a warning to other slaves.

Threats of insurrections on Montserrat also continued. The late 18th century witnessed rebellions of slaves across the Caribbean more widely, the most notable and successful of which (1791–1804) led to independence on Haiti.[45] In 1791 a rebellion on Dominica triggered great concern on Montserrat, where the government feared that their slaves might be inspired to rebel if word were to arrive about the Dominican uprising. In response, Lt. General Edward Mathew sent firearms and reinforcements to aid Montserrat's militia against any potential uprising—which, however, never occurred.[46]

Degrees of freedom in the decades before emancipation

In the years between the attempted St Patrick's Day uprising (1768) and emancipation (1834), the path to freedom for Montserrat's slaves was gradual, but nevertheless still punctuated by conflict and brutality. A class of Montserratians often overlooked in accounts of the St Patrick's Day uprising attempt, as well as being overall less visible in historical archives and the archaeological record, are the mixed race (mulatto) and free black populations who slowly, but steadily increased in numbers between the 1750s and emancipation in 1834. In 1754, Thomas Skerrett, Jr emancipated

---

[42] Letter from St Christopher's, August 29. In *The Virginia Gazette,* 22 September 1768 (*PS NEWS* 75): "A letter from St Christopher's advises that they are in terrible confusion at Montserrat, not only on account of the late conspiracy of the Negroes, but with civil discord and insurrections. There is a disagreement between the Governour and Assembly, and the people being dissatisfied with the delay in bringing the Negroes to trial, with the great and ruinous expense occasioned thereby, had risen in a body, destroyed all the habitations of the free Negroes, threatened to burn the gaol with all the Negroes in it unless immediately brought to trial, and the commissioners were in danger of feeling their vengeance."

[43] *PS NEWS* 76.

[44] *PS TNA* 95.

[45] Dubois and Garrigus 2006.

[46] *PS TNA* 93.

a "mulatto boy John Lewey", and two years later John Davis Molineux freed a "mulatto woman named Mary and her three children—a boy named Peter and two girls named Lucy and Mary".[47] In these two instances, it is quite possible that the estate owners were actually the fathers of the listed children, as white planters often had sexual relationships with enslaved women and gave them and their offspring special privileges.[48]

In other cases, slaves were manumitted by their owners because they earned their freedom, or on account of their age or health. In 1766, for instance, John Bramley of St Peter's Parish manumitted five of his slaves: Baba, Sarah, old Aucub, and Nell (all described as old women) and a man called old Cuffee.[49] But the most notable manumission during this period was of Gustavus Vassa, later known as Olaudah Equiano (ca. 1745–1797), who in 1794 went on to write an autobiographical account of his captivity, *The Interesting Narrative of the Life of Olaudah Equiano, or Gustavus Vassa, the African* (Fig. 82).[50]

Equiano spent most of his enslaved life working in England, where he became literate and gained mathematical skills. In the early 1760s he arrived on Montserrat as the slave of Captain James Doran, an English merchant, and he was soon thereafter sold to a Philadelphia-based Quaker merchant, Robert King, one of Montserrat's most successful traders at the time. King mentored Equiano's development as a merchant and accountant, and Equiano soon gained enough competency to work alongside him in business. King also permitted Equiano to conduct his own trading on the side, from which he generated a modest personal income. By the age of 20, in 1766, Equiano accumulated £70—enough to buy his freedom.[51] After his manumission, King invited Equiano to continue to work with him as a waged employee on Montserrat, but Equiano was rightly concerned about the possibility of being kidnapped and sold back into slavery, so he moved back to England, where he established a successful career and raised a family. Equiano's autobiography was one of the first narrative accounts of captivity authored by a former slave, and it became an influential source for English abolitionists in their campaign to pass the 1807 Slave Trade Act that outlawed trans-Atlantic human trafficking.

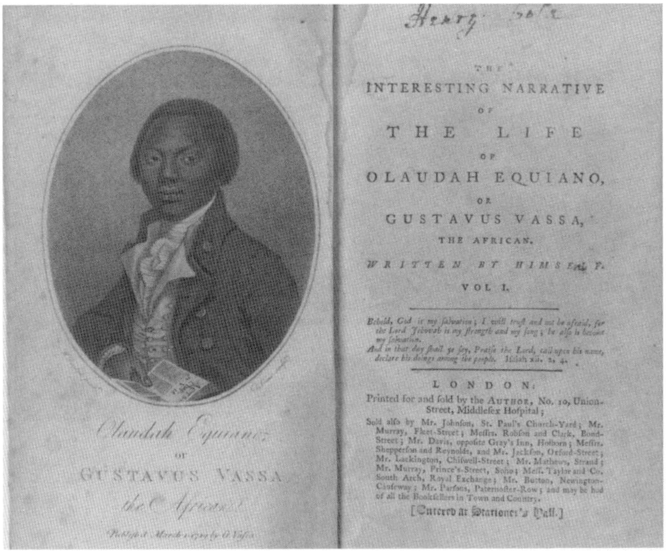

Fig. 82. Frontispiece of Equiano's 1789 autobiography, The Interesting Narrative of the Life of Olaudah Equiano or Gustavus Vassa, The African. *(The copy shown here is in the John Carter Brown Library.)*

---

[47] *PS LLA* 48; *PS LLA* 47.

[48] In some cases planters, like Thomas Thistlewood of Jamaica, even recorded in their personal diaries the graphic details of their frequent sexual contact with slaves, and some of these sources survive today; see Burnard 2004.

[49] *PS LLA* 52.

[50] Equiano *et al.* 1815.

[51] *PS MNT* 57.

Equiano did not live long enough to witness the successful passage of the Slave Trade Act just a few years after his death. But back in his former home of Montserrat, things were changing fast in the early years of the 19th century. Historian Riva Berleant-Schiller reports that between 1805 and 1822 Montserrat's white population was reduced by half, while the free colored population grew by 274%.[52] By 1828, six years before emancipation, there were actually 484 more free black Montserratians living on the island than white residents. Not only were the composition and status of the island's population changing rapidly, but both popular and political pressure was building back in England for the Parliamentary legislation that would, finally, emancipate the slaves held throughout Britain's Caribbean possessions.

[52] Berleant-Schiller 1996: 258.

9. Emancipation and its aftermath

Emancipation began in the British Caribbean islands on 1 August 1834. In some places, such as Antigua, former slaves were immediately freed and they established new villages on the outskirts of plantation estates. But on most other islands, including Montserrat, vestiges of plantation slavery persisted. In the years immediately following emancipation Montserratian laborers were bound to their former estates and masters under a system of "apprenticeship", which lasted until 1838. Apprenticeship was intended to gradually transition the new island society to an economy based on wage labor, diversified industries, and increased land ownership or tenancy by smallholders. The system was supposed to safeguard the new laboring class by ensuring that estate owners provided continued support in the form of either wages or subsistence. But in reality, apprenticeship on Montserrat was a device that restricted laborers' mobility, welfare, and opportunities for advancement.[1] This chapter uses primary historical documents, some of them only recently examined, and evidence from 19th-century archaeological sites to illustrate the conditions of the new Montserratian society that emerged in the first generations after emancipation, from 1834 until the turn of the 20th century.

In 1837, government officials counted 3,615 apprentices on Montserrat—nearly 2,600 fewer individuals than the 6,209 who were listed as slaves in 1830.[2] The discrepancy between these figures does not indicate that thousands of former slaves were already living outside of the apprenticeship system on Montserrat. Instead, it conveys the disorder and social upheaval that the entire island society was experiencing during these transformative years, from the government officials to the newly emergent laborer class. In their correspondence, officials admitted that under apprenticeship, the population of laborers on Montserrat was impossible to calculate. This uncertainty was due to the emigration of many former slaves off-island (especially to Demerara in Guyana and Trinidad), high child mortality rates, and the movement of laborers off or between estates, either as day-jobbers or squatters.[3] Because of these circumstances, the laboring population was in a constant state of flux during apprenticeship.

[1] Fergus 1994: 104–112.

[2] *PS BOA* 19:90; *PS BOA* 22:114; *PS ABNA* 14.

[3] Census and Blue Book records through the 1840s and 1850s calculate Montserrat's total population as around 7,000 individuals. These numbers do not differ greatly from the 1830 figure of 7,353 (*PS BOA* 18). The rate of depopulation that the reports suggest during the apprenticeship period was thus not as dramatic as the numbers make it seem.

Total disarray

Montserrat's apprentices were fully emancipated on 1 August 1838. The sudden introduction of thousands of new citizens to the island economy and social structure was unprecedented, and it was a process fraught with logistical difficulties and lingering prejudices. As a result, island society fell into a state of total disarray from which it would take more than a generation to rebound economically and socially.

In the years following emancipation, Montserrat's government could well be described as barely functional. Until the 1860s, Montserratians were actually unable to fill the 20 legislative seats and other official positions that were necessary for the local government to operate at its most basic capacity.[4] The main reasons for this shortfall were twofold: only white residents were allowed to serve in government positions, and most of the island population was illiterate. In fact, by 1850, out of a population of 7,000, only 85 people above the age of 21 could read or write: in other words, only 1.2% of the population was literate during the 1840s. Despite these limitations, the short-staffed government nonetheless succeeded in introducing harsh new restrictions and refusing material benefits to the island's recently-freed laboring class. Lingering race-based discrimination from the slavery era stymied the development of the island's post-emancipation governance, legal system, and other social welfare programs.

The generation following emancipation was perhaps the most miserable period in the island's history. Upon emancipation, the majority of estate owners left Montserrat, abandoning their estates in their wake, and the local government in the early 1840s was described as the most "turbulent and disorderly" in the region.[5] They left behind an economy that was severely depressed because of the devaluation of sugar and the demise of the slave labor-based system for its production. In 1837, for example, the local government was so poor that the Assembly resorted to selling the "old cannon scattered about various parts of the island".

In the decade after emancipation the entire island population suffered from impoverishment, political dysfunction, disease, and natural disaster. Conditions continued to be especially inhumane and unjust for former slaves. Montserrat's local government diverged from the British government in its views on how to manage post-emancipation society.[6] In particular, Montserrat was unwilling to comply with the British recommendation that encouraged the sale of small parcels of land to recently freed slaves, so that they could work as wage laborers, while also building their own houses and cultivating their own crops (a model that was successful on nearby Antigua). By 1832, all the British Caribbean colonies except Montserrat and St Kitts had purged their legal codes of race-based discriminatory laws, and allowed free men of color to serve in the government.[7] Montserrat's government was unwilling to change with the times. With support from the plantocracy, local leaders introduced restrictive legislation that limited the freedoms of laborers. One such law, introduced in November of 1838, was "An Act for the Punishment of Idle and disorderly persons, rogues, and Vagabonds, incorrigible rogues and other Vagrants in Montserrat". The local version of this Act required a punishment of a three-month prison term with hard labor, whereas an equivalent British Act of Parliament punished vagrancy with no more than 14 to 28 days in prison with hard labor.[8]

4 *PS CO* 34; *PS CO* 35; *PS CO* 39; *PS CO* 40.
5 *PS ABNA* 4.
6 Berleant-Schiller 2014.
7 Berleant-Schiller 1996: 264.
8 *PS CO* 6.

As a result of divergent legal perspectives, overseers and agents on Montserrat sanctioned the administration of violent punishments that were actually illegal under British law at the time. These violations were duly noted by colonial officials. In 1837, a Captain Graeme was sent by the Leeward Islands government to Montserrat as a Magistrate to report on and assist in preventing the illegal arrest and unjust imprisonment of apprentices. He compiled a "Return of Apprenticed Laborers Illegally Punished by the Local Magistrates of Montserrat", which detailed how five individuals had been publicly whipped for breaking sugar cane, and how others were accused of capital felonies, punishable by death, for acts of cattle theft and burglary, even though such draconian laws were no longer in existence in Britain.[9]

Post-emancipation political and social strains were compounded by droughts, natural disasters, and disease outbreaks in the 1840s and 1850s. The most difficult and destructive episode was the catastrophic earthquake of February 1843, which devastated Montserrat, causing widespread damage to its infrastructure, roads, and buildings. In the aftermath, Montserrat's government petitioned the Leeward Islands government for earthquake recovery assistance, but was only granted £15,000 of the £23,000 it requested. This sum was hardly adequate to rebuild the island, which then suffered a severe depression in 1846–1847. It would be decades, until 1873 in fact, before Montserrat was able to repay the Crown. In the intervening years colonial relationships were strained and Montserratians struggled simply to restore the island's basic functions and services.

In the decade following this earthquake, starvation, malnutrition, outbreaks of disease, and high infant mortality rates led to desperation for the laboring class. During times of economic downturn, agents managing estates often could not afford to pay their laborers. Wages were routinely withheld for more than six months, or paid in food and drink rather than currency.[10] By 1849 Montserrat's economy stalled to the point that foreign correspondence and trade came to a standstill: no British ships anchored in Montserrat that year, and no official mail boats arrived either. Colonial government correspondence from 1850 remarks on the "deplorable destitution" of the laboring classes, who, they reported, were naked and hungry.[11]

An economy in transition

Montserrat's economic dependence on sugar ended with emancipation. With West Indian sugar prices at record lows in the 1840s, estate managers could not profitably produce sugar and afford to pay wages to newly emancipated laborers. But sugar did remain in production on Montserrat, albeit in lesser quantities and on far fewer estates, throughout the 19th and into the 20th century.[12]

The decline of the post-emancipation sugar industry is well-documented in the abandonment and sale of indebted estates, especially in the decades following the widespread structural damage to sugar works caused by the 1843 earthquake. In 1841 half of the island's 70 estates were producing sugar, but by 1856 there were 15 fewer estates on the island.[13] Of the estates that remained, about the same percentage (53%) were under sugar cultivation, while eleven were uncultivated, seven produced

[9] *PS CO* 5.
[10] *PS CO* 32:123; *PS CO* 33:228.
[11] *PS CO* 34.
[12] Sugar and rum continued to be produced in smaller quantities on several estates into the 20th century. The last functioning sugar works was on Farrells Estate; it closed in 1972, as noted in *UPR* 30: 10.
[13] *PS BOA* 23.

Fig. 83. Olveston Estate in the 1890s. (Photo: Sturge Collection, MNT.)

provisions, three were dedicated to corn production, and two were pasture estates. Early attempts at citrus lime cultivation also appear in the same 1856 estate inventory; limes are listed as the primary crop at the estates of Lawyer's, Duberry, and Needsmust (later renamed Olveston) (Fig. 83).[14] Within a year, 18 of the 55 estates mentioned in the 1856 inventory were indebted to the point that they were sold under the provisions of the Encumbered Estates and Tax Acts. These estates included several in St Peter's Parish whose archaeological remains have been documented: Silver Hills, Underwood, Little Bay, and Geralds.[15]

In an effort to rebuild the island's fledgling post-emancipation economy, Montserratians attempted, without much success, to develop several new profitable industries during the 1840s. Entrepreneurs tried to establish industries based on the production of silk, coffee, vanilla, corn, cacao, bananas, vines, and olives.[16] But it would be the introduction of citrus lime cultivation to Montserrat by Francis Burke, with support from the Sturge family, in the early 1850s that would ultimately revitalize the island's economy in the second half of the 19th century. Citrus lime cultivation proved to be a profitable replacement for the declining sugar industry. It also provided the opportunity for estate managers, for the first time, to introduce a fair and structured wage labor system to the island. This had utterly transformative effects on both the local economy and the social welfare of the laboring class. The inspiration for Montserrat's wage labor system came from the prominent English abolitionist Joseph Sturge VI (1793–1859) (Fig. 84).

In 1836 Sturge and his fellow Quaker businessman, Thomas Harvey, journeyed to Montserrat and other West Indian islands to investigate the conditions of former slaves under apprenticeship. They reported their observations about the continued poverty and suffering of recently-freed slaves in their 1838 book, *The West Indies in 1837*, which immediately became a pivotal source in advocating for Parliament's early termination of the apprenticeship system in 1838.[17] Joseph Sturge VI would later purchase Bransby Estate (renaming it Elberton), with the intention of introducing the wage labor system to still-active sugar production there. Unfortunately, his death in 1859 prevented him from witnessing improvements to Montserrat's labor structures. It would be under the direction of his extended family members that the wage-based work system was implemented, alongside the expanded cultivation of citrus limes in the following decades.

[14] *PS BOA* 24.
[15] *PS CO* 36: 94, 184, 189–190.
[16] *PS CO* 31; *PS CO* 33.
[17] Sturge and Harvey 1838.

The first instance of lime cultivation associated with the Sturge family enterprises dates to 1852, when Joseph's brother Edmund contracted Francis Burke, a local Montserratian politician and entrepreneur, to cultivate limes at his estate in Woodlands. Sturge intended to use the lime juice processed at Woodlands as the basis for citric acid produced at the chemical works of J. & E. Sturge, in his family's hometown of Birmingham, England. Over the course of the 1850s and 1860s, the Sturge family increased their investments in Montserrat's former sugar estates, purchasing them through the Encumbered Estate Act auctions and then converting their infrastructure to accommodate citrus lime production. Burke managed the first two Sturge-owned estates, Elberton and Olveston.[18] Elberton estate occupied the buildings of the former Bransby sugar works, as well as lands from the Delvins Estate; Olveston was converted from the former Needsmust Estate (Fig. 85).

Lime juice production peaked in 1866, when 180,000 gallons were exported, and production remained steady until the hurricane of 1899.[19] In 1869 the Sturge family formed the Montserrat Company Ltd, and within a decade it was the largest landowner on the island, controlling over a dozen estates and cultivating in excess of 4,000 acres of lime trees.[20] The success of the citrus lime industry brought international fame to Montserrat in the second half of the 19th century, until blight and hurricane damage brought it to an end (Box K). The lime industry also allowed the island's wage laborers a semblance of financial stability. As they accumulated savings, former slaves were able, for the first time, to invest in the island's economy as they wished.

Fig. 84. Memorial statue of Joseph Sturge VI at Five Ways, Birmingham, England. The inscription reads: "He laboured to bring freedom to the Negro slave, the vote to British workmen, and the promise of peace to a war-torn world". (Photo: Sturge Collection, MNT.)

Fig. 85. Payday at Elbertons in the 1890s. (Source: Sturge Collection, MNT.)

[18] Notes from Mrs. John Edmund Sturge, Sturge Family website: http://sturgefamily.charlessturge.com/Discover/THE%20MONTSERRAT%20CONNECTION.htm
[19] Fergus 1982: 11.
[20] These include estates at Elberton, Olveston, Woodlands, Richmond Hill, Isles Bay, Delvins, O'Garra's, and Hope. *PS MNT* 61.

Box K: Montserrat's world-famous citrus limes

One traveler's account from 1903 described Montserrat as "The Lime Juice Island". Visitors at the turn of the 20th century marveled at how the island was "one vast garden of lime trees, and [how] nowhere in the world is there a finer sight than its thirty miles of orchards, laden with the fruit of the lime or fragrant with its blossoms."[i]

Fig. 86. Cover of promotional pamphlet about Montserrat's lime industry, first published in 1886 by Carlisle, H. Scott & Sons in England.[vii]

Citrus lime production began on Montserrat in the early 1850s, first with local planter Francis Burke, and then under the management of the Sturge family and The Montserrat Company Ltd. The Sturges were Quaker entrepreneurs from Birmingham, England, and their patriarch Joseph Sturge VI was a prominent abolitionist who petitioned Parliament to end the apprenticeship system on Montserrat in 1838. His brother, Edmund, established the family's first lime estates on Montserrat in 1855, combining the lands of Hope, Needsmust, and Freeman's into a plantation he called Olveston, after his English birthplace.[ii] Over the course of the next 80 years, Montserrat's lime industry revitalized the island's post-emancipation economy and attracted international fame.

Montserrat's limes were processed into juice, concentrate, and essence (oils). They were also pickled or traded fresh, as whole fruits. In 1886, during the crop's peak production, Montserrat exported 145,440 gallons of juice, 7,080 concentrated gallons, 26 cases of essence, 80 pounds of pickled limes, and 2,051 boxes of fresh fruit.[iii] Lime juice was used as the basis for chemicals, especially citric acid, but it was also marketed as a beverage, acclaimed for its unique flavor and medicinal qualities. Lime essence was converted into perfumes and soaps, which were then sold at high-end retailers, such as Harrod's in London.

The demand for Montserratian limes was truly international, as evidenced by later 19th-century advertisements in newspapers around the world—from London, New York, and Montreal, to Bombay, Detroit, and Shanghai. Montserratian lime juice appealed to teetotalers, and advertisers promoted it as "The Best Temperance Beverage", and as "a far more wholesome drink than any form of alcohol".[iv] Consumers were urged to drink it alone, mixed with water or soda water, and ice, if it was available. At the same time lime juice was also marketed as a mixer for alcoholic beverages, including a refreshing gin-based cocktail, topped off with a spot of Angostura bitters.[v] Chemists often emphasized the medicinal properties of limes, advertising the juice as "a blood-purifying drink of superior character".[vi] The British Navy followed suit and introduced Montserratian limes as a Vitamin C supplement, which sailors added to daily rations of grog (watered-down rum) to prevent scurvy, earning them the enduring nickname, "Limeys".

Fig. 87. Trade card advertising Montserrat Lime Juice, 1891. (Private Collection.)

i *PS NEWS* 81.
ii *PS MNT* 61.
iii Fergus 1982: 11.
iv *PS NEWS* 77:4; *PS NEWS* 78.
v *PS NEWS* 80.
vi *PS NEWS* 79.
vii Alexander 1886.

Archaeological sites associated with the citrus lime industry survive in a variety of industrial ruins, domestic settings, and public spaces.[21] Elberton's Estate, located 1 km east of Fox's Bay, is the best preserved citrus lime-processing complex. Historical photographs from the 1890s depict Elberton's laborers performing the steps involved in lime processing (Fig. 88). These photographs are especially valuable for seeing how the estate's structures, built for the sugar industry, were repurposed to suit lime production, and they also provide clues about what sort of by-products or portable objects associated with the lime juice production process might be encountered during archaeological excavations.

In 2017 the *SLAM* project documented this estate's standing building remains, which included an extant windmill base (with an internal diameter of 5.35 m), a former boiling house (28.6 × 12.3 m), two large stone cisterns lined with plaster (7.21 × 4.2 m), two stone outbuildings, a cattle pen (24 × 24 m), and seven fragments of stone retaining and boundary walls (Fig. 89).[22] No artifacts were visible during this archaeological survey, because volcanic ash deposits, over 1 m thick, entirely obscure the 19th-century ground surface.

In 1872, John Edmund Sturge and his wife Jane Richardson financed the construction of The Cot, a retreat on the lower slopes of Centre Hills above Olveston, where they resided until it was destroyed in the hurricane of 1899 (Fig. 90).[23] The remains of multiple structures and landscape features at the site have recently been relocated and documented. Foundations of the former dwelling, a two-storey stone-built structure, are well-preserved (Fig. 91). A formal driveway leading upslope to the front of the house (first noted in LiDAR imagery of the area) was explored during archaeological survey. In addition to small stone outbuildings adjacent to and behind the main house, residents at The Cot apparently enjoyed the luxury of a water feature (possibly a swimming pool), the concrete lining of

[21] The Montserrat Company also constructed the island's first non-denominational school in Olveston in 1875 for its workers and their children. There is speculation that the original school house occupied a stone-built historic structure in lower Salem, across from today's Olveston House, but this has not been confirmed by archaeologists or historical sources; see Ryzewski *et al.* 2018; *UPR* 24.

[22] *UPR* 24.

[23] *PS MNT* 61.

which survives intact.[24] In June and July 2018, the site was cleared of vegetation, mapped in detail, and test-excavated by Samantha Ellens, in the context of her research on the citrus lime industries of Montserrat and Dominica.

In 1903, the Montserrat Company expanded its agricultural industries on the island and planted 25 acres of Sea Island cotton. The environment turned out to be well-suited for cotton, and it soon became both the company's and the whole island's largest source of revenue. Sea Island cotton continued to be profitable until the mid-20th century.[25] Just as they had for citrus limes, the Montserrat Company converted former sugar-processing facilities to accommodate cotton gins and other processing machinery. Remains of cotton machinery and ginnery buildings have been documented by archaeologists at Blakes Estate and Waterworks (Fig. 92).

Fig. 88. Ecuelling limes at Elbertons, Foxes Bay, 1890s. (Source: Sturge Collection, MNT.)

Fig. 89. Interior of the boiling house at Elbertons, documented during archaeological survey in 2017. (Photo: Beau Kromberg.)

Living conditions

During the first two decades after emancipation, particularly between 1838 and 1860, historical and archaeological sources reveal that Montserrat's laborers mostly continued to live within the confines of the estates where they had previously been enslaved. Archaeologist Jean Howson's excavations of the slave-era plantation village at Delvins Estate (discussed in Chapter 8) also recovered artifacts associated with the post-emancipation community who lived there until 1856. These laborers were consuming both European-manufactured and locally-made goods.[26]

Beginning in the 1860s, the introduction of wage labor finally made it possible for the laboring class to establish themselves in villages or settlements beyond estate boundaries, and in some cases,

[24] *UPR* 15.

[25] Fergus 1982: 11. Arrowroot was also a profitable crop on Montserrat during this period; remains of an arrowroot processing site were documented by archaeologists on the Woodlands Estate. See *UPR* 9.

[26] Howson 1995: 320.

to purchase small plots of property. But the post-emancipation villages that emerged in places like Salem, Drummonds, and Rendezvous Village were not without their difficulties. In an 1862 report about living conditions on Montserrat, the Acting Registrar James W. Sheriff reported that "a large proportion of the population formerly resident on estates" had recently relocated to housing both in the town and in remote villages. The resettlement "led to a mischievous overcrowding of dwellings, sometimes situated in unfavourable localities, insufficiently drained, and giving rise to intermittent fever". Sheriff credited the seclusion of these villages with an increased "state of demoralization, as injurious to society as compromising to the character of the island".[27] In backwater enclaves such as Drummonds and Rendezvous Village, archaeologists have documented remains of dwellings and artifacts associated with the sorts of settlements to which Sheriff was referring. But rather than suggesting unfavorable and disorderly living conditions, they seem to have been well-positioned to take advantage of prevailing winds and local agricultural resources. At Rendezvous Village, for instance, a network of irrigation channels and several man-made ponds, whose use is dated by the 19th-century pottery and glass bottles found in association with them, document how the laborers who lived in these communities skillfully managed water to ensure that a sustainable supply was available for their own consumption, and for crops and livestock (Fig. 93).[28] Artifacts from Rendezvous Village show a marked increase during the post-emancipation period of English-made, decorated whiteware pottery, and

Fig. 90. The rear of "The Cot", the Sturge family home built above Olveston in 1872. The photo dates to the 1890s, shortly before the house and other outbuildings were devastated during the 1899 hurricane and afterwards abandoned. (Source: Sturge Collection, MNT.)

Fig. 91. Ruins of the rear of "The Cot" (pictured in Fig. 90). Parts of the window frames seen in the 1890 photograph survive, but deep ash deposits obscure other features such as the driveway and ornamental garden. (Photo: John Cherry, June 2018.)

[27] *PS CO* 38:81.
[28] *UPR* 7; *UPR* 9.

a decreasing reliance on locally-made coarse earthenware pottery.[29]

Fig. 92. Cotton processing machinery at Waterworks Estate used during the 19th and 20th centuries. (Photo: John Cherry, 2012.)

Social welfare

Religious and educational institutions were entwined with one another in 19th-century Montserrat. Following emancipation, churches and schools became the foundation of social welfare among the laboring classes. Beginning in the 1830s, Christian missionary societies arrived on the island to establish schools and to promote church attendance. Records from the late 1830s onwards record a widespread shift among the laboring class towards involvement in organized, Anglo-religious practices, as evident by the increasing numbers of apprenticed and freed laborers who appear in the returns of marriages and baptisms.[30] There have not yet been any archaeological investigations focused on historic churches on Montserrat. But survey and excavations conducted recently on Potato Hill has provided a glimpse into the development of educational institutions, and what the schooling experience was like, during the second half of the 19th century.

Fig. 93. Manmade waterhole (foreground), fed by irrigation channels on the slopes behind it, at Rendezvous Village. (Photo: John Cherry.)

Schooling after emancipation

Under slavery, education was regarded by the white plantocracy as irrelevant, even inimical, to slave society.[31] This attitude continued after emancipation, and the local Montserratian government refused to fund education for the laboring classes during the first three decades. But primary education was an important priority for the British colonial government and recently-freed Montserratians alike, and the laboring classes actively pursued it for their

[29] Although European-made pottery dominates post-emancipation artifact assemblages, the island's black inhabitants continued to manufacture coarse earthenware pottery in the second half of the 19th century. Davy 1854: 415 notes of Montserrat's black inhabitants that "In advance of some of the other islands, they are not altogether without manufactures, however rude; they make bark-ropes for sale and articles of earthenware".

[30] *PS ABNA* 13; *PS ABNA* 14.

[31] Fergus 1994; Ryzewski *et al.* 2018: 549.

children.[32] This is clearly evident in the immediate establishment of primary-level day schools for the laboring class; in 1838 there was only one, but by 1840 there were seventeen throughout the island.[33] For the rest of the 19th century Montserrat had an average of eleven religious-affiliated primary day schools in operation.

Before 1834, enslaved children and adults were permitted to attend regular Sunday schools, which were held at churches and on estates across the island. Some estate owners received contributions to establish Sunday schools for enslaved, and later free, black children on their properties. Charitable support for these schools came from the Wesleyan Methodist Church, the Mico Institution, and the Christian Ladies' Society. Initially, in the 1840s, the new primary day schools were also based on sugar estates, many of them having hosted Sunday schools prior to emancipation. Estates with schools in the 1830s and 1840s included Whites, Tar River, Farrells, and Galways.[34] In the course of the next two decades, schools gradually shifted away from estates to village centers and local churches, in a trend that was reflective of the broader demographic shifts of the island's laborer population. In 1858 only two schools still remained on working sugar estates, at Brodericks (31 students) and Galways (104 students).[35]

Methodist missionary Jonathan Cadman opened the first primary day school for freed laborers at Cavalla Hill, in St Peter's Parish, in 1838.[36] This 50-student school introduced basic formal instruction in writing, reading, scripture, and mathematics, as well as practical training in domestic tasks and agriculture. The curriculum aimed to instill both Methodist and English ideals of respectability and moral behavior among the new laboring class of black and mixed-race children.[37] Most of Montserrat's schools during the first two generations after emancipation were affiliated with the Anglican or Methodist churches. One Roman Catholic school also existed in Plymouth during the second half of the 19th century, and one private school, unaffiliated with any religious organization, operated during the 1860s.[38]

It took 29 years, from the opening of the first day school for laborers' children at Cavalla Hill in 1838 until 1867, for the Montserrat Government to invest in local education.[39] A major turning-point in Caribbean primary education was the passage of the Federal Education Act of 1874, implemented on Montserrat in 1875. This Act brought all Leeward Islands schools under the supervision of an inspector. Compulsory education for children between ages 5 and 12 was instituted on Montserrat in 1890, along with regulations that standardized primary schools.[40] The extent to which education had developed into an essential resource for all classes is evident by the government's recovery priorities after the hurricane of 1899: schools were the first public institutions to receive funds for repair.[41]

---

[32] In *PS CO* 35 the Rev. S. Smith, a Wesleyan missionary who was supervisor of those schools, reported, "The Wesleyan mission schools in this island continue to serve the great purpose for which they were instituted, affording as they do religious and secular instruction to hundreds of children, chiefly of the poor and laboring classes".

[33] *PS BOA* 21; *PS BOA* 22; Berleant-Schiller 2014.

[34] *PS BOA* 18; *PS BOA* 21; *PS BOA* 24.

[35] *PS BOA* 26.

[36] Berleant-Schiller 2014: 57.

[37] *PS CO* 35; cf. Olwig 1990.

[38] *PS CO* 41.

[39] *PS BOA* 27.

[40] *PS CO* 42:15.

[41] *PS BOA* 28.

A schoolhouse on Potato Hill

In 2015 and 2016 the *SLAM* project excavated the remains of a mid- to late 19th-century structure on Potato Hill in Little Bay that appears to have functioned in some capacity as a schoolhouse.[42] Disappointingly, despite extensive archival research, no records have yet been located about this school, its affiliation, or its history. Yet nearly 7,000 finds recovered during the excavations provide a reasonable basis for discerning the function, age, and activities involved in the educational activities that took place there. Diagnostic pottery found at the base of the structure's foundation walls shows that the building was constructed after the earthquake of 1843, and other finds help in clarifying its main period of use—for example, "BEST RING EDGE" copper-alloy buttons (whose manufacture began in the mid-1850s), and a bottle of Perry Davis's Vegetable Painkiller (with a design panel dating to 1855).[43] The frequency of artifacts with manufacturing ranges or peak market popularities between 1850 and 1860 suggests that the structure was most active during that timeframe. Quite possibly, the schoolhouse was destroyed by the hurricane of 1899, since an historic photograph of the hilltop taken some time around 1900 shows the area as unoccupied and without any

Fig. 94. Aerial shot of the Potato Hill schoolhouse, during excavation in 2016; white lines outline the exterior walls of the structure. (Drone photo: Matthew Pihokker.)

[42] For information on the Potato Hill excavations and artifact analysis, see *UPR* 17; *UPR* 22; *UPR* 27; Ryzewski *et al.* 2018.
[43] Ryzewski *et al.* 2018.

standing structures.[44] No other examples of schoolhouses have been located archaeologically on Montserrat.

The schoolhouse building's remains are located towards the eastern end of Potato Hill in Little Bay. Details of the building's architecture, as uncovered by excavation, shows it to be a large, sturdy, stone-founded rectangular structure whose ground-level footprint measured 5 × 7 m (Fig. 94).

Fig. 95. Examples of 19th-century pottery from the Potato Hill schoolhouse excavations. (Photo: Krysta Ryzewski.)

Based on the adjacent fallen stone rubble, it is estimated that the foundation walls were originally about 1 m or more in height. Along the exterior of the building's stone foundation were uncovered eight postholes, placed about 40 cm from the exterior walls and measuring 20–30 cm in diameter, each of them dug into bedrock. The posts that once stood in these holes would have supported substantial load-bearing timbers. Based on comparative examination of vernacular architectural styles on Montserrat, including the former Great Houses at Trants (Fig. 68) and Farm Estates, the structure on Potato Hill appears to have been built in the so-called "skirt-and-blouse" style, with a stone-built ground floor or basement supporting an elevated wood-framed structure above it, and perhaps also an overhanging roof or verandah. The architectural evidence suggests that the original building contained at least two fairly large rooms on the ground level. Immediately west of the structure are the remains of two water-catchment features: a large rock-cut cistern, 2.8 m in diameter, and a waterstone with a bowl-shaped depression that would have captured enough rainwater for drinking or for use in daily chores.

The majority (54%) of the items from the schoolhouse excavations were fauna (fish and animal bones), followed by metal (15%), pottery (14%), and other historic materials (glass,

44 *PS MNT* 61.

etc.). The most popular pottery types were 19th-century whiteware (60%) and locally-produced coarse earthenware (18%). From the 977 pottery sherds recovered, 214 individual vessels have been identified, mostly bowls, cups, and service vessels, the majority of them (76%) decorated; but matching sets were uncommon (Fig. 95). This trend is consistent with the pottery recovered from other post-emancipation settlements at nearby Drummonds, Rendezvous Bluff, Rendezvous Village, and Delvins, and it probably reflects a combination of the piecemeal market availability of European ceramics and the particular preferences of Montserratian consumers during this period.[45]

Fig. 96. Ruled writing tablets and slate pencil fragments excavated from the schoolhouse on Potato Hill. (Photo: Beau Kromberg.)

Among the 198 special finds excavated, many can be interpreted as objects associated with a variety of educational activities, including reading, writing, arithmetic, home economics, agriculture, and animal husbandry. Forty of them were writing implements—fragments of 11 slate writing-tablets with incised lines and 29 slate pencils—likely used by children practicing their writing and arithmetic (Fig. 96). Also present were five toys—two porcelain dolls, the head of a porcelain goose figurine, and two marbles (Fig. 97). Further indications of homemade playthings are six circular disks, refashioned from broken pottery and potentially used as gaming tokens (see Fig. 80).

Fig. 97. Toys excavated from the Potato Hill schoolhouse. (Photo: Krysta Ryzewski.)

Other artifacts reveal that young female and male pupils probably devoted some time to learning the skills required to perform domestic service: sewing, tailoring, cooking, and home

[45] Ryzewski and Cherry 2016.

maintenance. These interpretations are corroborated by historical descriptions in annual Colonial Blue Book abstracts and further supported by local oral histories. Older Montserratians recall that their great-grandparents learned basic sewing, cooking, and agricultural skills in primary school. Sewing supplies, buttons, and beads comprised nearly half of the special finds recovered at Potato Hill. Sewing-related artifacts included seven copper alloy thimbles, six eyelets, three buckles, and a straight pin (Fig. 98). Fifty-three buttons were recovered, in various materials: bone, brass, shell, fabric, ceramic, and copper alloy. It is rather unlikely that the buttons in the assemblage actually belonged to clothes worn by the schoolchildren themselves, since records from 1850 made a point of commenting on how poorly dressed the children on Montserrat were.[46] Of particular interest are the 12 four-hole copper-alloy buttons (mentioned above) molded with the generic slogan "BEST RING EDGE", and another button labeled "BEST SOLID EYELET". These types of items were manufactured in abundance in England from the mid-1850s onwards, and were designed for adult work clothing.[47] Often associated with military trousers, but also commonly used on men's work trousers and women's underskirts, they were designed for durability and were inexpensive. Montserrat's new laboring class, then, seems to have been adopting these buttons for their work clothing, and their presence in the schoolhouse suggests that children may have been involved in maintaining these garments (the finding of a clothing iron is perhaps telling in this regard).

Fig. 98. Thimbles excavated from the Potato Hill schoolhouse. (Photo: Beau Kromberg.)

More than half of all the finds from the schoolhouse were faunal remains. Alexis Ohman, who conducted their analysis, reports that they include a wide variety of domestic animals (most common were sheep/goat and pig), and local tropical fish and molluscs, presumably prepared at the school and eaten there.[48] Corroboration of local husbandry practices, perhaps undertaken as part of the educational curriculum, comes from the presence of eggshells, maybe from chickens kept on the premises. There is some evidence of a gate and fencing around the schoolhouse, presumably to keep at bay animals roaming nearby.

As already mentioned, and despite this richly informative body of archaeological evidence, archival research has so far failed to locate any mentions of either the name or affiliation of a

---

46 *PS CO* 34.
47 Lindbergh 1999.
48 *UPR* 34.

schoolhouse on Potato Hill. Still, the wide range of diagnostic artifacts strongly implies that the structure functioned at least in part as a schoolhouse. Like all other post-emancipation primary schools on Montserrat, the Potato Hill school was probably co-educational. It is conceivable, in fact, that this school was the one unnamed private school listed in the 1860 Blue Book, with 31 male and 36 female children enrolled; but, in the absence of more detailed historical records, this remains only speculation.[49]

The archaeological history of the Potato Hill schoolhouse shows the extent to which Montserrat's adult laboring class was eager to invest in a better future for their children, despite local government's failure to adjust to changing social needs. The parents of schoolchildren during the mid-19th century would have experienced tremendous economic hardships, government resistance, and little hope of upward mobility during their own lifetime; yet the rapid growth of schools shows how they looked forward to a better future for the generations yet to come. The resilience of the new laboring class ensured that by the 1890s primary education had become a mandatory rite of passage for all of the island's children, and a cornerstone of society as Montserrat entered the 20th century.

[49] *PS CO* 37: 65.

10. Disaster, destruction, and development: the future of the past on Montserrat

When we talk about catastrophic natural events such as earthquakes, hurricanes, and volcanic eruptions, we tend to recount them as isolated episodes: 18 July 1995 (the Soufrière Hills volcano begins erupting); 16 September 1989 (Hurricane Hugo strikes Montserrat); 8 February 1843 (a major earthquake devastates the island). In the immediate aftermath of these incidents, responses are consumed by dealing with the urgent matters of physical destruction and loss. This period, which might last a few days, weeks, or even months or years, is a time when the focus is on repairing damaged property, healing from injuries, and restoring basic necessities such as water and electricity. But the impacts of these events continue to unfold long afterwards; they do not necessarily end when we are able to return to some semblance of our former daily routines.

Disasters are not isolated episodes, nor is any so-called "natural disaster" entirely natural in the way it plays out. Of course, there is no question that tectonic or weather-related incidents are usually triggered by specific natural forces.[1] But the actual disaster is the long-term process of physical, economic, social, and psychological disruption that follows a forceful event. In recent years, social scientists in general, and archaeologists in particular, have begun to focus on the enduring effects of disasters. There is a growing consensus that disasters are never truly "natural", but rather are the product of a mixture of social, cultural, and environmental factors.[2] How populations in disaster-prone settings such as Montserrat respond to upheaval in the aftermath of catastrophic events depends on their ability, as a society, to prepare for, cope with, and recover from the disturbances that forceful natural events have caused.[3]

As two anthropologists have recently put it, "Disasters have pasts, presents, and futures".[4] Archaeology is especially well equipped to examine the life-cycles of disasters, because it employs a long-term temporal framework that views them as processes of preparing, coping, and rebuilding. This is especially relevant on Montserrat, where, from an archaeological perspective, we can observe how responses to the current volcanic disaster are either direct consequences of the eruptions, on the one hand, or rooted in pre-existing practices, on the other. For example, the major

[1] But in the current era, in which fracking for natural gas may be causing local earthquakes and storms of greater intensity are almost certainly the consequence of human-induced global warming, this is no longer entirely the case.
[2] Torrence 2019.
[3] Blaikie *et al.* 1994: 9; Sheets 2012; Torrence 2019: 258.
[4] Oliver-Smith and Hoffman 2002.

Fig. 99. The resettlement village at Lookout under construction in 2007. (Photo: Krysta Ryzewski.)

shift in settlement to the island's north, and the construction of resettlement villages at Lookout, Drummonds, and Davy Hill, are direct consequences of volcanic destruction (Fig. 99).

These recent settlements emerged because volcanic activity destroyed or rendered inaccessible villages in the southern half of the island, giving people no option but to relocate; in their present form, these communities simply did not exist prior to 1995. Other responses to disaster recovery on Montserrat, however, are rooted in history, derived from practices and priorities that existed before the start of the current volcanic activity. A prime example of this continuity and adaptability is the perpetual search for sustainable, profitable industries, which Montserratians need in order to establish a productive economic base. So, for instance, today concerted efforts are underway to expand mining of the new deposits created by pyroclastic flows. Exploration for geothermal energy sources also continues in earnest, although as yet without much success.

We could view these economic revitalization efforts as unique to the volcanic recovery process, but they do not really reflect new priorities. An archaeological and historical perspective helps situate them against a much longer background of ongoing economic struggles and renewal efforts. To cite an example from just three decades ago, the aftermath of another disaster—Hurricane Hugo in 1989—represents another moment when Montserratians urgently sought to rebuild their

Fig. 100. In Plymouth, the former capital, a vast landscape of ruination—comprised of scores of abandoned homes, public buildings, and infrastructure—was created by recent volcanic activities. How might archaeologists in the present and future learn from the remains of this contemporary disaster? (Photo: John Cherry.)

economy.[5] Having damaged nearly all of the island's properties, Hugo was also responsible for the termination of the island's legendary music recording industry housed at AIR Studios (see below), and the end of Radio Antilles, the station with the most powerful broadcasting signal in the region. Or we might locate efforts to revitalize the island's economy in the decades before World War II, when the citrus lime industry had faded from existence and Sea Island cotton production took center stage. We can go even further back, to the 1830s: sugar had become no longer profitable, and planters scrambled to find alternative sources of profit in the new post-emancipation world, experimenting—usually unsuccessfully—with all sorts of agricultural possibilities (silk, olives, vines, cacao, and so on). As archaeologists, the point we would emphasize is that a long-term perspective is vital for understanding the extent to which certain social, economic, and political processes in present-day Montserrat—or indeed in other disaster recovery settings—were in place

[5] On Hurricane Hugo's devastating impact on Montserrat, see Markham and Fergus 1989.

prior to the destructive event(s), or were a direct result of them.[6] Management plans and recovery strategies can surely only be enhanced and better informed by an awareness that other people, in other times, and in other places, have also grappled with similar challenges posed by disasters: knowing how they prepared, and how they coped, is part of what archaeology and history can bring to the table (Fig. 100).

This chapter, then, applies archaeology's long-term framework to understanding the impacts of disasters on Montserrat. It especially considers how disasters and Montserratians' responses to them affect the preservation of archaeological remains and heritage sites, either directly or indirectly. We begin with a summary of disastrous events on Montserrat and an example from a heritage site that shows responses to them. Next, we consider the direct impacts of the recent volcanic eruptions on the preservation of archaeological sites. We then discuss how archaeological heritage sites are also adversely affected by indirect responses to the volcanic activity, especially short-sighted development initiatives. In doing so, we draw attention to the irreversible consequences of destroying archaeological heritage in the process of disaster recovery. We conclude with recommendations for protecting archaeological resources, so that the past may be preserved for future generations.

Disasters strike Montserrat

Montserrat is unquestionably a disaster-prone island. From the time of the first historically-documented storm in 1638 until the present, Montserrat has been affected by over two dozen hurricanes.[7] Not infrequently, these have caused damage to nearly all of the island's buildings, as was the case three times in the course of the past century or more—in 1989, 1928, and 1899. A half-dozen major earthquakes, and countless smaller seismic tremors, have also repeatedly damaged island infrastructure. Several of these tremors have actually been associated with volcanic eruptions on other islands, such as in 1843, when La Grande Soufrière erupted on Guadeloupe and triggered a series of strong earthquakes throughout the region. Montserrat's villages have also suffered from the by-products of these meteorological and tectonic events, including ruinous floods, mudslides, lahars, and massive erosion. No matter the scale of devastation caused by these repeated catastrophes, Montserratians have, time and again, rebuilt their infrastructure and economy, and moved on, mindful of the potential threats of future disasters. In the process, they have also recognized the value of maintaining, preserving, or reconstructing certain heritage sites. One such example of this dedication and resilience is to be seen in the physical remains of St Anthony's Church in Plymouth, whose history extends back to the very first years of English settlement on Montserrat during the 1630s. This church has been rebuilt no fewer than six times in the aftermath of destructive events (Box L).

Volcanically-induced damage to archaeological sites

The volcanic crisis of the past two decades has directly impacted the survival of all types of archaeological sites on Montserrat. In 2006 and 2007, two pairs of archaeologists (David Miles and Julian Munby, and David Watters and Gillian Norton) documented the post-eruption survival

[6] Torrence and Grattan 2002: 7–11.

[7] See Wheeler 1988 for a chronology of natural disasters affecting Montserrat between 1638 and 1899.

Box L: St Anthony's Church, Plymouth

St Anthony's Anglican Church was one of the first public buildings constructed by English settlers on Montserrat. The ruins of this significant heritage site are still standing today in Plymouth. The church was originally built in 1635 by the island's first governor, Anthony Brisket, and was already in its third incarnation when it appeared on the 1673 Blathwayt map of Montserrat (see Box G). Over the course of Montserrat's nearly 400-year history as an English settlement, St Anthony's has fallen victim to many of the island's catastrophes. These include:

1666: Burned by the French and Caribs
1672: Destroyed by an earthquake on Christmas Day
1712: Leveled by French invaders after they used it as a barracks
1899: Destroyed by hurricane
1928: Destroyed by hurricane
1989: Damaged by hurricane
1995: Damaged by volcanic eruptions

Records indicate that the church was also impacted, if less severely, by other invasions and natural disasters at various points during its history. The church has been rebuilt on the same site no fewer than six times during the course of its history. Following the hurricane of 1928, which totally ruined the cross-shaped church (Fig. 101), construction workers encountered brick flooring from one of the 17th-century iterations of the building while they were digging a deeper foundation for the new nave.[i]

During the 1990s and early 2000s, St Anthony's Church was damaged over the course of successive volcanic episodes. Today the building sits without a roof, but many of its furnishings survive, including the pipe-organ, lectern, and pews, as well as monuments commemorating influential 18th- and 19th-century rectors and parishioners (Fig. 102).

In the yard behind the church is a burial ground with tombstones and mausolea belonging to the island's elite English planters and their families. This cemetery and the area around

Fig. 101. The ruins of St Anthony's church after the hurricane of September 1928. (Source: Peters 1928: 26.)

Fig. 102. St Anthony's church in June 2017, following 22 years of damage from the Soufrière Hills eruptions. (Photo: Miriam Rothenberg.)

the church are now deeply covered by volcanic ash, but many of the headstones are still partially visible above the ground surface.

Given the church's deep history of rebounding from catastrophic disasters, it is perhaps too soon to declare that the recent volcanic crisis has caused irreparable damage to St Anthony's.

[i] Peters 1928: 26.

rate of sites, both historic and prehistoric, in the Exclusion Zone. Their observations, helpfully, if also depressingly, confirm that many previously-known archaeological locations in the island's south have been buried, damaged, destroyed, or rendered inaccessible for the foreseeable future as a result of volcanic activity.[8]

In May 1995, just prior to the start of volcanic eruptions in July that year, Miles and Munby compiled a brief inventory of the island's sugar plantation ruins. Of the 50 historic sites they identified, 35 were close to the Soufrière Hills volcano. Watters and Norton's subsequent 2007 assessment of these and other sites documented how pyroclastic activity had destroyed, damaged, or cut off the majority of the 35 sites near Soufrière Hills (Fig. 103). Historic sugar estates at Tar River, Farrell's, Tuitts, Galways, Lees, and Gages were totally destroyed or buried. Roche's and Bethel partially survived, but were isolated from access by pyroclastic flows. Trants Estate was at first partially

[8] Miles and Munby 2006; Watters and Norton 2007.

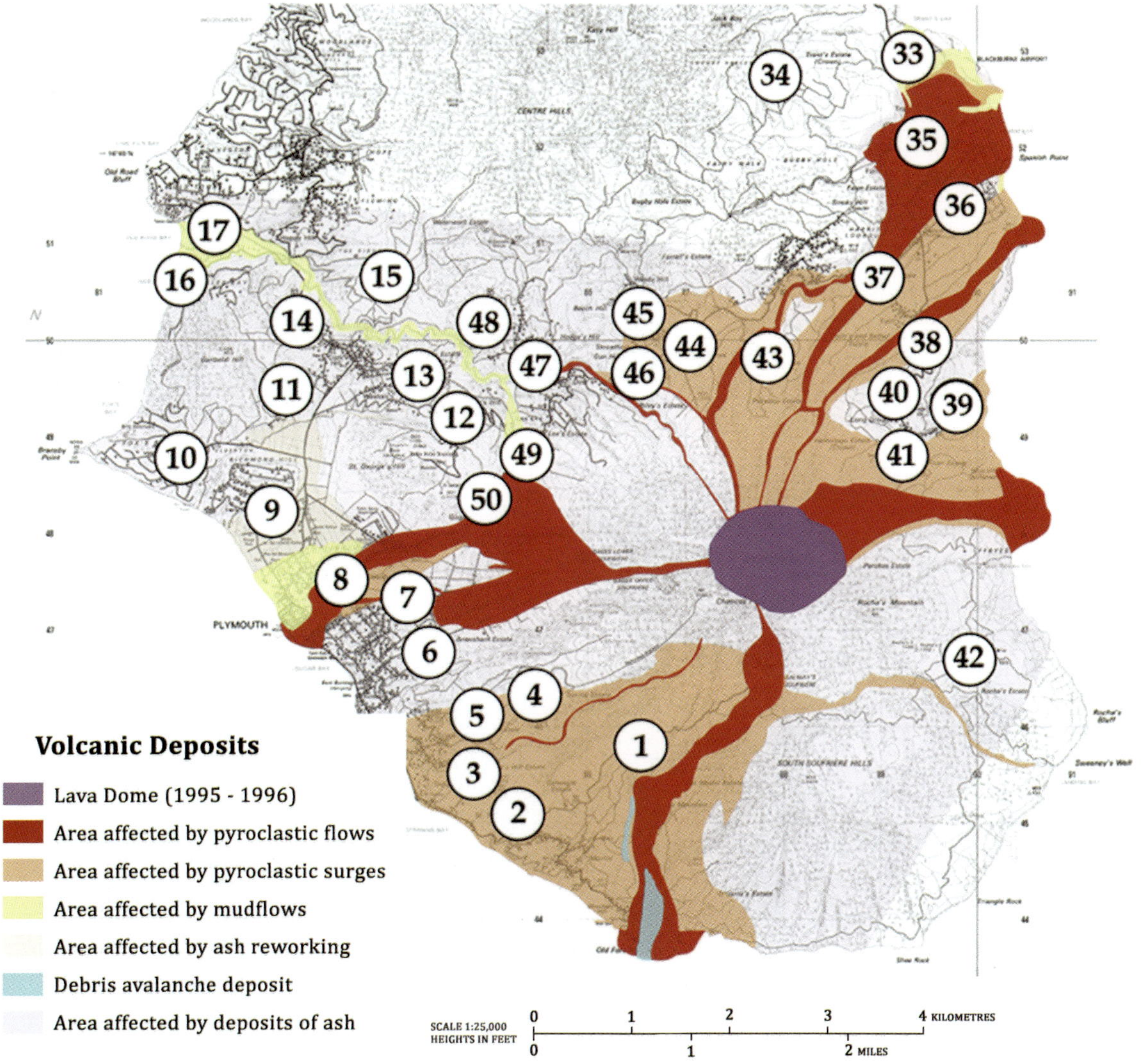

Fig. 103. The location of historic sugar estates and the extent of volcanic impacts on them as of 2007. (Adapted from Watters and Norton 2007: fig. 1.) Key to sites: 1, Upper Galways; 2, Lower Galways; 3, Reid's Hill; 4, Spring; 5, Broderick; 6, Amersham; 7, Parson; 8, Webb; 9, Richmond Hill; 10, Elberton; 11, Delvins; 12, St George's Hill; 13, Weekes; 14, Cork Hill; 15, Waterwork; 16, Isles Bay; 17, Old Road; 33, Trants; 34, Locust Valley; 35, Farm; 36, Bethel Yard (Spanish Point); 37, Tuitt; 38, White; 39, Mulcares; 40, Hermitage; 41, Tar River; 42, Roche; 43, Paradise; 44, Farrell; 45, Streatham; 46, Riley; 47, Hodge; 48, Molyneaux; 49, Lee; 50, Gages.

spared, but later massive eruptions in 2010 buried it almost entirely, along with the former Bramble airport nearby (Fig. 104). Only three of these sugar estates (Upper Galway, Delvins, and Trants) had seen systematic archaeological research before the start of the eruptions in 1995. Numerous villages with historic structures and known but unexamined archaeological sites were destroyed, most notably Kinsale and St Patrick's. Prehistoric sites at Radio Antilles, Trants, the Belham River golf course, Dagenham, and Spanish Point (the Farnsworth site) were also lost.

Over the course of the current volcanic crisis, the boundaries of the Exclusion Zone have changed many times. When the volcano was especially active, access to areas as far north as Olveston and Salem were prohibited; but in quieter periods it has been possible to gain daytime entry to Plymouth and full-time access to previously off-limit villages such Cork Hill, Weekes, and Richmond Hill. As Exclusion Zone boundaries have become relaxed, archaeologists from the *SLAM* project have been afforded the chance to expand their survey coverage into areas that had been directly impacted by ashfall, pyroclastic flows, and lahars as recently as 2010, in order to assess the preservation of archaeological sites there. As a result, it has been possible to document the survival of plantation remains at places such as Elbertons, Delvins, Weekes, and Richmond Hill (see Figs 1 and 45). In 2017–2018, survey was also extended into the current Exclusion Zone, and, with the co-operation of scientists from the Montserrat Volcano Observatory, it has been possible to document the current state of, for example, the Grove Agricultural Station, St Anthony's Church, and the Governor's mansion in Plymouth, and—relying on helicopter lifts—what remains of remoter upland villages such as Long Ground.

Fig. 104. The Trants Estate after the February 2010 eruption: only the boiling house's smokestack (center) and the circular top of the windmill tower nearby remain visible. This volcanic event pushed the shoreline about 650 m out to sea. (Drone photo: Matthew Pihokker 2016.)

Fig. 105. The recording studio at AIR Studios as it appeared in May 2010; all of the buildings were completely cleaned out in 2012. (Photo: Krysta Ryzewski.)

To turn to a more detailed example, perhaps the most nostalgic site examined by archaeologists in the former Exclusion Zone is AIR Studios. Active only between 1979 and 1989, this is hardly an ancient site; but its recent vintage makes it no less archaeological than the prehistoric site of Trants, more than 2,000 years old. We consider AIR Studios to be an example of a contemporary archaeology site, a place where the material remains of the house, recording studio, and materials from past activities that took place there survive alongside living memories from the people who once recorded, worked, or visited there in its heyday.[9]

AIR Studios Montserrat was a premier international recording destination, a satellite of the parent AIR Studios in London, owned and managed by Beatles manager Sir George Martin. Many of the world's most famous musicians of the 1970s and 1980s recorded there, including Dire Straits, The Police, Jimmy Buffett, The Rolling Stones, Elton John, Paul McCartney, and Duran Duran.[10] During its heyday, AIR boasted the most advanced recording technology of the era, including a 58-input Neve recording console. In 2010, with permission of its owner, the *SLAM* project conducted a contemporary archaeological survey and a small excavation at the AIR Studios recording complex (Fig. 105). The studio building and adjacent house had been abruptly abandoned after Hurricane Hugo in 1989 and never reoccupied.

Fig. 106. Inscriptions by band members and sound engineers in the courtyard of the AIR Studios guest house. (Photo: Krysta Ryzewski, 2010.)

At the time of the archaeological survey, the property had been recently subjected to heavy ashfall from the February 2010 eruption, but all sorts of materials relating to music production and the use of the house as an accommodation for musicians remained in place.[11] During the survey, *SLAM* archaeologists documented the layout and current conditions of the complex's spaces. In the ruins of the house, they recorded small finds such as cans of food, clothes hangers, and bathroom fixtures—hardly the stuff of legendary rock 'n roll parties, but indications nonetheless of the everyday living conditions they would have experienced when in residence. In the interior spaces of the recording studio and production rooms, considerable quantities of movable material culture related to the studio's music production activities were documented, including technical electronics manuals, reel-to-reel tapes, lights, wiring for sound, paper forms for booking artists, an empty guitar case, and microphone stands. In the interior courtyard garden, excavations removed concreted ash deposits to reveal signatures and hand-imprints made in freshly laid concrete by the musicians, producers, and sound engineers who recorded at AIR Studios over the years, including the members of the Climax Blues Band, the very first group to produce an album there in 1979 (Fig. 106).

These are, of course, unconventional archaeological remains, but they hold great interest for those with interests in music history and who remember AIR Studios Montserrat. The ruins of AIR Studios also present a poignant dilemma for preservationists. In 2012 the buildings were

---

[9] Harrison and Schofield 2010.

[10] A list of albums recorded at AIR Studios Montserrat, along with a description of the *SLAM* excavations there, appears in Cherry *et al.* 2013.

[11] In 2011 the buildings were totally emptied and stripped in anticipation of converting the space to function as a tourism site, but the building's owner, Sir George Martin, died in 2016 before any such plans were put into action.

stripped of all material traces of the musical talent that once filled their rooms. As of 2019, the buildings are in a state of utter dereliction and obscured by vegetation. Whether the derelict building complex is worth rehabilitating is a topic of debate that raises many questions about how sites so close to a still dangerous volcano might be managed or commemorated for future generations to enjoy as a heritage site.

Development and archaeology in the context of disaster recovery

Indirect impacts of volcanic activity, especially unchecked or short-sighted development plans, have resulted in damage to, or destruction of, a number of archaeological sites on Montserrat, especially in the years since the last major eruption in 2010. New buildings, roads, and infrastructure have (of necessity) been hastily constructed to serve the needs of the expanded population in the

Fig. 107. The proposed 2009 Master Plan for Little Bay envisioned a new capital settlement populated with luxury villas, government buildings, a boardwalk and market, green spaces, a cathedral, marinas, and a hotel and hillside villas atop Potato Hill. These plans were quickly replaced by other visions that have also not come to fruition.

Fig. 108. Part of the developments at Little Bay, seen from Potato Hill in 2015. Immediately above the cricket pitch is the new National Museum, with the Social Security Building under construction farther upslope; between them lies the Little Bay Estate heritage site. (Photo: John Cherry.)

island's north, yet almost always without recognition of potential or known archaeological resources that exist in the vicinity. The most notable transformation to the island's northern landscape has involved the extensive building projects at Little Bay, the area slated to become Montserrat's new capital town. Since 2006, the creation of this town at Little Bay has involved a series of ambitious planning schemes, none of which have been fully materialized. Some buildings, certainly, have been constructed there—for instance, the new port facility, the Montserrat National Museum, the Social Security Building, an indoor sports arena, a row of beachside restaurants, and (earlier) the Cultural Centre (Figs 107 and 108).

A number of the proposed construction projects have been taken just far enough to alter the landscape and impact archaeological heritage sites, before being postponed or abandoned. We have already mentioned the prehistoric site at Little Bay and the area of enslaved housing nearby at the Little Bay Estate, in both cases obliterated by road construction. A particularly dramatic example involved the remains on Gun Hill, at the south end of Carr's Bay, where *SLAM*, at the request of the MNT, discovered and excavated a well-preserved 18th-century stone cannon platform. Yet despite aspirations to preserve the site, Gun Hill and its platform were demolished shortly after excavations concluded, in order to make space for the proposed construction of a cruise liner berth, which has not yet come to fruition (see Box M). A further example, just a

Box M: The sad story of Gun Hill in Carr's Bay

In 2013 archaeologists from the *SLAM* project discovered the ruins of a substantial, well-constructed gun battery atop a headland in Carr's Bay on the northwest coast of Montserrat. Although this headland was known locally as Gun Hill, its use as a fortification from the sugar era—indeed its very existence—had long been forgotten.

Archaeological excavations on Gun Hill revealed a well-constructed stone platform, suitable for use as a cannon emplacement. By far the best-preserved example of 18th-century military architecture outside of the Exclusion Zone, the battery's platform was built with unusual precision and skill, almost certainly by enslaved laborers.[i] The Gun Hill battery was D-shaped and constructed of large, flat stones capable of supporting the weight of heavy guns. A low encircling parapet running along the coastal edge of the battery would have provided protection for the militia as they monitored or defended the more than 180-degree perimeter to the west, north and east. Excavations showed that the battery was constructed with considerable forethought, with walls continuing down 1 m below the surface, providing a very strong foundation. The stone paving itself was carefully designed, beginning by laying out three lines of individual larger stones running southwest–northeast, and another northwest–southeast, and the spaces in-between were infilled with smaller flat stones.[ii] Seventy historic-period artifacts were unearthed, including glass bottles, tobacco pipe-stems, and English-made pottery (creamware, white salt-glazed stoneware, and pearlware), the manufacturing dates of which were used to date the structure's use in the mid- to late 18th century.

The Gun Hill platform was probably constructed around 1756, when defenses across the island, including at Carr's Bay, were expanded in response to French threats in the region.[iii] The best parallels for the Gun Hill platform's architecture are at the Bransby Point Battery and the now-destroyed Power's Hill Battery (Old Fort Point).[iv] Both had the same D-shaped layout and low parapets.[v]

Excavations on Gun Hill were conducted as a brief "rescue" dig, rather than as a longer-term research or heritage preservation project. In Spring 2013, the Carr's Bay—Little Bay New Town Development Plan announced the intention to level most of Gun Hill as a step towards constructing a marina for luxury yachts and a berth for small cruise ships. Initially, there was no provision for involving preservationists or archaeologists in assessing the site and whether it might be preserved as part of this development. Then the Montserrat National Trust intervened and obtained permission for archaeologists to examine the site and to retrieve as much information about it as possible.

Ultimately, however, Gun Hill's historical merit was no match for the economic value promised by the proposed marina and cruise-ship berth. Developers did not see heritage preservation as compatible with economic interests. As a result, in the summer and autumn of 2013, Gun Hill—and with it, the historic cannon battery—was demolished down to sea level. Shortly thereafter, the development plans stalled. As of June 2019, seven years later, the former site of Gun Hill still remains undeveloped.

Fig. 109. The carefully constructed platform atop Gun Hill, uncovered by archaeological excavations, was positioned to command a sweeping view of the island's north. (Photo: Krysta Ryzewski.)

Fig. 110. Excavations in progress atop Gun Hill, May 2013. (Photo: John Cherry.)

Fig. 111. The former location of Gun Hill in 2018, five years after the hilltop was demolished in the name of development. This photograph was taken from a similar orientation as Fig. 110. (Photo: Miriam Rothenberg.)

The story of Gun Hill's destruction should be a cautionary tale. This site could perhaps have been Montserrat's equivalent (on a much smaller scale) to Shirley Heights in Antigua—a major historic attraction and a scenic overlook, enjoyed by locals and tourists alike. Unfortunately, this irreplaceable cultural resource fell victim to short-sighted development planners who held no regard for the island's past in their vision of its future. Increased attention to existing UK-based protective heritage legislation (see Chapter 2) and better coordination between developers and preservationists could prevent additional tragic and unnecessary endings to archaeological sites on Montserrat.

---

[i] Gun Hill does not appear by that name in any known historical records. Nothing is mentioned in the exceptionally thorough inventory by Crandall, 2000. The hilltop was situated directly above the Carr's Bay Battery and would have been associated with it during its use as a fortification in the 18th century. The Carr's Bay battery was established with two six-pounder cannon by order of the Council and Assembly of Montserrat in November 1693, and significantly upgraded by 1756 (see Chapter 7).

[ii] *UPR* 11

[iii] Crandall 2000: 341.

[iv] Crandall 2000: 344, 349.

[v] Unlike Gun Hill, they also had associated houses/powder magazines.

few hundred meters farther north, concerns Potato Hill, the flat-topped promontory that divides Carr's Bay from Little Bay. There, bulldozing and grading took place in 2013 to prepare the site for the planned development of a luxury gated villa complex or hotel. The machinery removed trees and scrub, slightly damaging an 18th-century structure in the process. The cleared area did provide archaeologists with an opportunity to conduct a gridded surface survey in 2013, which revealed traces of historic late 18th- and 19th-century structures, excavated in 2016 and 2017, as described in Chapter 2—one of them likely used as a schoolhouse in the post-Emancipation period (see Chapters 7 and 9). Another unfortunate episode occurred at Upper Blakes in 2017, when the central part of what was by then definitively known to be the oldest prehistoric site on Montserrat, one of Caribbean-wide significance (as discussed in Chapter 3), was casually destroyed, despite prior archaeological advice, in the course of civil engineering work to improve drainage and limit surface erosion. Further south, the ruins of the Great House at Weekes Estate were slightly damaged in 2016 by the placement of a geothermal drilling pad over part of the site (see Chapter 7). Damage to Upper Blakes and the Weekes Estate, where important archaeological sites were known to exist before construction began, could easily have been prevented in ways that did not adversely affect development plans, had construction workers been in consultation with appropriate heritage professionals beforehand.

To summarize, some 35 historic-era sites have been destroyed or impacted by volcanic activity since 1995 (Fig. 103), along with an additional eight prehistoric sites. A further half-dozen sites have been destroyed or seriously damaged by development activities since the volcanic crisis began (the slave village at Little Bay, the prehistoric site at Little Bay, the Archaic site at Upper Blakes, Gun Hill at Carr's Bay, Potato Hill at Little Bay, and the Weekes Estate).

What is the role of the past in the future of Montserrat?

On islands such as Antigua, Dominica, and St Kitts, the most accessible and enjoyable places for locals and tourists alike to visit are heritage sites—Nelson's Dockyard, the Cabrits, the Kalinago Reserve, and Brimstone Hill, to name but a few.[12] What might be Montserrat's equivalent heritage sites to showcase, as the economy grows and tourists begin to return to the island?

Plymouth? This would be the immediate answer given by most Montserratians and tourism consultants. We return to current discussions about converting Plymouth into a heritage/geological park momentarily. But first, we ask: why is there not as much interest in developing sites such as Valentine Ghaut, Potato Hill, Locust Valley Estate, or the Little Bay Estate for local educational purposes and tourism? Why wasn't there a public outcry when Gun Hill was demolished? When Upper Blakes was leveled? Or when the slave village at Little Bay was bulldozed?

The complicated answers are twofold. They may have to do, firstly, with a lack of direct connections to certain pasts, and, secondly, with a desire to create distance between present-day communities and the island's painful pasts, especially those of the plantation era. Interestingly, despite the evidence (discussed in Chapter 5) for entanglement and intermingling of native people with Europeans and Africans, Montserratians today do not appear to feel much affinity with an Amerindian heritage—as certain contemporary groups on other islands, for instance, self-identify

[12] With accompanying archaeological remains and, in some cases, museum exhibits.

Fig. 112. Pyroclastic flows and lahars from the Soufrière Hills volcano (background) have completely destroyed the capital city of Plymouth, burying the majority of the city center, as pictured here. (Photo: Miriam Rothenberg, 2017.)

as Taíno or Kalinago/Cayo—and so they show scant interest in prehistoric remains.[13] Likewise, the ubiquitous standing structures of the plantation works of the sugar and slavery era constitute a painful "dark heritage" for most Montserratians of African descent, who prefer not to explore the alternative histories of survival and resilience that are manifested by the material remains. Instead, interest is focused on efforts to trace individual family lineages via websites such as *ancestry.com* and records of slave shipments from Africa. To a considerable extent, as the Antiguan archaeologist Reg Murphy has written, the most meaningful heritage for many islanders may be the *intangible* heritage traditions of distinctive types of food and drink, music and song, dance, dress, and so on.[14] Might there be a way to better connect the prevailing local interests in intangible heritage

[13] Various groups in Puerto Rico, Cuba, Jamaica, and Dominica, as well as on the US mainland, currently identify as Taíno; a recent DNA study suggests that most Puerto Ricans have some degree of Taíno ancestry. On Dominica, the Kalinago maintain a 15 sq. km territory, granted to them by the British Crown in 1903, which supports a population of about 3,000 Carib descendants.

[14] Murphy 2011

with particular cultural and archaeological sites on the island's landscape, particularly outside the exclusion zone? This is a challenge that the next generation of Montserratians will face, especially as development continues to threaten archaeological sites.

When it comes to selecting places for tourism development, the current focus is on Montserrat's former capital city, Plymouth. It is frequently referred to as the "Pompeii of the Caribbean" because most of it is buried under thick volcanic deposits (Fig. 112).

Indeed, Plymouth and the many other communities within the Exclusion Zone that were destroyed during the volcanic eruptions present a unique opportunity for archaeologists of the recent past to examine responses to catastrophic events. Until 2017, these areas were totally off-limits for research, but the first contemporary archaeology documentation project began in 2018 with the fieldwork of Brown University doctoral student Miriam Rothenberg; she has been collecting information about the loss, decay, and reclamation of buildings and culturally modified landscapes in the Exclusion Zone (as well as in nearby villages, such as Cork Hill and Richmond Hill), in order to help inform interpretations of disaster responses in ancient societies, such as Pompeii or Herculaneum.

Recent proposals to turn Plymouth into a heritage tourism venue and/or a volcanological park raise intriguing possibilities, but also many difficult questions.[15] The remains of the buried city and its visible ruined buildings are striking and undoubtedly fascinating to gaze upon (Fig. 113).

Visiting Plymouth is without question an emotional experience, even for outsiders who have no prior memory of the town, when it was the bustling and vibrant central place on the island a generation ago. There are few places in the world that showcase the dramatic impacts of volcanic destruction on modern landscapes in the way that Plymouth does. But the long-term prospects for tourism-inspired development in the Exclusion Zone raise some fundamental safety, logistical, and ethical issues. First and foremost, Plymouth cannot be considered safe, so long as the volcano remains active: deadly gases from pyroclastic flows and dangerous lahars can reach Plymouth in a matter of minutes, with little or no advance warning, potentially trapping and injuring visitors. That is why the recently established tourist trips into Plymouth are allowed to take place only in the company of safety-trained taxi-van drivers, along with a police escort, and constant radio communication with the Montserrat Volcano Observatory. Second, the environment of Plymouth is obviously unsuitable for those with mobility concerns, asthma, or who are of certain age groups. It also presents hazards to tourists who might wander off designated routes: there are many buried buildings, no longer clearly visible on the current ground surface, whose roofs are liable to collapse. Third, consideration would need to be given to how Plymouth's disaster landscape might be "maintained" over the years, if the aim is to preserve the look of a city so dramatically and recently affected by ashfall and pyroclastic flows—the experience, presumably, that tourists would want to see. Vegetation has already overrun areas such as the Belham River, Sturge Park, and Richmond Hill, which were blanketed in ash and devoid of plant growth just a few years ago; it is encroaching on Plymouth too, even though high levels of atmospheric acidity impede vegetation. Would there be coordinated efforts to forestall the growth of vegetation over Plymouth in order to maintain the "authentic" look of the city in the immediate aftermath of its destruction?[16]

[15] As part of the development of the Little Bay/Carr's Bay area, there were plans to construct a volcano interpretation museum, immediately adjacent to the Montserrat National Museum and the Little Bay Estate Heritage site; but these appear to have stalled or been shelved.

[16] Such debates about authenticity are common in the museum community, especially when it comes to deciding how best to represent properties that have long-term histories.

Fig. 113. The ruins of the former Government House in Plymouth in 2018. (Photo: Miriam Rothenberg, 2018.)

The final (and certainly the most important) issue is whether it is really appropriate or respectful of the Montserratians who experienced so much loss in the eruptions to convert their damaged and abandoned homes, businesses, and other buildings into a tourist attraction. Is it too soon? Although the volcano has been quiet for nearly a decade, the pain from the destructions it caused are still raw—the psychological process of disaster recovery continues. Such sentiments are best illustrated in comments on social media posts, such as the "Archaeology on Montserrat" Facebook Page that the *SLAM* project and its affiliated archaeologists maintain. In one case, for example, a picture posted of the ruined houses in Windy Hill taken from the Montserrat Volcano Observatory's helicopter by John Cherry in 2018 generated a series of heartfelt, nostalgic comments from Montserratians living both in the diaspora and on the island. In the course of posting fond memories about the places they once called home, one woman summed up the lasting, lifelong feelings about Montserrat's volcanic crisis that many share, exclaiming, "What a pain to carry!". So, with these people and these sentiments in mind, are we comfortable converting Plymouth and other devastated villages into sights of ruin-gazing, where visitors might poke their heads into the windows of houses where the clothing belonging to people evacuated at a moment's notice still hangs in their closets? There are no easy answers to such questions.

Ultimately, the ruins of Plymouth are just one chapter in Montserrat's very long history. As the examples in this book have shown, there are dozens of heritage sites, both within and beyond the

Exclusion Zone, that have the potential to be maintained and promoted in ways that tell particular stories about the island, for the benefit of local enjoyment and tourism alike. These heritage sites can be presented in ways that recognize Montserratians' millennia of cultural contributions and resilience in the face of difficult social and environmental circumstances on a disaster-prone island.

Fig. 114. Local primary school students, during a SLAM *project classroom session, learn archaeological laboratory methods in the course of mending broken modern pottery vessels. (Photo: Emanuela Bocancea, 2011.)*

Unfortunately, calls of preservation-minded Montserratians and visiting scholars often fall on the deaf ears of those in government and of development authorities who prioritize economic revitalization above all else. To quote from our own experience, in advocating for archaeological and historic-site preservation on Montserrat, we have been told by a senior government official that "development always trumps heritage". Naturally, we do not agree with such a sentiment. The twin aims of cultural heritage management and development need not be mutually exclusive. Archaeologists and preservationists are not against sustainable economic development projects, and they do not request permission to conduct archaeological research as a tactic for stalling or impeding construction projects. On the contrary, our archaeological interests, and those of our preservation-minded colleagues, are not stuck in a past that has no regard for the future needs of Montserrat's economy and society.

Our concerns are with preserving and communicating about Montserrat's unique heritage and history so that it can inform and be appreciated and enjoyed by future generations (Fig. 114). For the foreseeable future, damage to Montserrat's archaeological sites is likely to continue, in the absence of a resident archaeologist to coordinate with developers and government planning officials and to help apply heritage management policies that are enforced island-wide. But it is surely the case that compromises made in the best interests of the island's economy and heritage can be reached between developers and preservationists—if there is co-operation and goodwill on all sides.

References

A. Primary sources (PS)

ABNA: Antigua and Barbuda National Archives

1. Acts of Montserrat 1835–1861, Book 310
2. Correspondence from England relating to Montserrat, 1834–1862, CO6
3. Dispatches from Downing Street, 1834–1862, CO6
4. Francis Burke to Speaker of the House, letter, 6 December 1838, Minute book of Montserrat Council and House of Assembly, 1814–1862, CO398
5. Governor Colebrooke to the President of Montserrat, letter, 29 August 1837, Minute book of Montserrat Council and House of Assembly, 1814–1862, CO398
6. Governor Colebrooke to the President of Montserrat, letter, 13 November 1838, Minute book of Montserrat Council and House of Assembly, 1814–1862, CO398
7. Governor William Woodley to Montserrat Assembly, letter, 22 March 1768, Montserrat Council and Assembly Minute Book
8. Letters Book: Out-letters to Montserrat from Antigua,1836–1842, File Box 34
9. Montserrat Council and Assembly: Minutes, 25 November 1693, CO155
10. Montserrat House of Assembly: Minutes, 12 August 1697, CO155
11. Montserrat House of Assembly: Minutes, 14 June 1698, CO155
12. Records of Enrollments 1818–1862: List of Estates Requesting Assistance Post-earthquake, 21 October 1845, Miscellaneous Papers from Montserrat 416
13. Records of Enrollments 1818–1862: Return of Marriages of Apprenticed Laborers Solemnized in Montserrat 1 Aug 1834 to 1 Aug 1837, Miscellaneous Papers from Montserrat 416
14. Records of Enrollments 1818–1862: Return of Number of Apprentices in the Island of Montserrat, 30 Nov 1837, Miscellaneous Papers from Montserrat 416

AGI: Archivo General de Indias AGI, Sevilla, Spain

15. Don Luis de Valdes, Gouverneur Capitaine Général de l'île de Saint-Martin, letter, 22 Août 1636, IG 1872
16. Du Gouverneur de Porto Rico à sa Majesté, letter, 10 Novembre 1560, Licencie Hachegoyan, Santo Domingo, SD 71
17. Du Gouverneur de Porto Rico à sa Majesté, letter, 27 Julliet 1566, Sevilla, SV 155, (doc. 174 verso)

BOA: British Online Archives

https://microform.digital/boa/collections/73/caribbean-colonial-statistics-from-the-british-empire-1824–1950

18. Caribbean Colonial Statistics for the British Empire: Montserratian Blue Book, 1830
19. *ibid.*, 1836
20. *ibid.*, 1837
21. *ibid.*, 1839
22. *ibid.*, 1840
23. *ibid.*, 1841
24. *ibid.*, 1848

25. *ibid.*, 1856
26. *ibid.*, 1858
27. *ibid.*, 1867
28. *ibid.*, 1900

CEN: Census records

29. Mounserrat, 1677–78, a census. In Vere L. Oliver (ed.) 1910, *Caribbeana: Being Miscellaneous Papers Relating to the History, Genealogy, Topography, and Antiquities of the British West Indies*, Vol. 2, London: Mitchell, Hughes and Clarke, 316–320; 342–347.
30. Mounserrat, 1729, a census. In Vere L. Oliver (ed.) 1916 *Caribbeana: Miscellaneous Papers Relating to the History, Genealogy, Topography, and Antiquities of the British West Indies*, Vol. 4, London: Mitchell, Hughes and Clarke, 302–311.

CO: Colonial Office, Great Britain

31. Report Exhibiting the Past and Present, State of Her Majesty's Colonial Possessions, 1845
32. *ibid.*, 1847
33. *ibid.*, 1848
34. *ibid.*, 1850
35. *ibid.*, 1854
36. *ibid.*, 1856
37. *ibid.*, 1860
38. *ibid.*, 1862
39. *ibid.*, 1865
40. *ibid.*, 1866
41. *ibid.*, 1869
42. *ibid.*, 1890

JCB: John Carter Brown Library, Brown University

43. *The Landing of Columbus*, unknown artist. From Theodor de Bry's edition of Girolamo Benzoni's *History of the New World*, Frankfurt am Mein, 1594 (Figure 38).
44. Map of Mountserrat, Blathwayt Atlas, 1673, file name 8189–30

LLA: Lamont Library Archives, Harvard University

45. Appraisal and Inventory of (Personal) Estate of Thomas Duberry Esq., 21 January 1764, Book of Deeds, August 1762–July 1771, Montserrat, Reel 6, 53–63
46. Deed of Sale for Old Road Plantation between Nicholas Tuite and James Doran, May 1764, Book of Deeds, July 1765–1767, Montserrat, Reel 7, 8–9
47. Emancipation of Slaves by J.D. Molineux, 10 April 1756, Book of Deeds, January 1755–February 1757, Montserrat, Reel 3, 147
48. Emancipation of Thomas Skerrett Junior, 28 July 1754, Book of Deeds, January 1755–February 1757, Montserrat, Reel 3, 146
49. Indenture between John Dyer, Mary Gerald and Edmund Akers, guardians of the Last Will and Testament of Joseph Gerald, 1 March 1756, Book of Deeds, January 1755–February 1757, Montserrat, Reel 3, 169
50. Indenture between Richard Tuite, Robert Skerrett and Nicholas Tuite of the first part, and Charles O'Garra, 1766, Book of Deeds, July 1765–1767, Montserrat, Reel 7, 1130
51. Inventory of Robert Tuite, Esq., 11 May 1763, Book of Deeds, August 1762–July 1771, Montserrat, Reel 6, 22
52. Manumission of Slaves by John Bramley of St. Peter's, 11 January 1766, Book of Deeds, July 1765–1767, Reel 7, 1103

LOC: Library of Congress, Washington, D.C.

53. Tuitts Estate Map, 1886, Court of the Commissioners for Sale of Encumbered Estates in the West Indies (Montserrat), Hards & Jenkinson, London, 2016586778
54. Weeks or River Head Estate Map, Encumbered Estates Act, 1870, Court of the Commissioners for Sale of Encumbered Estates in the West Indies (Montserrat), Hards, Vaughan, & Leifchild, London, 2016586629

MNT: Montserrat National Trust

55. Jane Liddell, Widow, petition, re Intestate Late Husband William, 22 August 1733, Register of Deeds, Montserrat: 1787–1792, Transcriptions of Deeds 1734–1739, 144
56. John Farrill to Dominick Trant, land deed, 1727, Book of Deeds, Montserrat: 1787–1792, Transcriptions of Deeds 1734–1739
57. Manumission for Gustavus Vasa [sic], Montserrat, 11 July 1766, D. Terry Legay
58. Nicholas Skerrett to John Blake, land deed, 1732, Book of Deeds, Montserrat: 1787–1792, Transcriptions of Deeds 1734–1739
59. Report on Measurement of Land Boundaries Pursuant to Judgement Granted to Mr Robert Piper against Mr Hugh Allen, 1737, Book of Deeds, Montserrat: 1787–1792, Transcriptions of Deeds 1734–1739
60. Somerville Papers, 1976. Delores Somerville, Unpublished Typescript, Montserrat National Trust
61. Sturge Family Papers, Documents, Letters, and Photographs, Boxes 1 and 2
62. Will of Edmond Murphy, 1685, Copied in Register of Deeds, Montserrat: 1787–1792, Transcriptions of Deeds 1734–1739
63. William Stapleton to Dennis Brennan, land grant, 1681, Copied in Register of Deeds, Montserrat: 1792–1793, Transcription of Deeds 1739–1749, 248

MPL: Montserrat Public Library

64. An Act Against Slaves Going from their Master's Plantation on the Lord's Day, and Against such as Entertain any Runaways, &c., 1668, Mountserrat Acts of Assembly, 1668–1740, John Baskett, London, 30
65. An Act for Condemning all Lands Lost to his Majesty in the said Island of Montserrat, 1668, Mountserrat Acts of Assembly, 1668–1740, John Baskett, London, 3
66. An Act for Quieting Possessions, and for the Better Securing and Confirming the Titles of Lands in this Island, 1705, Mountserrat Acts of Assembly, 1668–1740, John Baskett, London, 65
67. An Act for Reducing the Trade of this Island into Three Certain Towns in the Same, 1670, Mountserrat Acts of Assembly, 1668–1740, John Baskett, London, 19
68. An Act for the Speedy Erecting of Beacons in the Several Parts of this Island, 19 September 1668, Mountserrat Acts of Assembly, 1668–1740, John Baskett, London, 7
69. An Act to Prevent Clandestine Dealings with Negroes, 1702, Mountserrat Acts of Assembly, 1668–1740, John Baskett, London, 61–62
70. Dominick Trant, Joseph and Christopher Hixon and Thomas Meade, Plantiffs vs John Doe (Henry Dyett), 1780, Kings Book and Common Pleas, 1778–1788, Record 295, 82–105
71. Inventory of Buildings at Old Road Estate, Register of Deeds, Montserrat: 1886–1875, 163–165
72. Irish Connection Pays Off, *Montserrat Times*, 27 March 1986, 3
73. March 17th/Montserrat's National Day?, *Montserrat Mirror*, 17 March 1979, 1a
74. Preliminary Report: Visitor Expenditure and Motivational Survey, Montserrat, February–March 1979

NEWS: Newspaper sources

75. A Letter from St. Christopher's, 22 September 1768, *The Virginia Gazette*
76. Account of the Aftermath of the Intended Insurrection on St. Patrick's Day, May 26, 1768, *Pennsylvania Gazette*
77. Advertisement for Montserrat Lime Juice, *The Freeman*, 8 May 1885, 4
78. Advertisement for Montserrat Lime Juice, 3 November 1885, *The Indian Planters' Gazette*
79. Advertisement for Montserrat Lime Juice, *The Times of India*, 11 June 1879, 1

80. Advertisement for Montserrat Lime Juice, *The Times of India*, 29 September 1925, 12
81. The Lime Juice Island, June 1903, *Detroit Free Press*, 4

RLM: Rylands Library, University of Manchester

82. An Account of the Receipts and Payments of the Publick Stock there from the Year 1670 to the Year 1680, Stapleton MSS 2/3
83. An Act Against Tradeing with Negroes, 19 November 1683, Acts for Montserrat, 12–13, Stapleton MSS 2/5
84. By Divers Persons for their Slaves in Number hereafter Mentioned, 1672, Publique Account for the Island Montserratt 1674, Stapleton MSS 2/3
85. Levy of Slaves for the Publique of this island, 1672, Publique Account for the Island Montserratt 1674, Stapleton MSS 2/3
86. Levies Enacted on Thatched Houses and Corrupted Indigo, 1679, Stapleton MSS 2/3
87. Lieutant and Col. Wm Stapleton appointed Deputy Governor in ye Island of Montserrat, 1660. Stapleton MSS STP/1/1/1
88. Militia Rolls, Montserrat 1681, Stapleton MSS 2/6
89. Publique Account for the Island Montserratt 1674, Stapleton MSS 2/3
90. Pulique Stock of ye Island Montserrat 1678, 21 February, Stapleton MSS 2/3
91. William Stapleton to Sir James Russel, Lease for Waterworks Estate, 1 May 1678, Stapleton MSS

TNA: The National Archives, Kew

92. An Accounting of Sufferings and Losses Sustained by Residents During the Attack, 1716, CO 152/16
93. Lt. General Edw. Mathew to Right Hon. Lord Grenville, letter, 4 June 1791, CO 101/31
94. Map of Montserrat, 1734, MPG 1/90
95. Minutes of the Council of Montserrat 1768–1779: 18–21 March 1768, CO 412/462
96. Slave Registry of Montserrat, 1817, T71/447

B. Secondary sources

Akenson, D.H. 1997. *If the Irish Ran the World: Montserrat 1630–1730.* Montreal: McGill-Queen's University Press.

Alexander, J.R. 1886. *The Island of Montserrat: Its History and Development Chiefly as Regards its Lime Tree Plantations, with a Short Description of Lime Juice and its Use as a Medicinal Agent, and as a Beverage.* London: Carlisle, H. Scott & Sons.

Armstrong, D.V. 2010. Degrees of Freedom in the Caribbean: Archaeological Explorations of Transitions from Slavery. *Antiquity* 84: 146–160.

Bercht, F. (ed.) 1997. *Taíno: Pre-Columbian Art and Culture from the Caribbean.* New York: Monacelli Press.

Berleant-Schiller, R. 1989. Free Labour and the Economy in Seventeenth-Century Montserrat. *The William and Mary Quarterly*, 3rd Series 46(3): 539–564.

— 1996. The White Minority and the Emancipation Process in Montserrat, 1807–32. *Nieuwe West-Indische Gids/ New West Indian Guide* 70(3/4): 255–281.

— 2014. From Labour to Peasantry in Montserrat After the End of Slavery. In Karen Fog Olwig (ed.), *Small Islands, Large Questions: Society, Culture and Resistance in the Post-Emancipation Caribbean*, 53–72. Hoboken, NJ: Taylor and Francis.

Blaikie, P., T.P. Cannon, I. Davis and B. Wisner. 1994. *At Risk: Natural Hazards, People's Vulnerability, and Disasters*. London: Routledge.

Boomert, A. 1986. The Cayo Complex of St. Vincent: Ethnohistorical and Archaeological Aspects of the Island Carib Problem. *Anthropologica* 66: 3–68.

— 2016. *The Indigenous Peoples of Trinidad and Tobago from the First Settlers until Today*. Leiden: Sidestone Press.

Bridenbaugh, C. and R. Bridenbaugh. 1972. *No Peace Beyond the Line: The English in the Caribbean*. Oxford: Oxford University Press.

Bright, A.J. 2011. *Blood is Thicker Than Water: Amerindian Intra- and Inter-insular Relationships and Social Organization in the Pre-Colonial Windward Islands.* Leiden: Sidestone Press.

Brussell, D.E. 1997. *Potions, Poisons, and Panaceas: An Ethnobotanical Study of Montserrat.* Carbondale: Southern Illinois University Press.

Burnard, T. 2004. *Mastery, Tyranny, and Desire: Thomas Thistlewood and His Slaves in the Anglo-Jamaican World.* Chapel Hill and London: University of North Carolina Press.

Callaghan, R.T. 2001. Ceramic Age Seafaring and Interaction Potential in the Antilles: A Computer Simulation. *Current Anthropology* 42(2): 308–313.

Chase, A.F., D.Z. Chase and J.F. Weishampel. 2010. Lasers in the Jungle. *Archaeology* 63(4). archive.archaeology.org/1007/etc/caracol.html

Chase, A.F., D.Z. Chase, J.F. Weishampel, J.B. Drake, R.L. Shrestha, K. Clint Slatton, J.J. Awe and W.E. Carter. 2011. Airborne LiDAR, Archaeology, and the Ancient Maya Landscape at Caracol, Belize. *Journal of Archaeological Science* 38: 387–398.

Cherry, J.F. 2018. Insights from the Outside: Wider Perspectives and Future Directions in Caribbean Island Historical Ecology. In P. Siegel (ed.), *Island Historical Ecology: Socionatural Landscapes of the Eastern and Southern Caribbean*, 345–366. Oxford and New York: Berghahn Books.

Cherry, J.F. and K. Ryzewski. 2014. Montserrat. In B.A. Reid and R. Grant Gilmore III (eds), *Encyclopedia of Caribbean Archaeology*, 238–242. Gainesville: University Press of Florida.

— 2019. An Archaic Site at Upper Blakes on Montserrat: Discovery, Context, and Wider Significance. In C. Hofman and A. Antczak (eds), *Early Settlers of the Insular Caribbean: Dearchaizing the Archaic*, 231–244. Leiden: Sidestone Press.

Cherry, J.F. and T.P. Leppard. 2018. Patterning and its Causation in the Pre-Neolithic Colonization of the Mediterranean Islands (Late Pleistocene to Early Holocene). *Journal of Island and Coastal Archaeology* 13(2): 187–201.

Cherry, J.F., K. Ryzewski and L.J. Pecoraro. 2013. "A Kind of Sacred Place": The Rock-and-Roll Ruins of AIR Studios, Montserrat. In M.C. Beaudry and T.G. Parno (eds), *Archaeologies of Mobility and Movement*, 181–198. New York: Springer Verlag.

Cherry, J.F., K. Ryzewski and T.P. Leppard. 2012. Multi-period Landscape Survey and Site Risk Assessment on Montserrat, West Indies. *Journal of Island and Coastal Archaeology* 7(2): 282–302.

Cherry, J.F., R.S. Opitz and K. Ryzewski. 2017. Airborne LiDAR and the survey of historic era landscapes in central Montserrat. In C.B. Velasquez and J.B. Haviser (eds), *Proceedings of the 26th Congress of the International Association of Caribbean Archaeologists, Sint Maarten, July 19–25, 2015*, 1–16. Sint Maarten: International Congress for Caribbean Archaeology.

Cherry, J.F., T.P. Leppard and K. Ryzewski. 2014. The Prehistory of Montserrat: A Synthesis and an Update. In B. Bérard (ed.), *Proceedings of the 24th Congress of the International Association of Caribbean Archaeologists, Martinique, W.I., July 23–30, 2011*, 266–76. Martinique, W.I.: Université des Antilles et de la Guyane.

Cherry, J.F., K. Ryzewski, T.P. Leppard and E. Bocancea. 2012. The Earliest Phase of Settlement in the Eastern Caribbean: New Evidence from Montserrat. *Antiquity* 86 (Issue 334) *Project Gallery* (http://antiquity.ac.uk/projgall/cherry333/).

Coppier, G. 1645. *Histoire et voyage des Indes occidentales*. Lyon: Jean Huguetan.

Crandall, D.R. 2000. *A Military History of Montserrat, W.I.: Attacks, Fortifications, Cannons, Defenders, 1632–1815.* Privately published, Montserrat, W.I.

Crock, J.G. and R.N. Bartone. 1998. Archaeology of Trants, Montserrat. Part 4: Flaked Stone and Stone Bead Industries. *Annals of Carnegie Museum* 67: 197–224.

Cruxent, J. and I. Rouse. 1958–1959. *An Archaeological Chronology of Venezuela*, Vols 1–2. Social Science Monographs No. 6. Washington, D.C.: Pan American Union.

DAACS 2018. Digital Archaeological Archive of Comparative Slavery. https://www.daacs.org/

Davis, D.D. 1974. Some Notes Concerning the Archaic Occupation of Antigua. In *Proceedings of the 5th International Congress for the Study of the Pre-Columbian Cultures of the Lesser Antilles, Antigua, July 22–28, 1973*, 65–71. St. John's, Antigua: The Antigua Archaeological Society and The Antigua National Trust.

— 1993. Archaic Blade Production on Antigua, West Indies. *American Antiquity* 58(4): 688–697.

— 2000. *Jolly Beach and the Preceramic Occupation of Antigua, West Indies*. Yale University Publications in Anthropology 84. New Haven: Yale University Press.
Davy, J. (1854). *The West Indies, Before and Since Slave Emancipation, Comprising the Windward and Leeward Islands' Military Command, Founded on Notes and Observations Collected during a Three Years' Residence*. London: W. and F. G. Cash.
Deerr, N. 1949. *The History of Sugar*. London: Chapman and Hall.
Dennell, R.W., J. Louys, H.J. O'Regan and D.M. Wilkinson. 2013. The Origins and Persistence of *Homo floresiensis* on Flores: Biogeographical and Ecological Perspectives. *Quaternary Science Reviews* 96: 98–107.
Diderot, D. 1958 [1758]. *A Diderot Pictorial Encyclopedia of Trades and Industry, in Two Volumes*. Charles Coulston Gillispie (ed.). Originally published in French in 1758. New York: Dover Publications.
Donahue, J.D., D.R. Watters and S. Millspaugh. 1990. Thin Section Petrography of Northern Lesser Antilles Ceramics. *Geoarchaeology* 5: 229–254.
Donovan, A.R., M. Bravo and C. Oppenheimer. 2013. Co-production of an Institution: Montserrat Volcano Observatory and Social Dependence on Science. *Science and Public Policy* 40: 171–186.
Druitt, T.H. and B. Peter Kokelaar (eds) 2001. *The Eruption of Soufrière Hills Volcano, Monserrat, from 1995 to 1999*. Geological Society of London Memoir 21. London: Geological Society of London.
Dubelaar, C.N. 1995. *The Petroglyphs of the Lesser Antilles, the Virgin Islands and Trinidad*. Amsterdam: Foundation for Scientific Research in the Caribbean Region.
Dubois, L. and J.D. Garrigus. 2006. *Slave Revolution in the Caribbean, 1789–1804: A Brief History with Documents*. London: Macmillan.
Dukes, J.A. and E.J. Reitz. 1995. Use of Vertebrate Resources at Trants, a Saladoid Site on Montserrat. In R.E. Alegría and M. Rodríguez (eds), *Proceedings of the 15th International Congress for Caribbean Archaeology, San Juan, Puerto Rico, 25–31 July, 1993*, 201–208. San Juan: Centro de Estudios Avanzados de Puerto Rico y el Caribe.
Dunn, R.S. 2012 [1972]. *Sugar and Slaves: The Rise of the Planter Class in the English West Indies, 1624–1713*. Chapel Hill, NC: University of North Carolina Press.
Du Tertre, J.-B. 1667–1671. *Histoire générale des Antilles habitées par les Français*, 4 vols, Volume 4, 199–205. Paris.
Ellens, S. 2017. *Mapping Montserrat's Transition from Sugar to Limes: A Geosocial Landscape Approach*. Paper presented at the 27th Congress of the International Association for Caribbean Archaeology, St. Croix, July 26.
English, T.S. 1930. *Ireland's Only Colony: Records of Montserrat, 1632 to the End of the Nineteenth Century*. London: West India Committee.
Equiano, O., P. Wheatley and C. Tiebout. 1814. *The Interesting Narrative of the Life of Olaudah Equiano, or Gustavus Vassa, the African*. Halifax: J. Nichols.
Fergus, H.A. 1975. *History of Alliouagana: A Short History of Montserrat*. Plymouth, Montserrat: University Centre.
— 1982. Montserrat's Days of Lime and Cotton. *Caribbean Quarterly* 28(3): 10–18.
— 1994. *Montserrat: History of a Caribbean Colony*. London and Basingstoke: Macmillan.
Fitzpatrick, S.M. 2006. A Critical Approach to ^{14}C Dating in the Caribbean: Using Chronometric Hygiene to Evaluate Chronological Control and Prehistoric Settlement. *Latin American Antiquity* 17(4): 389–418.
— 2013. The Southward Route Hypothesis. In W.F. Keegan, C.L. Hofman, and R. Rodríguez Ramos (eds), *The Oxford Handbook of Caribbean Archaeology*, 198–204. Oxford: Oxford University Press.
— 2015. The Pre-Columbian Caribbean: Colonization, Population Dispersal, and Island Adaptations. *PaleoAmerica* 1(4): 305–331.
Galloway, J.H. 1989. *The Sugar Cane Industry*. Cambridge: Cambridge University Press.
— 1996. Botany in the Service of Empire: The Barbados Cane-Breeding Program and the Revival of the Caribbean Sugar Industry, 1880s–1930s. *Annals of the Association of American Geographers* 86(4): 682–706.
Giovas, C.M., M.J. LeFebvre and S.M. Fitzpatrick. 2012. New Records for Prehistoric Introduction of Neotropical Mammals to the West Indies: Evidence from Carriacou, Lesser Antilles. *Journal of Biogeography* 39(3): 476–487.
Goodwin, C.M. 1982. Archaeology on the Galways Plantation. *Florida Anthropologist* 35(4): 251–253.
— 1987. Sugar, Time, and Englishmen: A Study of Management Strategies on Caribbean Plantations. Unpublished PhD dissertation, Department of Archaeology, Boston University.
Graham, T. 2017. Apology to Liam Hogan. *History Ireland*. www.historyireland.com/liam-hogan/.

Grenham, J. 2015. Irish Roots: Were there Irish slaves in Barbados? *Irish Times*, June 12.

Gwynn, A. 1932. Documents Relating to the Irish in the West Indies. *Analecta Hibernica* 4: 139–286.

Hall, D. 1971. *Five of the Leewards 1834–1870: The Major Problems of the Post-Emancipation Period in Antigua, Barbuda, Montserrat, Nevis and St. Kitts*. Barbados: Caribbean Universities Press.

Harlow, V.T. (ed.) 2017 [1925]. *Colonising Expeditions to the West Indies and Guiana, 1623–1667*. London: Hakluyt Society.

Harrington, M.R. 1924. A West Indian Gem Center. *Indian Notes* 1(4): 184–189. New York: National Museum of the American Indian, Heye Foundation.

Harrison, R. and J. Schofield (eds) 2010. *After Modernity: Archaeological Approaches to the Contemporary Past*. Oxford: Oxford University Press.

Haviser, J.B. 1997. Settlement Strategies in the Early Ceramic Age. In S.M. Wilson (ed.), *The Indigenous People of the Caribbean*, 57–69. Gainesville: University Press of Florida.

Hayward, M.H., F.J. Schieppati and M.A. Cinquino. 2017. Lesser Antillean Rock Art: A Characterization. In C.B. Velasquez and J.B. Haviser (eds), *Proceedings of the 26th Congress of the International Association of Caribbean Archaeologists, Sint Maarten, July 19–25, 2015*. Sint Maarten: International Congress for Caribbean Archaeology.

Hayward, M.H., L.-G. Atkinson and M.A. Cinquino. 2013. Rock Art of the Caribbean. In W.F. Keegan, C.L. Hofman and R. Rodríguez Ramos (eds), *The Oxford Handbook of Caribbean Archaeology*, 486–503. Oxford: Oxford University Press.

Hincks, T., S. Sparks, P. Dunkley and P. Cole. 2005. Montserrat. In J.M. Lindsay, R.E.A. Robertson, J.B. Shepherd and S. Ali (eds), *Volcanic Hazard Atlas of the Lesser Antilles*, 148–167. St. Augustine, Trinidad and Tobago: Seismic Research Unit, University of the West Indies.

Hofman, C. and A. Antczak (eds) 2019. *Early Settlers of the Insular Caribbean: Dearchaizing the Archaic*. Leiden: Sidestone Press.

Hofman, C.L. and A. van Duijvenbode (eds) 2011. *Communities in Contact: Essays in Archaeology, Ethnohistory, and Ethnography of the Amerindian Circum-Caribbean*. Leiden: Sidestone Press.

Hofman, C.L. and M.L.P. Hoogland. 2016. *Saba's First Inhabitants: A Story of 3300 Years of Amerindian Occupation prior to European Contact (1800 BC–AD 1492)*. Leiden: Sidestone Press.

Hofman, C.L., A. Delpuech and M.L.P. Hoogland. 2014. *Espaces amérindiens: archéologie en Grande-Terre de Guadeloupe*. Le Moule, Guadeloupe: Musée Departemental Edgar Clerc.

Hofman, C.L., M.L.P. Hoogland and B. Roux. 2015. Reconstruire le táboüi, le manna et les pratiques funéraires au village caraïbe d'Argyle, Saint-Vincent. In B. Grunberg (ed.), *À la recherche du Caraïbe perdu: Les populations amérindiennes des Petites Antilles de l'époque précolombienne à la période coloniale*, 41–50. Paris: L'Harmattan.

Hogan, L., L. McAtackney and M.C. Reilly. 2016. The Irish in the Anglo-Caribbean: Servants or Slaves? *History Ireland* 24(2): 18–22.

Holliday, S.H. 2009. *Montserrat: A Guide to the Centre Hills*. St. John's, Antigua: West Indies Publishing.

Honychurch, L. 1997. Crossroads in the Caribbean: A Site of Encounter and Exchange on Dominica. *World Archaeology* 28(3): 291–304.

— 2000. *Carib to Creole: A History of Contact and Cultural Exchange*. Roseau, Dominica: The Dominica Institute.

— 2011. *The Archaeology of Dominica*. Self published.

Howson, J.E. 1990. Social Relations and Material Culture: A Critique of the Archaeology of Plantation Slavery. *Historical Archaeology* 24(4): 78–91.

— 1995. Colonial Goods and the Plantation Village: Consumption and the Internal Economy in Montserrat from Slavery to Freedom. Unpublished PhD dissertation, Department of Anthropology, New York University.

Hunt, G.M. 2013. *Desperate in Saint Martin: Notes on Guillaume Coppier*. Bloomington, IN: Trafford Publishing.

Jane, C. 1930–1931. *Selected Documents Illustrating the Four Voyages of Columbus*. Translated and edited with additional material, introduction and notes by Cecil Jane, 2 vols. Volume 1. London: Hakluyt Society.

Jönsson Marquet, S. 2002. *Les pétroglyphes des Petites Antilles Méridionales: Contextes physique et culturel*. BAR International Series 1051. Oxford: Archaeopress.

Keegan, W.F. and C.L. Hofman. 2017. *The Caribbean before Columbus*. New York: Oxford University Press.

Kirch, P.V. 2010. Peopling of the Pacific: A Holistic Anthropological Perspective. *Annual Review of Anthropology* 39: 131–148.

Knippenberg, S. 2006. *Stone Artefact Production and Exchange among the Northern Lesser Antilles*. Leiden: University of Leiden.

— 2011. Much to Choose From: The Use and Distribution of Siliceous Stone in the Lesser Antilles. In C.L. Hofman and A. Duijvenbode (eds), *Communities in Contact: Essays in Archaeology, Ethnohistory, and Ethnography of the Amerindian Circum-Caribbean*, 171–185. Leiden: Sidestone Press.

Kolchin, P. 1993. *American Slavery, 1619–1877*. New York: Hill and Wang.

LeFriant, A., E.J. Locl, M.B. Hart, G. Boudon, R.S.J. Sparks, M.J. Leng, C.W. Smart, J.C. Komorowski, C. Deplus and J.K. Fisher. 2008. Late Pleistocene Tephrochronology of Marine Sediments Adjacent to Montserrat, Lesser Antilles Volcanic Arc. *Journal of the Geological Society* 165(1): 279–289.

Lenik, S. 2012. Carib as a Colonial Category: Comparing Ethnohistoric and Archaeological Evidence from Dominica, West Indies. *Ethnohistory* 59(1): 79–107.

Leppard, T.P. and C. Runnels. 2017. Maritime Hominin Dispersals in the Pleistocene: Advancing the Debate. *Antiquity* 91: 510–519.

Lindbergh, J. 1999. Buttoning Down Archaeology. *Australasian Historical Archaeology* 17: 50–57.

MacLean, J.S. 2015. Sheltering Colonialism: The Archaeology of a House, Household, and White Creole Masculinity at the 18th-Century Little Bay Plantation, Montserrat, West Indies. Unpublished Doctoral Dissertation, Department of Archaeology, Boston University.

Major, R.H. (ed.) 2017. *Select Letters of Christopher Columbus: With Other Original Documents Relating to his Four Voyages to the New World*. London: Routledge.

Mann, R., L. Meadows, W.M. Bass and D.R. Watters. 1987. Description of Skeletal Remains from a Black Slave Cemetery from Montserrat, West Indies. *Annals of Carnegie Museum* 56: 319–336.

Mans, J.L.J.A. and L. Brock. 2017. Indigenous Movements and Social Transformations in the Lesser Antilles (post-1492). Paper presented at the 27th Congress of the International Association for Caribbean Archaeology, St. Croix, July 26.

Markham, E.A. and H.A. Fergus. 1989. *Hugo Versus Montserrat*. Coleraine and Boston: Linda Lee Books.

Mason, K. 1993. The World an Absentee Planter and his Slaves Made: Sir William Stapleton and his Nevis Sugar Estate, 1722–1740. *Bulletin of the John Rylands University Library of Manchester* 75: 103–131.

Mathews, T.G. 1969. The Spanish Domination of Saint Martin (1633–1648). *Caribbean Studies* 9(1): 3–23.

McAtackney, L., K. Ryzewski and J.F. Cherry. 2014. Contemporary 'Irish' Identity on the Emerald Isle of the Caribbean: St. Patrick's Day on Montserrat and the Invention of Tradition. In D.S. Nititham and R. Boyd (eds), *Heritage, Diaspora and the Consumption of Culture: Movements in Irish Landscapes*, 113–134. London: Routledge.

McCormack, M. 2017. The Irish and Slavery. Letter. *History Ireland* 25(5) September/October: 10–11 [Letter was removed from website in 2017, following formal apology from editor].

Messenger, J.C. 1975. Montserrat: The Most Distinctively Irish Settlement in the New World. *Ethnicity* 2: 281–303.

— 1994. St Patrick's Day in "The Other Emerald Isle". *Éire-Ireland* 29: 12–23.

Mickleburgh, H.L. and J.R. Pagan-Jimenez. 2012. New Insights into the Consumption of Maize and Other Plant Foods in the Pre-Columbian Caribbean from Starch Grains Trapped in Human Dental Calculus. *Journal of Archaeological Science* 39: 2468–2478.

Miles, D. and J. Munby. 2006. Montserrat before the Volcano: A Survey of the Plantations Prior to the 1995 Eruptions. *Landscapes* 7(2): 48–69.

Millard, M.E. 2017. The English Settlement of St Christopher, 1624–1629. Unpublished PhD dissertation, University of Plymouth.

Mol, A.A.A. 2013. Studying Pre-Columbian Interaction Networks: Mobility and Exchange. In W.F. Keegan, C.L. Hofman, and R. Rodríguez Ramos (eds), *The Oxford Handbook of Caribbean Archaeology*, 329–346. New York: Oxford University Press.

— 2014. *The Connected Caribbean: A Socio-material Network Approach to Patterns of Homogeneity and Diversity in the Pre-colonial Period*. Leiden: Sidestone Press.

Moreau, J.-P. 1992. *Les Petites Antilles de Christophe Colomb à Richelieu (1493–1635)*. Paris: Karthala.

Murphy, R. 2011. Antigua and Barbuda. In P.E. Siegel and E. Righter (eds), *Protecting Heritage in the Caribbean*, 73–79. Tuscaloosa: University of Alabama Press.

Nelson, E.C. 2001. Patrick Browne M.D. (c. 1720–1790), an Irish Doctor in the Caribbean: His Residence on St. Croix (1757–1765) and His Unpublished Accounts of Volcanic Activity on Montserrat. *Archives of Natural History* 28(1): 135–147.

Newsom, L.A. and E.S. Wing. 2004. *On Land and Sea: Native American Uses of Biological Resources in the West Indies*. Tuscaloosa: University of Alabama Press.

Odbert, H., P. Cole and A. Stinton (eds) 2011. *Island of Fire: The Natural Spectacle of the Soufrière Hills Volcano, Montserrat.* St. Augustine, Trinidad and Tobago: Seismic Research Unit, University of the West Indies.

Oliver-Smith, A. and S.M. Hoffman. 2002. Introduction: Why Anthropologists Should Study Disasters. In S.M. Hoffman and A. Oliver-Smith (eds), *Catastrophe and Culture: The Anthropology of Disaster*, 3–22. Santa Fe: School of American Research Press.

Oliver, J.R. 1999. The La Hueca Complex in Puerto Rico and the Caribbean: Old Problems, New Perspectives, Possible Solutions. In C.L. Hofman and M.L.P. Hoogland (eds), *Archaeological Investigations on St. Martin, Lesser Antilles: The Sites of Norman Estate, Hope Estate, and Anse des Pères*, 253–297. Leiden: ASLU.

Olwig, K.F. 1990. The Struggle for Respectability: Methodism and Afro-Caribbean Culture on 19th Century Nevis. *Nieuwe West-Indische Gids/New West Indian Guide* 64(3/4): 93–114.

Opitz, R.S., K. Ryzewski, J.F. Cherry and B. Moloney. 2015. Using Airborne LiDAR Survey to Explore Historic-era Archaeological Landscapes of Montserrat in the Eastern Caribbean. *Journal of Field Archaeology* 40(5): 523–541.

Pattullo, P. 2000. *Fire from the Mountain: The Tragedy of Montserrat and the Betrayal of its People*. London: Constable.

Peters, F.E. 1928. *Montserrat: Her Disasters. A Souvenir of the Great Hurricane of September 12th–13th*. New York: The Steber Press.

Petersen, J.B. 1996. Archaeology of Trants. Part 3: Chronological and Settlement Data. *Annals of Carnegie Museum* 65: 323–362.

Petersen, J.B. and D.R. Watters. 1988. Afro-Montserratian Ceramics from the Harney Site Cemetery, Montserrat, West Indies. *Annals of Carnegie Museum* 57: 167–187.

Petersen, J.B., R.N. Bartone and D.R. Watters. 1999a. Continuity and Syncretism in Afro-Caribbean Ceramics from the Northern Lesser Antilles. In J.B. Haviser (ed.), *African Sites Archaeology in the Caribbean*, 157–195. Princeton, NJ: Markus Wiener.

— 1999b. Pyroclastic, Storm Surge, and Saladoid Villager Deposits: The Archaeological and Geological Stratigraphy of the Trants Site, Montserrat. In *Proceedings of the 16th Congress of the International Association for Caribbean Archaeology*, vol. 2, 40–51. Basse Terre, Guadeloupe: Conseil Régional de la Guadeloupe.

Physical Planning Act. 2008. *Laws of Montserrat, Chapter 8.03: Physical Planning Act and Subsidiary Legislation (Revised Edition, 1 January 2008).* http://agc.gov.ms/wp-content/uploads/2011/10/Physical-Planning-Act.pdf

Price, R. 1966. Caribbean Fishing and Fishermen: A Historical Sketch. *American Anthropologist* 68(6): 1363–1383.

Pulsipher, L.M. 1977. The Cultural Landscape of Montserrat, West Indies, in the Seventeenth Century: Early Environmental Consequences of British Colonial Development. Unpublished PhD dissertation, Southern Illinois University, Carbondale.

— 1982. Resource Management Strategies on an Eighteenth Century Caribbean Sugar Plantation: Interpreting the Physical, Archaeological and Archival Records. *Florida Anthropologist* 35(4): 243–249.

— 1983. The Galways Plantation Project. *Caribbean Geography* 1(2): 141–142.

— 1986. *Seventeenth Century Montserrat: An Environmental Impact Statement*. Historical Geography Research Series No. 17. Norwich: Geo Books.

— 1987. Assessing the Usefulness of a Cartographic Curiosity: The 1673 Map of a Sugar Island. *Annals of the Association of American Geographers* 77(3): 408–422.

— 1990. They Have Saturdays and Sundays to Feed Themselves. *Expedition* (University of Pennsylvania Museum) 32(2): 24–33.

— 1991. Galways Plantation. In H.J. Viola and C. Margolis (eds), *Seeds of Change: Five Hundred Years Since Columbus*, 139–159. Washington, D.C.: Smithsonian Institution Press.

— 1994. The Landscapes and Ideational Roles of Caribbean Slave Gardens. In N. Miller and K. Gleason (eds), *The Archaeology of Garden and Field*, 202–221. Philadelphia: University of Pennsylvania Press.

Pulsipher, L.M. and C.M. Goodwin. 1982. A Sugar-boiling House at Galways: An Irish Sugar Plantation in Montserrat, West Indies. *Post-medieval Archaeology* 16: 21–27.

— 1999. Here Where the Old-time People Be: Reconstructing the Landscapes of the Slavery and Post-slavery Era in Montserrat, West Indies. In J.B. Haviser (ed.), *African Sites Archaeology in the Caribbean*, 9–37. Princeton, NJ: Markus Wiener.

— 2001. 'Getting the Essence of It': Galways Plantation, Montserrat, West Indies. In P. Farnsworth (ed.), *Island Lives: Historical Archaeologies of the Caribbean*, 165–203. Tuscaloosa: University of Alabama Press.

Purchas, S. 1906 [1625]. *Hakluytus Posthumus or Purchas his Pilgrims: Contayning a History of the World in Sea Voyages and Land Travells by Englishmen and Others*, vol. 18. Glasgow: MacLehose.

Rea, W.J. 1974. The Volcanic Geology and Petrology of Montserrat, West Indies. *Journal of the Geological Society of London* 130: 341–366.

Reitz, E.J. 1994. Archaeology of Trants, Montserrat. Part 2: Vertebrate Fauna. *Annals of Carnegie Museum* 63: 297–317.

Richardson, B.C. 2004. *Igniting the Caribbean's Past: Fire in British West Indian History*. Chapel Hill, NC: University of North Carolina Press.

Roe, P. 1995. Pottery Forms that Endure. In B. Braun (ed.), *Arts of the Amazon*, 24–29. London: Thames and Hudson.

Roobol, M.J. and A.L. Smith. 1998. Pyroclastic Stratigraphy of the Soufrière Hills Volcano, Montserrat: Implications for the Present Eruption. *Geophysical Research Letters* 25(18): 3393–3396.

Rouse, I. 1992. *The Tainos: Rise and Decline of the People Who Greeted Columbus*. New Haven: Yale University Press.

Rouse, I. and B.F. Morse. 1999. *Excavations at the Indian Creek Site, Antigua, West Indies*. Yale University Publications in Anthropology No. 82. New Haven: Peabody Museum of Natural History, Yale University.

Ryzewski, K. 2017. A Thorny Endeavor: Historical Archaeology and Diachronic Landscape Survey in the Caribbean Lesser Antilles. In A.R. Knodell and T.P. Leppard (eds), *Regional Approaches to Society and Complexity: Studies in Honor of John F. Cherry*, 225–245. Monographs in Mediterranean Archaeology. Sheffield: Equinox.

Ryzewski, K. and J.F. Cherry. 2012. Communities and Archaeology under the Soufrière Hills Volcano on Montserrat, West Indies. *Journal of Field Archaeology* 37(4): 316–327.

— 2015. Struggles of a Sugar Society: Surveying Plantation-era Montserrat, 1650–1850. *International Journal of Historical Archaeology* 19(2): 356–383.

— 2016. Surveying a Long-term Settlement on Potato Hill, Montserrat. In L.A. Bates, J.M. Chenoweth and J.A. Delle (eds), *Archaeologies of Slavery and Freedom in the Caribbean: Exploring the Spaces in Between*, 152–179. Gainesville: University Press of Florida.

— 2019. Archaeology across the Columbian Divide: Using Micro-regional Survey to Examine Montserrat's Island Communities (ca. 1000–1730 AD). In J.M. Torres and A.B. Persons (eds), *Proceedings of the 27th Congress of the International Association for Caribbean Archaeology, St. Croix, USVI, 24–28 July 2017*, 91–105. St. Croix: International Association for Caribbean Archaeology.

Ryzewski, K. and L. McAtackney. 2015. Contemporary Irish Identity on Montserrat, the "Emerald Isle of the Caribbean". In A. Donnell, M. McGarrity and E. O'Callaghan (eds), *Caribbean Irish Connections*, 119–139. Kingston, Jamaica: University of West Indies Press.

Ryzewski, K., J.F. Cherry and L. McAtackney. 2018. "The State of Decay into which the Island has Fallen": Education and Social Welfare on Montserrat after Emancipation. *International Journal of Historical Archaeology* 23: 543–567.

Saunders, N.J. 2005. *The Peoples of the Caribbean: An Encyclopedia of Archeology and Traditional Culture*. Santa Barbara, CA: ABC-CLIO.

Sheets, P.D. 2012. Responses to Explosive Volcanic Eruptions by Small to Complex Societies in Ancient Mexico and Central America. In J. Cooper and P. Sheets (eds), *Surviving Sudden Environmental Change: Understanding Hazards, Mitigating Impacts, Avoiding Disasters*, 43–63. Boulder: University Press of Colorado.

Shepherd, J.B., J.F. Tomblin and D. Woo. 1971. Volcano-seismic Crisis in Montserrat. *Bulletin of Volcanology* 35: 143–163.

Sheridan, R.B. 1974. *Sugar and Slavery: An Economic History of the British West Indies, 1623–1775*. Baltimore: Johns Hopkins University Press.

Siegel, P.E. 1989. Site Structure, Demography, and Social Complexity in the Early Ceramic Age of the Caribbean. In P.E. Siegel (ed.), *Early Ceramic Population Lifeways and Adaptive Strategies in the Caribbean*, 193–245. BAR International Series 506. Oxford: British Archaeological Reports.

— 2013. Caribbean Archaeology in Historical Perspective. In W.F. Keegan, C.L. Hofman and R. Rodríguez Ramos (eds), *The Oxford Handbook of Caribbean Archaeology*, 21–46. New York: Oxford University Press.

— (ed.). 2018. *Island Historical Ecology: Socionatural Landscapes of the Eastern and Southern Caribbean.* Oxford and New York: Berghahn Books.

Siegel, P.E. and E. Righter (eds). 2011. *Protecting Heritage in the Caribbean.* Tuscaloosa: University of Alabama Press.

Siegel, P.E., C.L. Hofman, B. Bérard, R. Murphy, J. Ulloa Hung, R. Valcárcel Rojas and C. White. 2013. Confronting Caribbean Heritage in an Archipelago of Diversity: Politics, Stakeholders, Climate Change, Natural Disasters, Tourism, and Development. *Journal of Field Archaeology* 38(4): 376–390.

Siegel, P.E., J.G. Jones, D.M. Pearsall, N.P. Dunning, P. Farrell, N.A. Duncan, J.H. Curtis and S.K. Singh. 2015. Paleoenvironmental Evidence for First Human Colonization of the Eastern Caribbean. *Quaternary Science Reviews* 129: 275–295.

Singleton, T.A. 2015. *Slavery Behind the Wall: An Archaeology of a Cuban Coffee Plantation.* Gainesville: University Press of Florida.

Skinner, J. 2004. *Before the Volcano: Reverberations of Identity on Montserrat.* Kingston, Jamaica: Arawak Publications.

Smith, A.L., M.J. Roobol, J.H. Schellekens and G.S. Mattioli. 2007. Prehistoric Stratigraphy of the Soufrière Hills–South Soufrière Hills Volcanic Complex, Montserrat, West Indies. *Journal of Geology* 115: 115–127.

Southey, T. 1827. *Chronological History of the West Indies*. 3 vols. London: Longman.

Steadman, D.W., D.R. Watters, E.J. Reitz and G.K. Pregill. 1984. Vertebrates from Archaeological Sites on Montserrat, West Indies. *Annals of Carnegie Museum* 53: 1–30.

Strasser, T.F., E. Panagopoulou, C.N. Runnels, P.M. Murray, N. Thompson, P. Karkanas, F.W. McCoy and K.W. Wegmann. 2010. Stone Age Seafaring in the Mediterranean: Evidence from the Plakias Region for Lower Palaeolithic and Mesolithic Habitation of Crete. *Hesperia* 79: 145–190.

Stine, L.F., M.A. Cabac and M.D. Groover. 1996. Blue Beads as African-American Cultural Symbols. *Historical Archaeology* 3(3): 49–75.

Sturge, J. and T. Harvey. 1838. *The West Indies in 1837: Being the Journal of a Visit to Antigua, Montserrat, Dominica, St. Lucia, Barbadoes, and Jamaica: Undertaken for the Purpose of Ascertaining the Actual Condition of the Negro Population of Those Islands.* 2nd edn, London: Hamilton, Adams and Co.

Torrence, R. 2019. Social Responses to Volcanic Eruptions: A Review of Key Concepts. *Quaternary International.* 499(B): 258–265.

Torrence, R. and J. Grattan. 2002. The Archaeology of Disasters: Past and Future Trends. In R. Torrence and J. Grattan (eds), *Natural Disasters and Cultural Change*, 1–18. London and New York: Routledge.

van den Bel, M. 2015. Description des Caraïbes cannibales ou des Îles sauvages à 1627. Un routier néerlandais des Petites Antilles collationné par Hessel Gerritsz. *Bulletin de la société d'histoire de la Guadeloupe* 171: 1–53.

Van Gijn, A.L. 1993. Flint Exploitation on Long Island, Antigua. *Analecta Praehistorica Leidensia* 26: 183–197.

Wadge, G., B. Voight, R.S.J. Sparks, P.D. Cole, S.C. Loughlin and R.E.A. Robertson. 2014. An Overview of the Eruption of Soufrière Hills Volcano, Montserrat, from 2000 to 2010. In G. Wadge, R.E.A. Robertson and B. Voight (eds), *The Eruption of Soufrière Hills Volcano, Montserrat from 2000 to 2010*, 1–39. Memoirs of the Geological Society of London 39. London: Geological Society of London.

Waldron, L. 2011. Geographic Distributions of Zoomorphic Motifs in Saladoid Ceramics. *Caribbean Connections* 1(2): 1–25.

— 2016. *Handbook of Ceramic Animal Symbols in the Ancient Lesser Antilles*. Gainesville: University of Florida Press.

Watters, D.R. 1980. Transect Surveying and Prehistoric Site Locations on Barbuda and Montserrat, Leeward Islands, West Indies. Unpublished PhD dissertation, University of Pittsburgh.

— 1981. A Turlington Balsam Phial from Montserrat, West Indies: Genuine or Counterfeit? *Historical Archaeology* 15(1): 105–108.

— 1987. Excavations at the Harney Site Slave Cemetery, Montserrat, West Indies. *Annals of Carnegie Museum* 56: 289–318.
— 1994a. Archaeology of Trants, Montserrat. Part 1: Field Methods and Artifact Density Distributions. *Annals of Carnegie Museum* 63: 265–295.
— 1994b. Mortuary Patterns at the Harney Site Slave Cemetery, Montserrat, in Caribbean Perspective. *Historical Archaeology* 28(3): 56–73.
— 2010. Supplementary Sources of Archaeological Data for Montserrat. In *Proceedings of the 22nd Congress of the International Association for Caribbean Archaeology*, 778–788. Kingston, Jamaica: Jamaica National Heritage Trust.
— 2015. Belham Valley (MS-A46): Montserrat's Third Saladoid Site. In *Proceedings of the 25th Congress of the International Association for Caribbean Archaeology*, 126–144. San Juan, Puerto Rico: International Association for Caribbean Archaeology.
Watters, D.R. and G.E. Norton. 2007. Volcanically Induced Loss of Archaeological Sites in Montserrat. In B. Reid, H. Petitjean Roget and A. Curet (eds), *Proceedings of the 21st Congress of the International Association for Caribbean Archaeology*, Vol. 1, 48–55. St. Augustine, Trinidad: University of the West Indies.
Watters, D.R. and J.B. Petersen. 1999. Trants, Montserrat: The 1995 Field Season. In *Proceedings of the 16th Congress of the International Association for Caribbean Archaeology*, vol. 2, 27–39. Basse Terre, Guadeloupe: Conseil Régional de la Guadeloupe.
Watters, D.R. and R. Scaglion. 1980. Utility of a Transect Survey Technique in Caribbean Prehistoric Studies: Applications on Barbuda and Montserrat. In S.M. Lewenstein (ed.), *Proceedings of the 8th International Congress for the Study of Pre-Columbian Cultures of the Lesser Antilles, St. Kitts*, 338–347. Tempe: Arizona State University.
— 1994. Beads and Pendants from Trants, Montserrat: Implications for the Prehistoric Lapidary Industry of the Caribbean. *Annals of Carnegie Museum* 63:2 15–237.
Wheeler, M.M. 1988. *Montserrat, West Indies: A Chronological History*. Montserrat: The Montserrat National Trust.
Wilson, S.M. 1989. The Prehistoric Settlement Pattern of Nevis, West Indies. *Journal of Field Archaeology* 16(4): 427–450.
— 1994. The Cultural Mosaic of the Indigenous Caribbean in Europe and America. In W. Bray (ed.), *The Meeting of Two Worlds: Europe and the Americas 1492–1650*, 37–66. Proceedings of The British Academy 81. Oxford and New York: Oxford University Press.
Zacek, N. A. 2010. *Settler Society in the English Leeward Islands, 1670–1776.* Cambridge: Cambridge University Press.
Zellmer, G.F., C.J. Hawkesworth, R.S.J. Sparks, L.E. Thomas, C.L. Harford, T.S. Brewer and S.C. Loughlin. 2003. Geochemical Evolution of Soufrière Hills Volcano, Montserrat, Lesser Antilles Volcanic Arc. *Journal of Petrology* 44(8): 1349–1374.

C. Unpublished reports

[Note: In the Endnotes, these reports are referred to by number: Unpublished Report 1 = *UPR*1.]

(i) Reports on file at the Montserrat National Trust, Olveston, Montserrat

1. Platt, C. 1970. *Trial Excavations at the Golf Course.*
2. Zabawski Gundy, E. 1984. *Archaeology of Bransby Point: A Report of the 1983 Fieldwork.*
3. Bell, B. 1985. *Preliminary Study of the Dagenham Beach Site (MS-A2): A Prehistoric Burial and Occupation in Plymouth, Montserrat.*
4. Mann, R. 1987a. *An Analysis of Human Skeletal Remains from Dagenham Beach (MS-A2), Montserrat, West Indies.*
5. Mann, R. 1987b. *An Analysis of Human Skeletal Remains from Trants Bay (MS-G10), Montserrat, West Indies.*
6. Beaudry, M.C. and L.M. Pulsipher. 2007. Narrative Report of March 2007 Archaeological Investigations at the Montserrat National Trust Heritage Site at Little Bay.

7. Ryzewski, K. and J.F. Cherry. 2010. *Survey and Landscape Archaeology on Montserrat: A Report on the First Field Season, June–July 2010.*
8. Ryzewski, K. and E. Bocancea. 2011. *Report on the Montserrat National Trust Collections: Storage Conditions, Collections Management, and Projections of Future Needs.*
9. Ryzewski, K., J.F. Cherry, T.P. Leppard and E. Bocancea. 2012. *Survey and Landscape Archaeology on Montserrat: Narrative Report on the Second Field Season, June–July 2011.*
10. Pecoraro, C. 2012. *Little Bay Carr Plantation Archaeology and Heritage Project Archival Report.*
11. Cherry, J.F. and K. Ryzewski. 2013. *Report on the Survey and Excavations at Gun Hill, Montserrat, May 2013.*
12. Ryzewski, K. and J.F. Cherry. 2013. *Survey and Landscape Archaeology on Montserrat: Narrative Report on the Third Field Season, May–June* 2012.
13. Ryzewski, K. and J.F. Cherry. 2013. *Report on the Survey and Excavations at Potato Hill, Montserrat, May 2013.*
14. Bocancea, E., K. Ryzewski and J.F. Cherry. 2013. *Report on the Archaeological Excavations at the Valentine Ghaut Site, Rendezvous Bay, Montserrat, Conducted by the Survey and Landscape Archaeology on Montserrat Project (SLAM) from 2010–2013.*
15. Moloney, B., K. Ryzewski and J.F. Cherry. 2014. *Airborne LiDAR Groundtruthing Report, Survey and Landscape Archaeology on Montserrat Project (SLAM), May–June 2014.*
16. Cherry, J.F., K. Ryzewski, B. Doucet, A. Zissis, S. Ellens and C.L. Brace VI. 2015. *Report on LiDAR Survey and Fieldwork in the Centre Hills Region, Montserrat, May–June 2015.*
17. Brace VI, C.L., K. Ryzewski and J.F. Cherry. 2015. *Archaeological Excavations on Potato Hill, Montserrat, May–June 2015.*
18. McAtackney, L. 2015. *Report on Archival Research Conducted in Association with the Survey and Landscape Archaeology on Montserrat Project, May 2015.*
19. McAtackney, L. 2016. *Report on Archival Research Conducted at the Montserrat National Trust, Olveston, SLAM Project, May–June 2016.*
20. Rothenberg, M.A., B. Doucet, J.F. Cherry and K. Ryzewski. 2016. *Report on 2016 Survey Operations (May–June), Survey and Landscape Archaeology on Montserrat Project.*
21. Ryzewski, K. and J.F. Cherry. 2016. *Report on the Soldier Ghaut Petroglyphs, Survey and Landscape Archaeology on Montserrat Project.*
22. Ellens, S., K. Ryzewski and J.F. Cherry. 2016. *Archaeological Excavations on Potato Hill, Montserrat, May–June 2016.*
23. Cherry, J.F. and K. Ryzewski. 2017. *Survey and Landscape Archaeology on Montserrat Project: Archaeological Fieldwork at Upper Blakes, 2012, 2016 and 2017.*
24. Ellens, S. 2017. *Report on the Elberton Estate (Site 36) Survey, ET 99, May 20, 2017.*
25. Cherry, J.F. and K. Ryzewski. 2017. *Survey and Landscape Archaeology on Montserrat, 2017 Excavations at Indian Creek (Site 15).*
26. Ryzewski, K. and M.A.W. Rothenberg. 2017. *Report on the Archaeological Survey of Weekes Estate (Site 48), 2017.*
27. Ryzewski, K., A. Zissis and J.F. Cherry. 2017. *Report on Artifact Analyses from Potato Hill, Montserrat (Features 16 and 298).* Revised edition, November 2017.
28. McAtackney, L. 2017. *Montserrat National Trust (MNT) Archival Report, 2017 Season.*

(ii) Other unpublished reports

29. Watters, D. 1995–1996. *Archaeological Impact Assessment, Blackburne Airport, Montserrat, Interim Reports 1–3.* Submitted by the Carnegie Museum of Natural History to the British Development Division in the Caribbean/Overseas Development Administration.
30. Oxford Archaeological Unit (OAU). 1995. *Historic Buildings at Trants Estate and Other Estate Sites on Montserrat.* Unpublished report prepared for the Government of Montserrat in advance of the Blackburne Airport Development, under assignment from the Overseas Development Administration.
31. Moloney, B., K. Ryzewski and J.F. Cherry. 2014. *Airborne LiDAR Ground-truthing Report, Survey and Landscape Archaeology on Montserrat Project (SLAM), May–June 2014.* Unpublished report submitted to the

Spatial Archaeometry Research Collaborations Program (SPARC), Center for Advanced Spatial Technologies (CAST), University of Arkansas.
32. Howard, J.L. 2015. *Geomorphology and Soils at Archaeological Sites on Montserrat.* Unpublished report, Department of Geology, Wayne State University, Detroit.
33. Rothenberg, M. 2015. *Geological Survey Conducted at Thatch Valley, Potato Hill and Valentine Ghaut, Montserrat, British West Indies.* Unpublished report, Joukowsky Institute for Archaeology and the Ancient World, Brown University.
34. Ohman, A. 2016. *SLAM 2015, Potato Hill Faunal Report.* Unpublished Report on File at the College of William and Mary.

Index

Figures in *italics*; n refers to note